D1156684

Bloody Promenade

THE AMERICAN SOUTH SERIES
Edward L. Ayers, Editor

Bloody Promenade

STEPHEN CUSHMAN

University Press
of Virginia
*Charlottesville
and London*

Reflections on a Civil War Battle

The University Press of Virginia

© 1999 by the Rector and Visitors of the University of Virginia

All rights reserved

Printed in the United States of America

First published 1999

∞ The paper used in this publication meets the minimum requirements of the American National Standard for Information Sciences—Permanence of Paper for Printed Library Materials, ANSI Z39.48-1984.

Library of Congress Cataloging-in-Publication Data

Cushman, Stephen.

    Bloody promenade : reflections on a Civil War battle / Stephen Cushman.

        p.   cm. — (The American South series)

    Includes bibliographical references and index.

    ISBN 0-8139-1874-X (cloth : alk. paper)

    1. Wilderness, Battle of the, Va., 1864—Historiography.

2. Wilderness, Battle of the, Va., 1864—Miscellanea. 3. United States—History—Civil War, 1861–1865—Influence. I. Title.

II. Series.

E476.52.C88   1999

973.7´36—dc21   99–11730

                                                      CIP

For my sons.
May nothing like it happen in your time.

Students of war, let me suggest that once in a while as you study battles that you take Imagination's offered hand; she will lead you through simple height-gaining paths till at last fife and drum die away and lo! you are in a blessed company charged to convert what is earthly into what is spiritual.

Morris Schaff, *The Battle of the Wilderness* (1910)

... the bloody promenade of the Wilderness. . . .

Walt Whitman, *Memoranda during the War* (1875)

Contents

Illustrations

Acknowledgments

Thanks to the people who helped in so many different and crucial ways: Edward Ayers, Susan Bacik, John Burt, Douglas Chambers, Roberta Culbertson, Anne Cushman, Bigelow Cushman, Charlotte Cushman, Sandra Bain Cushman, Brady Earnhart, Mark Edmundson, William Frassanito, Gary Gallagher, Jon Guillot, Scott Hennessey, Dick Holway, Felicia Johnson, Courtney McIntosh, Ervin Jordan, Pat Michaels, Stephen Railton, Jahan Ramazani, Perry Roland, Mary Lee Settle, Ann Southwell, Jerry Stenger, Robert Talbot, Widdy Tazewell, John Toffey, Frank Walker, Rod Waterman, Gavin Watson, Charles Wright, Andrew Wyndham; the Shannon Center for Advanced Studies at the University of Virginia; the staff and fellows of the Virginia Foundation for the Humanities; the staff of Special Collections at Alderman Library, University of Virginia; the University of Virginia Small Grants Committee; the staff of the Deer Isle–Stonington Historical Society, Deer Isle, Maine.

"Whenever I Smoke a Cigar" first appeared in *Hayden's Ferry Review* 21 (Fall/Winter 1997). "Skirmish at Rio Hill" first appeared in *Westview* 17, 1 (Fall/Winter 1997). I am grateful to the editors of both these journals.

"Except I Shall See" first appeared in the *Southern Review* 30, 3 (Summer 1994) and is reprinted from *Blue Pajamas* (Baton Rouge: Louisiana State University Press, 1998) by permission. For the title, see John 20:25 (King James Version). " 'War, Effect of a Shell on a Confederate Soldier' " first appeared in *Poem* 75 (May 1996) and is also reprinted from *Blue Pajamas* by permission.

The Library of Virginia provided the copy of Edwin Forbes's "Waiting for the Enemy."

Winslow Homer's *Skirmish in the Wilderness* is reproduced with the permission of the New Britain Museum of American Art, New Britain, Connecticut.

The photograph with the caption "Remains of the Dead at Chancellorsville" is reprinted by permission of Russell & Volkening as agents for Roy Meredith. Copyright © 1946 by Roy Meredith, © renewed 1974 by Roy Meredith.

Maps of the Wilderness and central Virginia were prepared with the assistance of Perry Roland, Digital Media and Music Center, Clemons Library, University of Virginia. For permission to adapt George Skoch's mapping of the battle in Gordon Rhea's *The Battle of the Wilderness, May 5–6, 1864* (1994), I thank Louisiana State University Press.

I am grateful to Suzanne Wolk, who copyedited the manuscript, and to Brooks Moriarty, who prepared the index.

In Lieu of a Label

I F A B O O K were a box of cereal, a list of ingredients would appear on its label. Just as shoppers read labels to avoid too much salt, too much sugar, or too many preservatives, readers could use labels to steer clear of too much irony, too much bias, or too many clichés.

This book contains three main ingredients that may not be completely apparent from the title or the table of contents. The first is the Battle of the Wilderness, fought in central Virginia on Thursday, May 5, and Friday, May 6, 1864. This book is not another history of the battle. Many fine histories already exist, and the reader who turns this page, peeks at the table of contents, and sees that one of the chapters is called "Histories" may guess, correctly, that that chapter talks about the various ways people have written histories of the Battle of the Wilderness. Likewise, chapters on "Newspapers," "Weeklies," "Memoirs," "Fictions," and "Poems" consider the ways people have written about the battle in these respective genres and media. If this book is the history of anything, it's the history of verbal and visual images of a single, particularly awful moment in the American Civil War. I've chosen this moment not because I'm especially fond of the particularly awful but because I live near the Wilderness and can't help thinking about it. Readers who already know a great deal about the battle will find here, I hope, another approach to what they already know, and readers who know nothing will find most of what they need to know in the brief description of the battle that appears at the end.

The second main ingredient is reflection or meditation on the war itself, particularly on the war as it continues to confront us in our everyday lives here at the turn of the century. To write a professional history of any aspect of the Civil War, one has to turn back from everyday life and dig into materials from the past. In the course of reflecting or meditating I've done a good bit of that digging. But to understand and interpret various images of the war, one has only to look around at the newest book or film or monument or reenactment to begin the process of contemplation. Larger reflections on the war, as they appear in chapters such as "The Book" or "Buff" or "Ancestors" or "Reenactment" or "Acoustic Shadow," usually include images of the Battle of the Wilderness, but they also circle restlessly around and move beyond those images. Much of the rhythm of this book emerges from shuttling back and forth between the specific instance of May 5–6, 1864, and the general contexts of both then and now.

The third main ingredient is myself. As Thoreau puts it wryly on the first page of *Walden,* "I should not talk so much about myself if there were anybody else whom I knew as well." But I haven't written this book about myself. There's nothing here, for example, about what I eat for breakfast or how I do at my job or what kind of physical exercise I prefer. Instead I've used myself, along with an informal, first-person voice, simply as a way of approaching material that otherwise would be mostly unapproachable, at least for me. As a reader of professional histories, I've come to admire objectivity and detachment, but as a reader of many other things, as well as a viewer of drawings and photographs and films, I also value the forcefulness of subjectivity and engagement. Writing in the first person from my own point of view has helped me balance subjectivity with objectivity, engagement with detachment. In some chapters, such as "The Ground," or in the poems at the end of "Poems," the subjectivity will be most obvious. If I were a novelist or a better writer, I might have found a way to introduce subjectivity apart from myself. But I'm not.

Bloody Promenade

Reflections on a Civil War Battle

ONE

Signs

A T THE LAST light before home, waiting for a left-turn arrow, I have a minute or two to lift my eyes to the hills above the shopping center on my right, above signs for the bank and burger place, car wash and insurance agency, and to find, if the leaves have fallen, the white dome of Monticello, which from this angle looks nothing like the back of a nickel. When the turn arrow shines, homebound traffic makes the sharp left north, jockeying from two lanes down to one, and soon a small green sign, which identifies Route 20 as "The Constitution Route," shoots by. It's called the Constitution Route because just south of Orange, Virginia, it runs past James Madison's Montpelier. Next, in quick succession, come the no-littering and speed-limit signs, both of which I obey, and after them the large green mileage sign I can't pass without feeling spooked. The white letters of its bottom line read, "Wilderness 51."

> Thursday 5th. A and O rode down to the F[ederal] pick-
> ets. hear musketry and see clouds of smoke going up from
> the artilery. There is skirmishing going on this afternoon;
> now about 1 oclock.

In the spring of 1864, from May 4 through May 22, Katherine Couse wrote a twelve-page letter to some friends who have not been identified. She wrote the letter in diary form, inserting the dates to help her friends follow the chronology of what we now call the Battles of the Wilderness (May 5–6) and Spotsylvania (May 8–21). Originally from New Jersey, Katherine moved with her family to Laurel Hill, Spotsylvania County, Virginia, before the war. Although we don't know for sure where her house stood, her letter mentions both "Alsops" and "the Court-House road," references that locate Katherine near the area that the National Park Service identifies as the site of the "Laurel Hill Engagement," where the Battle of Spotsylvania opened on May 8. Wherever the house stood in the Laurel Hill area, which lies about five or six miles southeast of the tactically crucial unfinished railroad cut that runs through the Wilderness, two of the bloodiest battles of the Civil War erupted around Katherine's house.

> later between 3 and 4 oclock
> sharp skirmishing on the Court-House road. we heard the
> yells and the pop and the crack of musketry made me feel
> faint, it continued some time Confed soldiers around. this
> eve three Fed soldiers came galloping up. we went out to
> see them. shook hands with the officer and told him we
> were glad to see them. smiled and said he was glad they
> had some friends here, charming weather.

Helpful people in the State Climatology Office found the meteorological journal of the observatory in Washington for May 5 and 6, 1864, and the records show that by the time Katherine was chatting with the Federal officer, a lovely spring day had passed in northern and central Virginia, moving from a low in the forties toward a high in the seventies, with light winds from the northwest keeping the early morning clear before they shifted to the south or southeast and blew in a little haze. Mr. Eastman, the man who made the observations, or at least the one who signed them, noted at the bottom of the page, "A few faint shooting stars about midnight."

> Friday, May 6th, 1864. heard the cannon the first thing.
> they jar the house continually. lovely morning. The whole
> outdoors alive with voices of soldiers. hear waggons and
> cannon moving, rumbling. the country is now all excite-
> ment. I feel so nervous. Oh! so anxious.

One day this past summer a sonic boom broke over Charlottesville, rattling the windows and scaring everyone in the house to death. If one sonic boom several miles away can send the heart rate soaring, what would two days of continuous cannon fire in the immediate neighborhood do? Histories of the Battle of the Wilderness tend to repeat the accepted wisdom that Lee wanted to force Grant to fight in the thick woods in order to offset the Northern numerical advantage and to keep him from enjoying the benefits of his superior artillery force. One doesn't need a degree from West Point to understand that cannons can't do their best (or worst) firing from low-lying swamps and thickets into more low-lying swamps and thickets. At least with so-called light artillery, cannoneers prefer to fire from elevated positions that look down on clear fields, as they did at Malvern Hill in 1862 or on the third day of Gettysburg in 1863. For this reason, Lee's thinking makes perfect sense and probably saved the Army of Northern Virginia many casualties it could hardly afford. But as Katherine's letter makes clear, the Battle of the Wilderness still included more than enough artillery fire to fray a civilian's nerves.

> A rough Federal scouting party came up and acted very badly this morning. They took nearly all our little corn, and a good many fowls—all remonstrance was vain. The crash of musketry is terrific pop pop pop. The cannon shake the very foundations of the house. Two southern soldiers just now came, first one side then the other. now we hear the shells whistling at a terrific rate Oh, it makes me so weak so generally wretched. heard the southern bugles, we are surrounded—yankees on one side southern soldiers on the other pickets and vidette on all sides Confeds are coming up all the time. very warm. They tell us they have taken 3 thousand yankee prisoners. the Court House road is alive with yelling soldiers hear skirmishing at intervals all day up there, charging soldiers this eve late yelling no firing.

Katherine's Northern sympathies don't protect her from the treatment received by many other Southern civilians at the hands of the Federals and a few Northern ones at the hands of Confederates. Throughout Civil War writing, in letters, diaries, memoirs, histories, novels, short stories, and poems, the scene of Federal troops taking food, supplies, and booty from Southern civilians recurs. Union plundering provides Margaret Mitchell's *Gone with the Wind* (1936) with one of its more dramatic moments, for example. Like Mitchell, other Southern women writers have built fictions around pillaging scenes, among them Alberta Pierson Hannum in "Turkey Hunt" (1937), which also appeared in *The Best Short Stories of 1938,* and Caroline Gordon in "Hear the Nightingale Sing" (1945). Even Stephen Crane's *Red Badge of Courage* (1895), written by a Northern male and otherwise focused exclusively on Henry Fleming's experience of combat, depicts the intrusion of military need or greed upon the domestic sphere when in a memorable scene a member of Fleming's New York regiment badly underestimates the determination of a young Virginia girl to keep the horse he tries to steal from her, as his comrades cheer for the girl and make fun of him. More recently, Robby Henson's powerful film *Pharaoh's Army* (1996) and Charles Frazier's best-selling novel *Cold Mountain* (1997) have dramatized Yankee foraging. But the irony in the case of Katherine Couse, a stranger in a strange land whose food is stolen by her former compatriots, adds unusual complexity to the familiar scene.

In fact, in the turbulence of the fighting, what side she favors loses all significance, as both sides swirl around a house that suddenly finds itself, on the warm afternoon of May 6, in the unmediated presence of what Crane called "the red animal" and "the blood-swollen god." In these circumstances, partisanship dissolves, and civilian nerves have all they can do to hold on.

> there has been terrible fighting going on in the Court
> House road since 3 oclock it sounds almost at the house, it
> is soul sickening to listen to the continual crack of small
> arms, then the loud resounding cannon, shell whizzing
> balls whistling, soldiers yelling and hollowing as they rush
> on Oh! God human beings killing each other. this wicked
> war will it never come to an end.

Last fall I went to a college football game with my friend Mack. The stadium holds forty-four thousand, and when it's full it helps me imagine things I find hard to imagine. Forty-four thousand would be about the size of two army corps during the Civil War. Lee brought to the Wilderness slightly fewer than one and a half times this many people, Grant a little more than two and a half times this many. After two days in the Wilderness, more than half of these people would have been killed, wounded, captured, or missing. Way more than half. Say everybody on my side of the stadium and behind both end zones. That man there. The lady with the red scarf. This boy beside me. By the end of May

1864, after Spotsylvania and North Anna, Grant alone had lost nearly enough men to fill this place. When they complete the planned addition to the stadium, I'll have to start thinking about June, beginning with Cold Harbor. Before the game, as we were standing in the parking lot, somebody close by set off a volley of loud fireworks. When I opened my eyes, Mack had his hand pressed to his chest, looking a little shaky. Mack was Eighty-second Airborne in Vietnam.

> Grant, we beseech thee, Almighty God, that like as we do
> believe thy only begotten Son our Lord Jesus Christ to
> have ascended into the heavens; so we may also in heart
> and mind thither ascend, and with him continually dwell,
> who liveth and reigneth with thee and the Holy Ghost, one
> God, world without end. Amen

When I look up the Wilderness in James Robertson's *Civil War Sites in Virginia: A Tour Guide* (1982), it tells me that in 1864, May 5 and 6 "saw 182,000 men viciously fighting in woods often set afire by bullets" in a struggle that "produced 26,000 casualties and was little more than a momentary check to Grant's advance." The guide also tells me, "Regrettably, only pieces of the Wilderness battlefield survive today." Sifting through the surviving pieces of the Battle of the Wilderness isn't easy, especially for an outsider with no formal training in history and nothing but an urge to know something of what the Civil War was like before it became history. The pieces to sift include all kinds of materials, some of them words, some of them pictures, and some of them moments in day-to-day life in the United States now.

But Robertson's *Tour Guide* doesn't tell me that Thursday, May 5, 1864, was Ascension Day, the fortieth day after Easter on which, according to the first chapter of Acts, Jesus "was taken up, and a cloud received him" out of the apostles' sight. In fact, nothing I've read ever mentions that on May 5 the devout Lee, who had camped the night before near Mrs. Rhodes's house at New Verdiersville, would have ridden into the Wilderness having read the collect above, as would have many others on both sides. I've taken the collect from an edition of the Book of Common Prayer published in New York in 1846, the same year Lee began using the Philadelphia edition that he read until 1864, when he exchanged it because its type was too small for him to read. According to Douglas Southall Freeman, the most heavily worn page in the book, which Lee marked with a strip of paper, contains the Psalter for Day 30, which begins with Psalm 144: "Blessed be the Lord my strength: who teacheth my hands to war, and my fingers to fight." For Ascension Day, the Psalter reading combines slightly modified excerpts from Psalms 24 and 47, including this verse from the former:

Who is the King of glory? The Lord strong and mighty;
even the Lord mighty in battle.

and this from the latter

O clap your hands together, all ye people; shout unto God
with the voice of triumph.

New Verdiersville is too small to appear on any green sign, and there is now a beauty salon near the spot where Lee camped, but it's also on the Constitution Route, a little more than ten miles beyond Orange, right where county road 621, the old Orange Plank Road, diverges from Route 20, the old Orange Turnpike, and makes its own way into the Wilderness, the way Lee took with A. P. Hill's Third Corps, his mind's ear perhaps hearing in the solemn opening of the collect, *Grant, we beseech thee,* the faint trace of an echo, *Grant, Grant.*

TWO

The Book

PERHAPS THERE WAS a boy born in, say, 1859, a boy who turned five on May 5, 1864. Perhaps this boy lived in Orange or Spotsylvania County, Virginia, and knew Katherine Couse, who meant to send him some small present for his fifth birthday and would have done so if she hadn't been distracted by nearly two hundred thousand men, along with their horses, mules, wagons, and cannons, converging on her neighborhood. Perhaps the boy, after the sun set on that clear spring Thursday, came out of hiding from a house that had shaken and rattled all day, helped a mother or older sister draw water from the well, and carried buckets to a nearby company of exhausted, thirsty soldiers, say, Company G, Mount Jackson Rifles, Thirty-third Virginia. After some hard fighting that afternoon near Saunders' Field, now traversed by Route 20, the Constitution Route, perhaps Captain David B. Huffman accepted the water gratefully and passed it along to his men, many of them badly dehydrated by bleeding or diarrhea or both. And although he didn't mention the boy in the letter he wrote the next day to his sister Bettie, perhaps he spoke kindly to the child, who never forgot him or the battle in his backyard.

Suppose the boy survived into adulthood and in his fifties fathered his eleventh child, also a boy. That son, having heard many times about the battle, the buckets, and the kind captain who wished his father a happy fifth birthday, would be somewhere around ninety by the end of the twentieth century. Anyone who spoke to this elderly gentleman, with his kind eyes and soft Virginia accent, would be speaking to someone who had spoken to someone who was there. So long after the Wilderness, it would be impossible to get much closer to living memory of the fighting.

Although I've made up the particular details of the five-year-old boy in the Wilderness, I haven't made up the case of someone born in 1859 who took water to soldiers in Virginia and who later fathered a child who is still alive. I know the son personally. I also know a woman whose grandfather, still alive during her childhood, fought for the Seventh Maine. The grandfather, formerly a sailor from Sedgwick, Maine, and twenty years old in May 1864, was wounded at the Wilderness on May 6, having squared off the day before against Confederates near the Culpeper Mine Ford (also called the Spotswood) Road, just north of Saunders' Field and the Orange Turnpike. In fact, the regiment of the Maine man, Asa Candage, belonged to a brigade under Brigadier General Thomas H. Neill that made up part of the Second Division of John Sedgwick's Sixth Corps and fought just two brigades to the north of the one facing David B. Huffman's Stonewall Brigade, under Brigadier General James A. Walker and a part of Edward Johnson's Division of Richard Ewell's Second Corps.

I don't believe that my knowing two people who knew people who experienced the Civil War firsthand makes me unique. My guess is that plenty of people have similar stories and that more people might if they did some investigating. But I do believe that once these special links with the past have died in their turn, our relation to the war cannot help but change. When the last veteran, Walter Washington Williams, died in 1959, we lost access to the first group of witnesses. When the last civilian who could have had even childhood memories of the war also died, a death that may have occurred as late as the 1980s and probably went unrecognized for what it was, we lost a second link. Soon, with the passing of those who knew members of either of these groups, we will lose a third.

With each group lost, the remoteness of the Civil War increases not arithmetically but geometrically. With each group lost it becomes harder and harder to say to the past with the same assurance Walt Whitman radiates in the 1855 preface to *Leaves of Grass,* "Rise and walk before me that I may realize you." With each group lost, we depend more heavily on records, representations, reproductions, re-creations, and reenactments of one kind or another. Certainly this dependence has its compensations. Chief among them is the close attention we have no choice but to pay, after the participants themselves are gone, to the extravagant abundance they left us, an abundance not only of places to visit and objects to contemplate but also of their writings, sketches, paintings, photographs, and songs, all of which help us recover the events and conditions that recede from us steadily in time. In turn, these firsthand materials have produced a second layer of extravagant abundance, since during the remainder of the nineteenth century and throughout the twentieth they have produced so much more writing, visual art (including public monuments and film), and music, a surprising fraction of which is both good history and good art.

As interest in the Civil War grows the further it slides into the past, people spend more time commenting on and trying to explain this interest. In *Drawn with the Sword* (1996), for instance, James McPherson, who has spent as much time trying to explain the war to the nonacademic laity as anyone of his generation, argues that the most important reason people are interested in the war is that great issues were at stake in it. McPherson elaborates that liberty and the "multiple meanings of freedom" provide "the central meaning of the war for the American experience." Such an ambitious, comprehensive generalization resounds with rhetorical charisma, although without much stretching one could also argue that great issues, including the multiple meanings of freedom, inform our descriptions of the American Revolution or World War II or even Vietnam, though in a complicated way. Still, whatever the objections one might raise to his generalization, no doubt McPherson is right about many people's interest in the Civil War.

But in my own case, and I have a strong hunch I'm not alone, interest in the war began not with anything as abstract as great issues and the multiple meanings of freedom but with something very concrete: a book. In fact, I'll bet my case is typical of many who didn't grow up with first- or secondhand witnesses to hear from. For us the flood of Civil War images, which continues to rise and shows no sign of cresting, is not the effect of interest in the war but is itself the cause. Whether or not we have gone on to understand and appreciate the larger issues and implications behind the images, we got hooked on the images because they were perhaps beautiful, horrifying, comic, pathetic, sublime, ugly, realistic, romantic, ironic, surprising, infuriating but almost always arresting and unforgettable.

The book appeared in 1960, four years after I did and, not accidentally I'm sure, on the eve of all the centennial anniversaries that helped push the war into the awareness of many who previously had managed to live without giving it much thought. Titled *The American Heritage Picture History of the Civil War*, it measures 8½ by 11½ by 2 inches, has blue cloth binding with THE CIVIL WAR in gold letters on the spine, and runs over six hundred pages. So many years after the book first came into my hands, I can now appreciate the excellence and pleasures of Bruce Catton's lean narrative, which he also published separately

in a small volume called *The American Heritage Short History of the Civil War,*
reprinted in 1987, but as a child I knew only that between the blue covers lay a
strange, frightening, fascinating country, a country I walked into then and
haven't emerged from since. I've had the book longer than any other I now own.
It has been rebound once and gives off a rich, musky smell.

The book first came to my attention two or three years after its publication
when I saw an advertisement for it in a magazine, an advertisement that consisted of text I couldn't read very well, if at all, and a photograph I've never forgotten. The photograph, which is in color and is credited in very small letters
to David E. Scherman, shows the black silhouette of a man looking at the sunset. Scherman took the photograph from behind the man, a little to his left and
from an angle that looks up at him. The man rests his left hand on the handle
of a sword sheathed at his side. His right arm bends at the elbow, and the right
hand is hidden from the camera by his body. He wears boots, a hat with a brim,
and a beard that the turn of his head makes visible in profile.

Why did this image grab me? Was I merely the naive young dupe of crafty
advertising? Although McPherson doesn't list it among the major explanations
for widespread interest in the Civil War, we shouldn't underestimate the role of
shrewd, aggressive advertising in stirring up and maintaining that interest. In
fact, if we read the Civil War through the eyes of Karl Marx, who published several acute articles about it in the *New York Tribune* and the Vienna daily *Die
Presse* during the first two years of fighting, we see it as a conflict between two
social systems that could no longer coexist peacefully on the North American
continent—and the victory of the Northern social system has entailed, among
other results, an even greater emphasis on manipulative advertising to stimulate
the economic consumption without which free-market capitalism cannot survive. According to this point of view, which those who believe the war was
mostly about freedom will find too cynical, a boy who responds to an advertisement for a book about the Civil War helps fuel the economic system that has
dominated the United States since the Civil War.

Or was I unconsciously manipulated by the aesthetic qualities of the photograph, a striking image of a solitary man lost in contemplation of a magnifi-
cent vista? Scherman snapped his picture at precisely the moment when the
western sky showed the full spectrum of color, from the deeper blues at the top
edge, down through light green, yellow, and orange, to the near red of the land.
Although I couldn't have known it at the time, the location of the photograph
in the book produces an instructive irony about the strategies of composition,

since Scherman's beautiful color plate faces a page that includes Alexander Gardner's famous black-and-white photograph of the baby-faced Devil's Den sharpshooter at Gettysburg, a photograph that William Frassanito has shown Gardner composed with his assistants by first dragging the body forty yards from where they found it.

Perhaps I was both the dupe of advertising and a sap swooning over a pretty picture. But if so, I think that another element, a personal one, also played a part in capturing my attention forever. In one of her prose memoirs, Elizabeth Bishop tells of being a young child who, having just moved from Nova Scotia to Massachusetts, misunderstands a line of "My Country 'Tis of Thee." When she heard the line "Land where my fathers died," she thought it went, "Land where my father died," and took it to refer to her own father, who had died in the United States when she was eight months old. Something similar happened to me when I saw Scherman's photograph, since at some level I associated the dark man who had his back turned to me with my own mother's father, who left Ohio in 1942, when she was six, and died two years later in fighting at Anzio, Italy. I didn't know much about him then, but I did know that he had been a soldier and that my mother lost him when she was approximately my age. In some way, then, Scherman's photograph must have struck me as an image of fatherlessness, and in some way my first understanding of the Civil War, such as it was, must have had something to do with fatherlessness. I can't say for sure whether I feared it when I saw the photograph or felt relieved from that fear by seeing an image of the missing father. After all, he looked strong, self-reliant, unthreatened, and calm. Of course, my association of the war with fatherlessness, while admittedly personal, is hardly unusual. McPherson estimates that the war produced two hundred thousand widows and perhaps twice that many fatherless children. Added together, these numbers approach the total of the dead for both sides. For the widowed and fatherless, as for me both at age six and now, the distinction between military and social history didn't and doesn't mean much.

At any rate, I wanted the book, and I wanted it bad. As luck would have it, sometime during that first half of 1963, when people who already knew about the war were observing the centennial anniversaries of the Emancipation Proclamation, the battle at Murfreesboro or Stone's River, Burnside's Mud March, the signing of the Federal Draft Act, the Richmond Bread Riot, the battle of Chancellorsville, Stonewall Jackson's death, and the beginning of the siege of Vicksburg, I underwent a standard medical rite of passage for children of my generation and had my tonsils removed. In their anxiety before the surgery, my poor parents had promised me a present to be opened after the operation, and I asked for the book. Sure enough, when I awoke from anesthesia to an ice pack around my neck and the Goliath of all sore throats, they had it waiting for me. With the book to stare at and the promise of all the soothing ice cream I could eat, I never thought about the grisly aptness of beginning my study of the Civil War in a hospital bed, and it would be many more years before I ran across this small, precious passage in Walt Whitman's *Memoranda during the War* (1875):

> Ice Cream Treat.—One hot day toward the middle of June [1864], I gave the inmates of Carver Hospital a general ice cream treat, purchasing a large quantity, and, under convoy of the doctor or head nurse of each Ward, going personally through the Wards to see to its distribution.

The book taught me much about the war, including the identity of the blackly silhouetted man staring at the sunset. It turned out that my image of fatherlessness was the statue of Union General Gouverneur Warren, who, as the caption puts it, "stands guard on Little Round Top" at Gettysburg. People who have read Michael Shaara's *Killer Angels* (1974) or seen *Gettysburg* (1993), the film based on the novel, will recognize Little Round Top as the scene of the charge of the Twentieth Maine, led by Joshua Lawrence Chamberlain. In fact, a close look at the Little Round Top scenes in the film reveals the Gouverneur Warren statue incompletely hidden by leaves and branches placed there to conceal it. At Gettysburg Warren was Meade's chief topographical engineer, and his statue faces west toward Seminary Ridge because it represents Warren in the act of seeing and recognizing the vulnerability of the Union left caused by the advance of Sickles's Third Corps toward the Wheat Field and the Peach Orchard. In his right hand, hidden from Scherman's camera, Warren holds the crucial tool of his trade, a pair of field glasses. Less than a year after Gettysburg, where he was wounded, having commanded the Union Second Corps in Winfield Scott Hancock's absence during the Mine Run Campaign (November–December 1863), Warren would take command of the Fifth Corps and lead it into the Wilderness.

A book with a reproduction of a photograph of a statue of a man amounts to an image of an image of an image, and yet to me as a young reader, or viewer, the pictures in the *Picture History* were worth at least a thousand words apiece because they initiated me not just into the world of Warren and Longstreet and Meade and Lee and Lincoln and Davis but also into the world of Alexander Gardner, Timothy O'Sullivan, James Gibson, George Barnard, Alfred Waud, Edwin Forbes, and Winslow Homer. If the first group of names were men who had a direct influence on the sequence of events, the second group were men who shaped our perception and imagination of those events. For many of us there would be no Civil War, let alone interest in the Civil War, without them.

For reasons I can't be sure of, the Wilderness section of the *Picture History* always left me with mixed feelings. Flipping through the book, I have to admit that I tended not to stop at the color photographs of trees. I could accept photographs without action, since wartime photographs needed long exposures and modern photographs had no action to photograph, and I could accept photographs without people, since images of buildings, either under construction (the Capitol) or in ruins (the Gallego flour mills on the Richmond waterfront), have their uncanny appeal. But the two-page spread entitled "Impressions of the Wilderness," which consists of color plates of leafy trees, pink wildflowers, a pink lady's slipper, dried leaves, a hollow log, and the top half of a horse's skull, seemed to belong on the pages of a Sierra Club calendar and to have next to nothing to do with the Civil War, the horse's skull perhaps excepted. Now these photographs interest me more, both for their own merits and for what they show about the Wilderness itself.

For one thing, the area is hard to represent photographically. The same conditions that made the fighting hellish also impinge on photographic composition, both wartime and modern. Thick woods don't give photographers much chance to compose the dramatic long shots characteristic both of the Gardner team's work at Sharpsburg-Antietam or Gettysburg and of Scherman's shot of the Warren statue. For another thing, wartime photography required that all fighting have ended and that the photographer's side remain in possession of the battlefield, so that he could make his long exposures in peace. As Frassanito points out, Timothy O'Sullivan, who by the spring of 1864 had emerged as one of the best in the business, was the only photographer traveling with the Army of the Potomac. That he took no photographs between May 4, when the army crossed the Rapidan, and May 19, when he finally found it possible to take pictures of Confederate dead behind Union lines, tells us much about the pace and intensity of the fighting during those two weeks. The blank gap in the photographic record of the war serves as a fearsome image of the new kind of warfare emerging in the eastern theater.

In light of this gap, it makes sense to try to represent the Wilderness with a series of pastoral images that point both reassuringly to the restorative powers of seasonal cycles and ironically to the incongruity of men killing each other in the woods of central Virginia as pink lady's slippers, which flourish in the wet, woodsy conditions inhospitable to combat, bloom around them.

But if the photographic record of the Wilderness is insufficient, the sketched and painted record is impressive. The drawings of Forbes and Waud have particular power, as we shall see later, but predictably their small black-and-white subtleties failed to hold my gaze as long as did Homer's dramatic painting, *A Skirmish in the Wilderness* (1864), which the editors of the *Picture History* reproduced so that it extends across all of one page and part of a second. Now part of the collection at the New Britain Museum of American Art in New Britain, Connecticut, this oil on canvas measures eighteen inches by twenty-six inches, its surface area about four times that of the front cover of the book in which I first saw it. I didn't know or care that the painting came out of a significant phase of Homer's development, the artist having shifted his focus from illustration to oil-painting, beginning with an oil called *The Yankee Sharp-shooter*, which had appeared as an illustration in the November 15, 1862, *Harper's Weekly*. I also didn't know that in *Skirmish in the Wilderness* Homer came as close as he ever did to painting an actual battle scene, preferring instead to paint individuals and actions on the margins of combat—a sharpshooter, a group of prisoners, soldiers being punished for intoxication, a soldier standing on earthworks inviting a shot from the enemy, a soldier meditating beside a grave. I couldn't have said what "genre" meant or what a landscape was.

But I knew that the *Picture History* had no other images like this one and that the war it depicted didn't look much like the war depicted elsewhere in the book. Where was the field in this battlefield? In the center of the painting half a dozen dark-uniformed soldiers cluster beside a large, leafless tree brightly lit on its right side by a shaft of sunlight. The brightest and biggest object in the painting, the tree dwarfs the men at its base, men who are facing toward the left margin as one fires toward an unseen enemy, one reloads, one looks on, one sits hatless against the tree, perhaps wounded, and one or two crouch in shadow. To the right of this group, a larger mass of soldiers follows an officer with sword drawn into the clearing, presumably to reinforce the smaller central group. The forms of the reinforcing soldiers are indistinct, but the barrels of the rifles on their shoulders bristle vertically above them. The officer has a red insignia on his hat. In the background to the right of the big tree an even more indistinct group of soldiers has just fired a volley toward the same unseen enemy beyond the left edge of the painting. The smoke from this volley forms a small white cloud immediately behind the heads of two of the members of the central cluster, the man reloading and the man looking on. In the center foreground an indistinct figure crawls on his hands and knees toward the viewer. To his left a few patches of orange-red color the ground and the tree at the right margin. Otherwise various shades of blue, green, and yellow fill the painting.

This much I could see, even as a six-year-old, and this much was enough to stir up a fascination with Homer's woods, so lovely, dark, and deep, with his play of light and shade around the central group, and with the unsettling combination of openness in the clearing and claustrophobic enclosure by the surrounding woods. The painting neither glorifies war nor renders it particularly horrible, since none of the soldiers seems to be dead, and we can't see the one or two wounded men clearly enough to know how badly they are bloodied. In fact, for a representation of such a bloody battle, *Skirmish in the Wilderness* is a curiously bloodless picture. Although it strikes no heroic poses that might appeal to the romantic imaginings of a child, it mutes and softens the hard edges of battle, making the whole affair feel rather small compared to the thick woods that seem to be the real subject of the painting.

But later, with adulthood, have come more questions about this painting, questions about its intentions and effects. For openers, how closely could Homer have observed this scene? The central group looks no more than fifty yards away, but even at twice that distance, a civilian would have no business being in the vicinity. If *Skirmish in the Wilderness* exemplifies realism, that realism is highly selective. Where, for example, is the smoke from the shots fired by the central cluster of men? And what about the large, brightly lit central tree, which Homer paints with realistic clarity while he renders much of the surrounding scene as an impressionist would? Is it dead, or has it, like the somewhat smaller tree to its left, somehow not leafed out by early May in central Virginia? In the second-growth woods of the Wilderness, such a large tree, perhaps a sycamore, would have been rare. Then there is the source of light for the painting. Is it coincidence that light comes from the same direction as the blue soldiers? If not, is Homer patriotically associating light with the Union, or is he commenting more subtly and skeptically on the nature of a war in which what one is fighting against often stays hidden and refuses to come to light? What about the role of red paint in this composition? Is Homer touching the woods up with a few autumnal tints that don't belong, or is he trying to represent one of the great horrors of the battle, the fires that engulfed so many wounded men? Is the red at the same time an oblique allusion to the thousands of pints of blood spilled by more than twenty thousand bodies in the Wilderness, and does the red insignia on the officer's cap refer to the First Division of the Second Corps, commanded in the Wilderness by Francis Channing Barlow, a distant relative of Homer's? Barlow appears in Homer's later painting *Prisoners from the Front* (1866), in which the red trefoil of this division is visible on both a white flag and a soldier's cap.

Finally, how should we read the title of the painting? On one level, it makes plenty of literal sense. In Civil War battles, standard practice called for a small group or line of so-called skirmishers to precede the advance of a larger body, such as a regiment or brigade, in order to probe an enemy's position. The small central cluster of men may have been just such a group, and Homer shows them at a moment when they have engaged unseen Confederates, stopped advancing, and are being joined by the unit they preceded. Alternately, they may not be skirmishers who have stopped advancing but soldiers on picket duty at an outpost now threatened by a Confederate advance. Homer's decision to focus on a small group of skirmishers, rather than on, say, hundreds of men in close combat (as he does in *The War for the Union, 1862—A Cavalry Charge,* a drawing published in the July 5, 1862, issue of *Harper's Weekly*), confirms his preference for representing the war from its margins. But on another level, the title seems strange, as a skirmish is a small battle and the one represented in the painting is about to get much bigger. Furthermore, beyond the local significance of this particular part of the action, the title takes on a grotesquely ironic charge, since what erupted in the Wilderness was anything but a skirmish. In this larger context, Homer's title has the same kind of gruesomely understated quality as the imaginary title *A Little Misunderstanding at Normandy* (1944).

Homer's painting is only one of hundreds of memorable images in the *Picture History of the Civil War,* and if the editors hadn't included it, I still would have had plenty of others to stare at and study. But I wonder what would have happened if I had not come across this particular book when I did. The year after the one in which the last veteran died and the year before the centennial of Fort Sumter and First Manassas–Bull Run, 1960 included the publication of two other important works on the war, Bruce Catton's *Grant Moves South,* which follows Grant from Illinois into Kentucky and Tennessee and through the Vicksburg campaign, and Allan Nevins's *The War for the Union: War Becomes Revolution, 1862–1863*. But despite the great achievement of both books, it would be a rare six-year-old who would date his or her interest in the Civil War from the reading of either one. If there had been no *Picture History,* when would I, who had been living in Wisconsin and would move to Delaware later in 1963, have come across the stories and images of the Civil War? I dimly remember an episode of the *Walt Disney Show* that dramatized the story of John Clem, the ten-year-old drummer boy of the Twelfth Michigan who earned the nickname "Johnny Shiloh," but Ken Burns's documentary wouldn't air for another quarter century, and when it finally did, I wonder how many six-year-olds helped make up the audience of forty million. I can't remember anything about the Civil War from either my eighth-grade study of American history or from the required course in American history I took in high school, and both were good courses taught by good teachers. As for reading Crane's *The Red Badge of Courage* in high school, I didn't, not because I was lazy but because it wasn't assigned.

Although it no longer includes *Skirmish in the Wilderness,* the *Picture History* is still available, having been revised in 1996 and beefed up with an accompanying CD-ROM. Perhaps somewhere a first or second grader is learning about the war from it. But if parents can't afford the high price tag, or a school system strapped for funds can't add the electronically enhanced text to its resources, perhaps there is another book that will hook the rising generation of readers as the *Picture History* hooked me and mine. Perhaps it will be the volume *What Your Fifth Grader Needs to Know,* edited by E. D. Hirsch, Jr., and published in the somewhat controversial Core Knowledge Series. Having decided that a child doesn't need to know much about the war until fifth grade, Hirsch and his associates foreshadow their narrative of the war beginning with the volume for second graders. In a paragraph entitled "A Dark Time," the second grader learns that after the Mexican war many people did not want slavery to spread to the new territories and other people wanted slavery to end everywhere. "This conflict led to a war," the book explains, and a second grader could be excused for thinking that "this conflict" refers to one between free-soilers and abolitionists, since the paragraph politely refrains from saying that some people did want slavery to spread into the new territories and definitely did not want it stopped everywhere. The paragraph then concludes with an ominous sentence that I, for one, find moving:

Many American lives were lost in that war, and you will
learn more about it when you study that dark time in a later
grade.

With the warning that the story of "the worst time in our history" lies
ahead, the child learns the definition of a civil war in third grade during the
study of ancient Rome ("a civil war is a war between different parts of one country") and then in fourth grade concludes a section on reform movements with
the sentence, "In the next book in this series, you will read about how our country was torn in half—the North against the South—in the bloodiest war in our
history, the Civil War." When the narrative of the war finally comes, it takes the
student through sections that include the Missouri Compromise, Harriet
Beecher Stowe's *Uncle Tom's Cabin* (1852), the Dred Scott decision, the Lincoln-Douglas debates, John Brown's raid at Harpers Ferry, the argument over
states' rights, Lincoln's election and Southern secession, Fort Sumter, Lee and
Grant, the Emancipation Proclamation, black soldiers, the Fifty-fourth Massachusetts, Gettysburg and Lincoln's address there, Sherman's March to the Sea,
the fall of Richmond, the surrender at Appomattox, and the assassination of
Lincoln. Along the way, the fifth grader looks at maps, drawings, paintings, and
photographs, including one of Grant taken at his Cold Harbor headquarters
about six weeks after the Wilderness. The student won't learn much about the
war in Virginia during 1864 ("In the spring of 1864, the Confederates continued
to hold back Union troops in Virginia"), and nothing about the Wilderness, but
in a mere twenty-four pages the people at the Core Knowledge Foundation have
done an excellent job of painting the war in primary colors. The fifth grader
who reads and absorbs all twenty-four pages will know much more about such
complex issues as the argument over states' rights or the enlistment of black
troops than I did at nine or ten years old.

But before children reach the fifth grade, they could well come across
another book, one that my own six-year-old boy brought home from his school
library. As we read it together, I could see the story and pictures of this book
digging themselves into his attention and his memory as those of the *Picture
History* had dug into mine. Patricia Polacco's *Pink and Say* (1994), a brightly
illustrated book with a front cover the exact size of that of the *Picture History*,
could be tough going for many young readers, although I have to say that by the
end of the book the tears were in my eyes, not in his, perhaps because the first
time I skipped the details about the death by hanging of Pinkus Aylee, the for-

mer slave boy, at Andersonville. It could also be tough going for many parents, especially those who identify themselves with the Lost Cause of the Confederacy, since Polacco tells the story of her own great-great-grandfather, Sheldon Russell Curtis, a fifteen-year-old boy in the Twenty-fourth Ohio, and the story contains no attractive portraits of Southerners. When that story opens, Sheldon, nicknamed Say, is lying wounded in a pasture in Georgia. A young soldier in the Forty-eighth Colored Infantry, Pinkus, nicknamed Pink, finds him and takes him to the house of his mother, Moe Moe Bay. For the young reader, Polacco's book offers not only the vivid illustrations but also a story of the friendship between the two boys, some wisdom from Moe Moe Bay about courage (like Henry Fleming, Say ran from battle), an introduction to the history of black troops and their motivations, and some no-nonsense instruction about memory and memorializing:

> This book serves as a written memory of Pinkus Aylee
> since there are no living descendants to do this for him.
>
> When you read this, before you put this book down, say
> his name out loud and vow to remember him always.

Just as certain aspects of Homer's *Skirmish in the Wilderness* didn't mean anything to me until much later, so certain aspects of Polacco's *Pink and Say* will only become apparent to my son years from now, if ever. At the moment he doesn't care that Pink and Say probably meet somewhere in Georgia during Sherman's Atlanta campaign, which opened the same day that fighting began in the Wilderness. He doesn't care that neither boy's regiment appears among the units listed in the tables Sherman includes in his *Memoirs* (1875) or that the story of Sheldon Russell Curtis contains notable variations on familiar themes in its representations of slavery and soldiering, since, for example, Pink can read but Say cannot, and it is the son who loses his mother to war rather than the other way around. He doesn't care that the parents of some of his classmates might find Polacco's retelling of her great-great-grandfather's story inflammatory or one-sided. For now he cares only that he's found a book that tells him he must remember something important about the Civil War, and for now that's enough.

THREE

Buff

SOME WORDS or phrases imply assumptions I happen to disagree with. In the context of the Civil War, "home front" is an example. To speak of the "home front" in connection with the Civil War is to use an anachronism, since the phrase came into our language during World War I, when a distinction between people who lived at home in peace and people who faced the "red animal" across an ocean actually meant something. But to Katherine Couse, cringing at Laurel Hill in May 1864, or to Jennie Wade, killed in her kitchen at Gettysburg, this distinction meant nothing. Well, of course, some might argue, but doesn't the distinction between war front and home front hold wherever civilians do not confront actual combat, as in most of the North?

I don't believe so. In fact, one of the ways to think about "civil war," a way that perhaps still acknowledges the long history of Southern discomfort with the term, is to think of it as war in which the boundaries between war front and home front are anything but stable and clear. True, more fighting happened in the South than in the North, much of it in Virginia alone, and so the name "War of Northern Aggression" has some appeal, especially if one ignores the firing on Fort Sumter. But the fact is that effects of warfare, whether actual fighting between armies, the threat of actual fighting (as in the minds of the citizens of Harrisburg or Philadelphia after Lee invaded Pennsylvania in 1863), or the violent and destructive consequences of actual fighting (the New York draft riots of July 1863 or the Confederate raid on St. Albans, Vermont, in October 1864, a raid that many would now consider terrorism), extended far beyond the battlefield. Furthermore, and more important, beyond the worrying and nursing and grieving and mourning and financing and supplying and laboring and cheering that have made up the work of noncombatants during the later wars abroad, civilians during the Civil War, both North and South, felt deeply uncertain about the future shape of what they called home, about exactly where its front would be. When the phrase "home front" was coined fifty years after Appomattox, it was coined to describe a realm in which people *don't* feel deeply uncertain about the future shape of home.

Some people might disagree about this particular phrase, and I can accept their disagreement with something like respectful detachment. But in the case of certain other words or phrases my respectful detachment collapses, since those words or phrases imply assumptions I cannot stand. In the context of the Persian Gulf War, "collateral damage," an Orwellian euphemism for civilians killed in the bombing of Baghdad, would be an example. In the context of the Civil War, one of the worst offenders is *buff*, when used as a noun to mean someone interested in the events, conditions, and legacies of the years 1861 to 1865. Of course, there is at least one big difference between "collateral damage" and "buff." Whereas "collateral damage" disguises the killing of innocent civilians in neutral, bureaucratic language, most people who use the term *buff* have no conscious intent to obscure or conceal. The term does, however, obscure and conceal, just as it illuminates and reveals, much that is important.

Different dictionaries emphasize different aspects of the word, but the ones I looked at all point to the association of *buff* with firefighting and firefighters. Significantly, the closest relevant definition in the second edition of *Webster's New International* (1960) does not imply any necessary connection with interest in the Civil War ("An enthusiast about going to fires"), but the *Third New International* (1986) includes the etymology of the word (from "the buff overcoats worn by volunteer firemen in New York City" about 1820) and makes the connection implicit ("FAN, ENTHUSIAST, DEVOTEE"). The second edition of the *Oxford English Dictionary* (1989) gives no examples that involve the Civil War, but both the first edition of the *American Heritage Dictionary* (1969) and the second edition of the *Random House Dictionary* (1987) do:

> a devotee or well-informed student of some activity or subject: *Civil War buffs avidly read the new biography of Grant.* (*American Heritage*)

> *Informal.* One who is enthusiastic and knowledgeable about a given subject: *a Civil War buff.* (*Random House*)

What's the matter with these definitions? Who could object to being called "well-informed," "enthusiastic," and "knowledgeable"? Although the *Oxford English Dictionary* gives examples of usages from 1931 to 1968 that include "police buff," "choo-choo buff," "hi-fi buff," "disarmament buff," "ballet buff," and "sports buff," it's pretty clear from the history of the *Webster's* definition, as well as from the examples given in the two other dictionaries, that, at least in the United States, the Civil War centennial has tinged the term *buff* with particular associations. Regardless of the examples in the *Oxford English Dictionary,* which is English, after all, my bet is that when asked to fill in the blank in the phrase "so-and-so is a _____ buff," most Americans would supply "Civil War." Or, to design the test differently, if asked to complete the sentence, "My friend who visits all the battlefields is a Civil War _____," more Americans would volunteer *buff* than *fan, devotee,* or *enthusiast.* Although the dictionaries show that there have been other kinds of buffs since 1900, the centennial made the phrase "Civil War buff" idiomatic and in doing so reflected the emergence of a new attitude toward the war.

What's wrong with the definitions above, or, more accurately, what is incomplete about them, immediately becomes apparent when we try to use *buff* as though it were merely a neutral synonym for a well-informed, enthusiastic, knowledgeable person. If, for example, one were to call a well-informed, enthusiastic, knowledgeable student of Christianity "a Jesus buff," that epithet would sound disrespectful and offensive to many ears. Or if we called a passionately committed specialist in the history of the Nazi concentration camps "a Holocaust buff," the tasteless trivializing behind the phrase would be palpable. We would never think of describing Abraham Lincoln as "a Union buff," Jefferson Davis as a "states' rights buff," or Frederick Douglass as "an abolition buff."

The ludicrousness of these examples shows the difference between what calling a person "a Civil War buff" denotes and what it connotes. What it denotes is someone well informed, enthusiastic, and knowledgeable, but what it connotes is that this well-informed, knowledgeable enthusiasm is not really serious but a little quirky and eccentric, a harmless private hobby on the order of collecting bottle caps or matchbooks from around the world. It also reveals a distance in time and mind from events and conditions, including some of the ghastliest that the nineteenth century produced. It shows that the renewed interest accompanying the Civil War centennial was wide but not necessarily deep. In fact, it may have been wide and continue to be widening precisely because the distances in time and mind guarantee that it cannot be deep, or at least not so deep that it could interfere with one's enjoyment of the domestic prosperity and relative peacefulness of the United States before and after Vietnam.

When Patricia Polacco closes *Pink and Say* by telling us to say the name of Pinkus Aylee out loud and to remember it always, is she telling us how to be good Civil War buffs? I don't think so. If we return to the precentennial definition in *Webster's,* "[a]n enthusiast about going to fires," the adoption of *buff* to describe one interested in the Civil War should make us uncomfortable. On the one hand, fires, especially large fires, are beautiful, sublime, and hypnotic, except perhaps for those who are phobic about fire. Quite understandably, some people might be enthusiastic about watching one. On the other hand, large fires necessarily involve the destruction of property or the environment and often involve injury or loss of life. How can one be enthusiastic about these things, unless one is some kind of ghoul or sadist? War has the same two-sidedness, a doubleness that Whitman captures perfectly in his *Memoranda.* In an entry for July 3, 1863, immediately preceding one about Gettysburg, he describes watching "long strings of cavalry" pass from north to south along Fourteenth Street in Washington: "How inspiriting always the cavalry regiments! . . . This noise and movement and the tramp of many horses' hoofs has a curious effect upon one." But this exhilarating spectacle soon gives way to another that moves from south to north, the geography of its movement replicating in miniature the constant flow of bodies back from the fighting:

> Then just as they had all pass'd, a string of ambulances
> commenced the other way, moving up Fourteenth street
> north, slowly wending along, bearing a large lot of
> wounded to the hospitals.

One can be a buff about the cavalry pageant but not about the ambulance convoy or about a boy hanged and thrown into a lime pit. When Polacco tells us to say the name Pinkus Aylee and remember it always, she charges us with a deep memorializing that is the very opposite of chasing after fire trucks for the thrill of watching buildings burn.

Here then is the problem with *buff.* Its employment after 1960 to describe interest in the Civil War confirms that the boundary between war and peace within the United States feels so secure that people who want to can cross that boundary for their own amusement. In places and times where the boundary between war and peace feels insecure, interest in war is not a form of amusement. There were no Civil War buffs in Atlanta in 1865, no World War II buffs in London in 1945, no Vietnam War buffs in Saigon in 1975. McPherson may be right when he claims that many people fascinated with the Civil War are preoccupied with the multiple meanings of freedom, but a country in which there are two million copies of *Killer Angels* in print, a country in which supposedly nobody reads anymore, is a country that feels stable enough to entertain itself, while commuting to work or lounging at the beach or before turning out the light at night, with a story of a battle that involved over fifty thousand killed, wounded, and missing people.

It is only in the safety of peace that people can have fun with war. When a man plasters his pickup truck with bumper stickers reading, "Happiness Is a Northbound Yankee," "I had rather be dead than a Yankee," "Keep the history, heritage and spirit of the south flying [with picture of the Confederate battle flag]," "Forget, Hell!," "Send more Yankees / They are delicious [with picture of mosquito]," "Lest we forget the Civil War; America's Holocaust," "American by birth / Southern by the grace of God," "Welcome to the South / Now go home," and "When I'm old / I'll move up North / & Drive like I'm dead!," he appears to be carrying out a kind of deep memorializing that keeps the war present in his mind and that of anyone who sees his truck. But in fact he's having it both ways, since it is only because the war is so long gone and absent from most people's awareness that he can afford to brandish these inflammatory slogans. He appears to urge remembrance, but he does so in terms that depend on forgetting. If the Yankees who have overrun his Southern home felt as ardently as he about keeping sectional tensions alive, he might think twice about the possible effects of those bumper stickers on his insurance premiums.

In all fairness, many of those whom other people label *buffs* are committed to deep memorializing rather than to amusing themselves. Describing three different audiences for Civil War history, McPherson's essay "What's the Matter with History?" distinguishes among professional historians, the general readers who bought six hundred thousand copies of his Pulitzer Prize–winning *Battle Cry of Freedom* (1988), and those he calls Civil War buffs, including under this heading the members of two hundred Civil War roundtables, forty thousand reenactors, and two hundred fifty thousand subscribers to four popular Civil War magazines. Although McPherson charges the last group with ignoring political and social issues in their preoccupation with military matters, it is not at all clear to me that many of his general readers aren't out for their own amusement or that many of his so-called buffs aren't doing what they do in deep remembrance of realities that are anything but amusing.

But it's hard to know for sure. In the same spirit that, according to Corwin Linson's memoir *My Stephen Crane* (1958), led Crane to "wonder that *some* of those fellows don't tell how they *felt* in those scraps!" I often wonder how each of the two million owners of *Killer Angels* feels about the book or how each of the professional historians feels about devoting a life to Civil War history or how each of the forty thousand reenactors feels about reenacting. I even wonder how a genuine buff, someone who looks to the Civil War for amusement, feels about that amusement. Is he or she really amused? How and by what?

As for me, though I confess there are many moments when I can manage to forget the war and think about something truly amusing, the war itself is not a source of amusement. I'm not enthusiastic about chasing firefighters, and the word *buff* does not describe me. For one thing, I don't feel as secure about the boundary between war and peace as I'd like to, for reasons I'm still trying to discover. In the meantime, what word does describe my condition and that of people like me, however many or few we are? I'm not sure, but I think it might be the word "sufferer," as in the phrase "allergy sufferer." I think I must be a Civil War sufferer. How else can I explain the itchy throat and watery eyes when I pass the Wilderness sign?

FOUR

Ancestors

ALTHOUGH I WOULDN'T call my interest in the Civil War a form of amusement, I don't deny that the war produced humor. I have on my shelf, for example, a book called *Wit and Wisdom of the Civil War*, edited by Nick Beilenson and published in 1987. It's a very short book, only sixty-four pages, and the section titled "Civil War Humor" is very short indeed, filling fourteen pages thanks only to some generous spacing. Within these fourteen pages, there are few examples of humor about the Civil War itself, as Beilenson's criterion for inclusion seems to be merely that a quip have originated around the time of the war. But there are some exceptions.

> Crops around Washington are looking well. Winter wheat, crocusses and indefinite postponements were never in a more thrifty condition.

> It is said, my boy, that the celebrated Confederacy will resent the Proclamation by raising the Black Flag. It is common belief, that if such be the case, it will be the duty of our generals to raise the blacks without flagging.

One doesn't have to be especially bad-humored to deny these witticisms a place among the world's greatest jokes. But then again it isn't fair to conclude from Beilenson's meager sampling that the war hasn't made anyone chuckle. Who can read Lincoln's exasperated messages to or comments about McClellan without at least an inward smile? And what about the perfectly controlled irony of his January 26, 1863, letter to Hooker? "What I now ask of you is military success, and I will risk the dictatorship." Who can read Shelby Foote on the subject of Grant's distinctive quirks, or listen to Ken Burns's narrator, David McCullough, telling the one about Grant knowing only two tunes—one "Yankee Doodle," the other not—without pleasure?

But we don't have to confine the hunt for Civil War humor to one-liners and anecdotes. James Thurber's little gem, "If Grant Had Been Drinking at Appomattox," which first appeared in the December 6, 1930, issue of the *New Yorker,* succeeds by turning the contrast between the elegantly restrained Lee and the more informal Grant into irreverent caricature. Thurber also treats the war humorously in his autobiography, *My Life and Hard Times* (1933), the first page of which introduces the figure of a senile grandfather whose recollections of the years 1861 to 1865 deflate any idealized image of the Civil War as a holy war: "(On these occasions he was usually gone six or eight days and returned growling and out of temper, with the news that the federal Union was run by a passel of blockheads and that the Army of the Potomac didn't have any more chance than a fiddler's bitch.)"

So far my examples of humor have reflected a Northern point of view or, in the case of Shelby Foote's stories about Grant, Northern subject matter. For obvious reasons the war doesn't receive as much treatment as a laughing matter in the South. A comment like that of Thurber's grandfather gets a laugh, in part, because it prophesies failure where there was eventually success. If we substitute "Confederacy" for "federal Union" and "Northern Virginia" for "the Potomac," we get a statement every bit as true as the original must have seemed in May 1863, after Chancellorsville, but not at all funny from the perspective of 1933. Meanwhile, whatever his other strengths, Jefferson Davis does not show in his writings anything like Lincoln's dry, wry sense of humor, and although it seems perfectly acceptable for Northerners and Southerners alike to tell jokes about Grant, few of either would feel as comfortable joking about the unassailable Lee. We can see the bumper stickers plastered on the Southern pickup truck as a form of humor, but if so, we also have to distinguish between the self-deprecating humor Northerners direct at themselves and the angry humor a Southerner directs at Northerners. The former is a luxury of winning, the latter a barely concealed continuation of hostilities.

But Civil War humor doesn't have to come from the North. Fred Chappell's short story "Ancestors" (1995) combines humor, a Southern point of view, and implicit commentary on the difference between interest in the Civil War as amusement and interest in the Civil War as costly memorializing. Set during the 150th anniversary of the war (2011–2015), "Ancestors" tells the story of a comfortably middle-class North Carolina couple motivated by "that most destructive of all human urges[,] the desire for self-improvement." This desire prods the couple to sign up for the Ancestor Program of the Living History Series, a program sponsored by the U.S. Archives and History Division of the Department of Reality. Having signed up for the program, Harry and Lydie Beacham receive visits from three genetically reconstructed "sims," or simulacra, the third of whom represents Chappell's clever send-up of Walt Whitman as Wade Wordmore.

First, however, the Beachams must survive lengthy visits from two of Harry's Confederate ancestors, Lieutenant Edward Aldershot and Private William Harper, both of the Army of Northern Virginia. In the course of these excruciating visits, we discover that "Harry's knowledge of history was by no means as profound as his enthusiasm for it." Set up by Chappell as an exemplary buff, Harry must endure first Aldershot's "vivid and particular" accounts of bloodshed, "accounts that made the *Iliad* seem vague and pallid," and then Harper's sanguine reenactment of his death at First Manassas–Bull Run. Exhausted and sickened by the ancestors' visits, Harry and Lydie realize that their naive curiosity about Civil War ancestors has forced upon them a bigger dose of reality than they bargained for. Midway through Private Harper's visit Lydie, sounding more like a weary Scarlett O'Hara than a twenty-first-century enthusiast, admits, "I'm tired of hearing about that ugly old war." As the Beachams hear and watch Aldershot tell about the war, Chappell dramatizes the price of memory for both descendant and ancestor, commenting that "remembering had taken too much out of him." At the end of the story, Lydie admits pathetically that their desire to know more about Harry's ancestors "wasn't such a good idea."

Good idea or not, the search for Civil War ancestors is big business, and advertising beckons the fresh-faced in language that the Department of Reality could hardly surpass. The front cover of Bertram Hawthorne Groene's *Tracing Your Civil War Ancestor* (1973) promises a "complete guide to tracking down your ancestors' Civil War adventures, North and South," while the back cover invites the buyer to "[s]olve the mystery of your family's role in America's greatest struggle." The back cover continues, "It is tantalizing to speculate about the role your ancestors may have played in the great national drama of the Civil War" and concludes that most of all Groene's guide "is of inestimable practical value to family historians, North and South, who are discovering the pleasure and satisfaction of compiling an accurate family history."

Adventures? Mystery? Tantalizing? Pleasure? Satisfaction? Where do I sign up? But it's too easy to make fun of fatuous advertising copy, especially when it comes nowhere near describing the profound and sometimes complex satisfactions that many people experience from genealogical investigation. Dabbling in Civil War history from the complacent safety of his well-furnished house, Harry Beacham would prefer that reality not interfere too much with his comfort. But the members of a black family who use the national archives to discover that their ancestors had any recorded role in the war at all stand to recover much that really is of inestimable value, much that doesn't necessarily fall under the heading of adventure or mystery or tantalizing pleasure.

In trying to satisfy my own curiosity about ancestors, I used neither Groene's book nor the national archives. Instead, I stuck to family records, letters, and documents, and I used the *OR,* historians' shorthand for the "official records" collected in the 128-volume *War of the Rebellion: A Compilation of the Official Records of the Union and Confederate Armies* (1880–1901). Unlike the Beachams' investigations, my researches into ancestry didn't lead to anyone's bleeding to death before me, but like them I did make some sobering and instructive discoveries.

The first ancestor I ever heard about was a great-great-grandfather on my mother's side, the grandfather of the man killed at Anzio in 1944. Named John James Toffey, this ancestor came from New Jersey and served with two different regiments, first in the eastern theater from August 25, 1862, until June 15, 1863, and then in the western theater until November 1863. In the east Toffey served with Company C, Twenty-first New Jersey, and saw action at both battles of Fredericksburg (December 1862 and May 1863) and at Franklin's Crossing, Virginia, June 5, 1863. At Second Fredericksburg, which Sedgwick's Sixth Corps was fighting while the rest of the Army of the Potomac fought a few miles west at Chancellorsville, Toffey's regiment belonged to Neill's Brigade, which also included the Seventh Maine, the regiment of Asa Candage, grandfather of the woman I know. In his study of Chancellorsville (1996), Stephen Sears quotes Toffey's description of the fighting on May 4, 1863.

> We fought there about an hour and a half, the balls flying
> thick as hailstones. I no more expected to get out of that
> place than I expected to fly.

As it turns out, if he hadn't gotten out of that place, somewhere between what is now Route 3 and the Rappahannock fords to the north, I wouldn't be writing these words. But he did get out, although slightly wounded in the ankle.

Later in 1863, Toffey became a first lieutenant in Company G, Thirty-third New Jersey, a part of the Eleventh Corps, the so-called German Corps routed by Jackson at Chancellorsville, hammered again at Gettysburg, transferred west to the Army of the Cumberland in September 1863, and finally absorbed by the reorganized Twentieth Corps, Army of Georgia, in April 1864 for Sherman's Atlanta campaign. But Toffey didn't march into Georgia under Sherman; he was wounded at Missionary Ridge, November 23, 1863: "gun shot through the right hip, shell through the left hip, and gun shot in the back," according to a document examined by my uncle, another John James Toffey, who provided me with many of these details.

Because Lieutenant Toffey had been entrusted with the command of two companies that had lost their captains and was leading these companies in an attack across open ground when he was hit, he later was awarded the Congressional Medal of Honor. After he recovered sufficiently from his wounds, he received a commission in the Veterans Reserve Corps in May 1864 and was assigned to non-combat duty around Washington, mostly at Lincoln Hospital. Did he happen to see Asa Candage, who was recovering at Lincoln from the wound he received in the Wilderness? Did he ever cross paths with Walt Whitman? His letters don't mention either of these men, but they do show that he was in Ford's Theater the night Lincoln was shot, searched twenty-three houses for the assassins, and witnessed both the trial and the hanging of the conspirators.

What a great ancestor. If I had discovered him by using Groene's book, I would have thought the money it cost me well spent and the advertising on the covers more than justified. In Toffey's story I had plenty of adventures to savor and more than my share of pride in the congressionally honored role he played in the great national drama. What's more, he recovered from his wounds and survived the war, so if I ever get a visit from his sim in the twenty-first century, I won't have to watch him bleed to death in my living room, as Harry and Lydie Beacham had to watch William Harper do. Of course, the woundings at Fredericksburg and Missionary Ridge could prove unpleasant to see reenacted, but Toffey had no limbs amputated, and the relatively happy ending of his story would go a long way toward easing both his discomfort and mine. Unlike the

Beachams, I wouldn't come away from his visit with the bone-tired feeling of having lost the war. If I had quit my genealogical research there, it would have given me nothing but pleasure and satisfaction.

But I didn't quit there. The next stop on my genealogical tour took me to my father's side and his mother's grandfather, Samuel Estabrook Paine. Born in 1825, Paine was a farmer from Bentonsport, Iowa, who volunteered in 1862 and became captain of Company I of the Nineteenth Iowa. Later that year he went down into Arkansas and was wounded at the battle of Prairie Grove on December 7, 1862. When I visited Prairie Grove several years ago, I purchased a small booklet containing an account of the battle written by Samuel Jones, a Confederate major general, and issued in 1885. Jones's description includes this reference to the Nineteenth Iowa: "The slaughter in this charge and countercharge was very great—the ground was thickly strewn with the killed and wounded, among the killed being Colonel McFarland commanding the Nineteenth Iowa." E. B. Long's *The Civil War Day by Day* (1971) describes Prairie Grove as "a confusing battle" involving about twenty thousand soldiers. During the fighting, "Confederates held their position but bitter winter weather forced them to withdraw during the night." Long gives the number of Federal wounded as 813, one of whom was my great-great-grandfather. His letters have come down to my father, and the one that describes what happened after his wounding, written January 25, 1863, from the hospital at Fayetteville, Arkansas, provides a memorable glimpse into the strange fraternity of enemies.

> you wish to know if I lost my sword. I did not loose it
> exactly but the Rebs took it off from me after I was
> wounded on the battle field, saying I would not need it any
> more, and not feeling much like disputing with them about
> it at the time, I did not object, or blame them, for I would
> have done the same to them, they was very kind to me. they
> came along as I lay on the ground + gave me water, which
> was worth a dozen swords to me at that time + said they
> would come + take care of me after the battle if our men
> did not + said I should not be harmed by them— give my
> love to all + kiss my darling children for me. Good Bye my
> dear wife. Your Husband + father.
>
> S. E. Paine

The spelling, punctuation, and capitalization are Paine's, but his narrative of simple humanity is for everyone who cannot imagine war apart from accounts of atrocities and war crimes, such as the one called "A Glimpse of War's Hell-Scenes" in Whitman's *Memoranda*.

> No sooner had our men surrender'd, the rebels instantly
> commenced robbing the train, and murdering their prison-
> ers, even the wounded. . . . The wounded had all been
> dragg'd (to give a better chance also for plunder,) out of
> their wagons; some had been effectually dispatch'd, and
> their bodies lying there lifeless and bloody. Others, not yet
> dead, but horribly mutilated, were moaning or groaning.
> Of our men who surrender'd, most had been thus maim'd
> or slaughtered.

Whitman's narrative of the incident at Upperville, Virginia, depends on infor-
mation he got from soldiers who were there, but the stern interpretation of the incident is wholly his own: "Multiply the above by scores, aye hundreds . . . and you have an inkling of this War." Whitman's prescription is strong medicine for anyone with idealized or sentimental notions of the Civil War, and those whose genealogical research led them to the Fort Pillow Massacre (April 1864) or to the prisons at Elmira or Andersonville would have a considerably darkened view of their ancestors' adventures.

But in this case my genealogical research led to something like a glimpse of war's heaven scenes, if there can be such a thing. For one thing, Paine was not taken prisoner, although he had fallen into the hands of his enemy. Presumably any Confederate soldiers who had the time to stop and talk with him also had the time to take him prisoner. But they didn't, perhaps because they felt they could not be bothered with nursing a wounded Federal soldier. As for the kind treatment of the wounded man, some might argue that this incident occurred early in the war and that atrocities became more common as the war got fiercer and uglier. For example, both the Fort Pillow Massacre and Whitman's incident at Upperville occurred in 1864, the same year that Grant made the exchange of prisoners much more difficult and Henry Wirz became commandant of Andersonville. But the old gentleman who narrates John Peale Bishop's story "The Cellar," included in *Many Thousands Gone* (1931), claims exactly the opposite.

That is why most of the atrocities—those that are actually
committed—occur in the first few months of a war. The
troops are still a conglomeration of badly scared individuals, wretched in their uniforms, frightened of their own
arms. A nothing will start their terror.

By the end of "The Cellar," Bishop's readers have reason to question the narrator's judgment, but the letter from my great-great-grandfather confirms the
old veteran's initial statement, "I have seen soldiers do the gentlest things."
What's confusing is that we also need to multiply Paine's incident by scores and
hundreds to get some inkling of the Civil War.

Not all the letters written by Captain Paine are comforting, however. Three
weeks after his wounding—apparently the wound involved a leg because he
refers to being on crutches—he writes about that most familiar of Civil War
scenes, amputation.

Harrison O. Harra has got to have his leg taken off, to day. I
am sorry for him. They are cutting off Legs + arms here
every day at the different hospitals. The Doctors are now
amputating some poor fellows leg now in sight of my window I can write no more now, as I must lay down.

In this brief account Paine's use of the present tense, intensified by the repeated
"now" in "now amputating some poor fellows leg now," has the same overwhelming quality that it does in Katherine Couse's letter, and whenever I read
this passage I can't help wondering if his abrupt discontinuation, "I can write
no more now, as I must lay down," signals his feeling suddenly overcome by
what he sees from his window. It sounds as if, although for the moment he still
has his leg, he realizes he cannot count on keeping it.

Like Lieutenant Toffey, Captain Paine survived both his wounds and the
war. In a long letter of April 25, 1865, written from New Orleans, he deplored
the assassination that Toffey sat or stood so close to. After the war he went
home to the farm his wife had been managing and resumed his life. He didn't
win or leave behind the Congressional Medal of Honor, but I do have an old
envelope that contains a dark blue square of wool cloth from his military dress
coat and sixteen brass buttons. Although Corwin Linson's memoir of Stephen

Crane makes fun of emotionless Civil War narratives that tell what happened "down to the last belt and button," I can't help pausing over one of these buttons. On its front it has the raised image of an eagle, olive branch in one set of talons, arrows in the other. Set into the eagle's body is a shield with the letter "I" in it. I don't know whether the "I" stands for Iowa or for Company I of the Nineteenth Iowa Volunteers, but I do know that it doesn't signify the first-person pronoun. On the back of the button is the name "W. G. Mintzer" and the abbreviation "Phild." One could choose to see an Iowa button manufactured in Philadelphia as an irony or as an economic literalization of an abstract Union, but either way the button is a complicated emblem.

My genealogical research, or at least its pleasures and satisfactions, became even more complicated when I came across a small diary kept by Samuel Paine's wife, Mercy, whom he had married on November 26, 1849, in Providence, Rhode Island. I say "more complicated" because she is my ancestor, too, but her life at home in Bentonsport, Iowa, didn't have much to do with adventures in a great national drama or with solving tantalizing mysteries. I had already gotten a glimpse of her life in a letter that Paine wrote her from Florida on November 15, 1864.

> If you think there is danger of Bush Whakers robing you
> had better put those bonds in some other place in the
> House, as they would be easily found in the desk. also your
> silver ware.

So much for the distinction between an embattled Southern war front and a tranquil Northern home front. But bushwhackers were not Mercy's only challenge, as her diary soon made clear.

Mercy's diary is bound in black leather and measures 3 by $4\frac{1}{2}$ by $\frac{1}{4}$ inches. Inside the front cover my great-grandfather, Albert Bigelow Paine, has written, "Mother's diary while Father was in the Civil War," and noted, "I was one year old." The first page reads simply, "M C Paine / Bentonsport / Iowa / 1862." The diary runs thirty-five pages, beginning with August 25—by a strange coincidence the same day John James Toffey joined the Twenty-first New Jersey—and ending abruptly in the middle of an entry for October 29, 1862. Mercy made entries nearly every day for about two weeks, then every few days for another month, and then left a three-week gap in October shortly before the diary ends.

> Does anybody wonder so many women die? Grief and con-
> stant anxiety kill nearly as many women as men die on the
> battlefield.

This is Mary Chesnut in an entry dated about two and a half months before Mercy Paine began her diary. In his index to *Mary Chesnut's Civil War* (1981), C. Vann Woodward lists the page number for this passage under "Women, Southern, effect of war on"; yet for all their differences in class, education, and geographical allegiance, Mary Chesnut's sentences could easily serve as the epigraph for Mercy's diary. From the first entry on, loneliness and worry beset her.

> I am feeling quite sad for my husband has been gone one
> week and I miss him very much there are many things
> besides the loss of his society I have many cares out of
> doors as well as in the house my [hired] boy is no account
> (August 25)

> I feel lonsome tonight for it is dark and rainy where is my
> dear husband tonight they have left Camp Lincoln for St
> Louis (September 4)

> I am lonsome tonight for I am all alone all in bed but me and
> sundy is a lonsome day (September 7)

> I feel disappointed tonight because I have not heard from
> my husband in one week today I am afraid he is not well this
> anxiety is enough to kill any one (September 25)

For all her loneliness Mercy is no whiner, and although she frankly confesses her sadness and fear, her diary demonstrates that she has a generous supply of strength, determination, and faith to help her along.

> I believe I will try to get along and do all myself (August 25)

> I love to work it keeps me from thinking of my lonlyness
> (August 28)

made soap, cut corn; but as my brother sais we must be
willing to make some sacrifice for our country mine is
greater than any one can tell but I give him willingly (September 9)

I am afraid he worries about us I hope he will not for we
can get along very well so long as I am well I will do the
best I can but he needs his thoughts for those new cares he
has taken upon himself I will not go to him with my trou-
bles and cares (September 15)

For me these passages recall the final chapter of Sherman's *Memoirs,* in
which the general defines what he calls "true courage" with respect to men in
battle.

All men naturally shrink from pain and danger, and only
incur their risk from some higher motive, or from habit; so
that I would define true courage to be a perfect sensibility
of the measure of danger, and a mental willingness to incur
it, rather than that insensibility to danger of which I have
heard far more than I have seen. . . . I would further illus-
trate my meaning by describing a man of true courage to be
one who possesses all his faculties and senses when serious
danger is actually present.

The utter sobriety of Sherman's notion of courage in battle raises some interesting questions in the case of Stephen Crane's Henry Fleming, for when Fleming actually does act courageously, he does so precisely because he has left
behind a "perfect sensibility of the measure of danger" and entered what Crane
calls "his wild battle madness," in which, if he still possesses his faculties and
senses, he possesses them as "a savage, religion-mad." Although Crane never
saw combat and Sherman did, Sherman's version of courage sounds suspi-
ciously rational in the smoky, shaking, deafening chaos of a Civil War battle.

But what, if anything, does Sherman's notion of courage for men in battle
have to do with women at home? However idealized and rational it may be,
does Sherman's description help us understand the courage of women like
Mercy Paine? I think it does. The dangers of loneliness and anxiety may take

longer to make themselves felt than the dangers of bullets and shells, but over a period of months or years their effects can be comparably devastating. In the case of Mary Chesnut, for example, anxiety often led to "nervous fainting fits" (entry for February 11, 1862), which she treated with opium or morphine.

> It excited me so—I quickly took opium, and that I kept up.
> It enables me to retain every particle of mind or sense or
> brains I ever have and so quiets my nerves that I can calmly
> reason and take rational views of things otherwise madden-
> ing. (March 18, 1861)

We can't know whether Sherman would have seen Chesnut's drug use as evidence that her courage had faltered. On the one hand, her own testimony claims that she took opium to preserve the faculties and senses that Sherman valued so highly. She does not say, for example, that she used drugs to produce hallucinations so as to avoid confronting danger. On the other hand, I can't help feeling that Sherman would have distinguished between Mary Chesnut's courage, which is often undeniable, and that of Mercy Paine, whose only remedies for quelling anxiety seem to have been day-to-day work and service.

Of all the entries in Mercy's diary, those that record news of battle dramatize her struggle with fear and anxiety most vividly.

> today a letter came from him he was well and had marched
> all the way they are almost to Springfield where one deadly
> battle has been fought I pray there may not be another
> such an one but we shall have what is for us (September
> 30)

To some, Mercy's acknowledgment that "we shall have what is for us" might sound like thoughtless rationalization, to others like stoic resignation. As she shows less than a week later, after receiving news of fighting at Corinth, Mississippi, religious faith did not necessarily make bad news easier to bear or neatly resolve her feelings of distress.

> God only knows he will order things as he sees fit we got a
> letter tonight a great battle has been fought at Corinth
> Charlie [her brother?] is wounded I don't know how bad

O how can we wait for more news from him the time will
seem long (October 6)

The June 14, 1862, issue of *Harper's Weekly* published an engraving of
Winslow Homer's *News from the War,* which consists of a montage of seven different scenes. The largest of these, subtitled "Wounded," appears in the center
of the upper half of the montage. In it a dark-haired woman sits alone in a room
at a small table over which she slumps, her head cushioned by her right hand
and wrist. In her left hand she holds against the folds of her hooped skirt the
open letter that gives her the news she has been dreading. The understated simplicity of the picture is startling. Homer has hidden the solitary woman's face
from us, so we cannot measure the effects of grief in her expression. We cannot
hear her weep or see her frame shaking. Because she is alone, her reaction has
no theatrical quality intended for others. Instead, Homer shows us that the
weight of the news is sufficient to press the woman's head against the table. In
her complete stillness, she shows few signs of life and suggests that the caption
"Wounded" refers as much to her as to the man she has read about.

A three-week gap in the diary follows the news of Charlie's wounding at
Corinth. When Mercy resumes, it is obvious that something significant has
happened to her. In an entry written two days before the diary ends and about
six weeks before her husband is wounded at Prairie Grove, she moves from
news of battle to a vision of the kinship among all women, North and South,
who have to keep working at home while they wait for information about their
men.

there has been a fight in Arkansas but I don't think our
folks were in it but while I feel thankful for it I think there
is many sad hearts for it is some ones friend when I think
of the Corinth fight and there was two thousand killed and
wounded I shudder (October 27)

Although Mercy's own anxieties momentarily subside with the thought that no
one she knows was in the fight, her gratitude is mixed with a keen awareness of
others' losses. To borrow Sherman's phrase, her "mental willingness to incur"
pains that are not immediately hers, pains that she can imagine now that she has
suffered them herself, shows undeniable courage.

It's hard to think of shuddering with anxiety for three years as constituting

Winslow Homer, "Wounded" from *News from the War. Harper's Weekly,* June 14, 1862.
Courtesy of Special Collections, Alderman Library, University of Virginia.

an adventurous role in the great national drama, and discovering evidence of
that shuddering in my great-great-grandmother's diary hasn't solved any mysteries for me or given me any particular pleasure or satisfaction. But in getting
to know this ancestor better, I have found someone whose experiences of the
war come closer to my own than do those of the two men who fought in it.
Although she lived through the years 1861 to 1865 and I didn't, Mercy's knowledge of the war came from letters, from newspapers that often reported half-
truths, from silences, and from her own imaginings. When John Toffey writes
of getting shot through both hips or Samuel Paine of watching an amputation
through his window, he might as well be writing about the surface of the moon,
as far as my ability to understand him goes. But when Mercy thinks about the

casualties at Corinth and shudders, she does the same thing that I do when I pass the Wilderness sign. We in the present have a distant, oblique relation to the Civil War that is analogous to the relation that many of the women of the past had to the fighting. Like them, we live amidst absences and sift through the aftermath.

If my genealogical research had stopped there, I could have retired with my Northern credentials well established and unchallenged. Whatever benefits one can derive from pure partisanship might have been mine. I could claim a point of view and produce a pedigree to prove it. And in fact I didn't go looking for any more ancestors. The next one, if he is one, came to me.

Before he arrived, I had begun to wonder about ancestors who might have the same last name I do. Where were they? I had found my mother's paternal great-grandfather and my father's maternal great-grandparents, a Toffey and two Paines, but where were the Cushmans? Although I have a copy of the Cushman genealogy, which begins with Robert Cushman, a Puritan, in 1617, it doesn't help much because it only comes down to 1855, the year Whitman brought out the first edition of *Leaves of Grass*. Still, by the time it ends, the genealogy has reached the tenth generation and inventoried over three thousand Cushmans. Somebody had to have fought in the war.

Although I wondered about this blank, I didn't do much to try to fill it in. Instead, I kept on reading books about the war until I found myself going through Thomas Wentworth Higginson's *Army Life in a Black Regiment* (1869). Previously, I'm afraid I had thought of Higginson primarily as the poor dolt who didn't have the poetic acumen to recognize the genius of Emily Dickinson when she sent him a batch of her poems in 1862. Now, as I read through *Army Life*, I realized that Higginson had a lot more on his mind in 1862 than playing epistolary hide-and-seek with the dissembling Emily. In that year Higginson assumed command as colonel of the First South Carolina Volunteers, afterwards the Thirty-third United States Colored Troops, which he proudly describes as "the first slave regiment mustered into the service of the United States during the late civil war." (Higginson bases his description on the claim that older Louisiana regiments raised by Butler in New Orleans consisted mostly of freemen and that the First Kansas, which was the first black regiment to be engaged in combat, had a later muster date than the First South Carolina.) Higginson's account of the regiment contains much that's important—for example, the makers of the film *Glory* (1989) give Robert Gould Shaw of the

Fifty-fourth Massachusetts lines transposed from *Army Life*—but the passage that most startled me appears in the penultimate chapter, "The Negro as a Soldier."

> A few men, I remember, who belonged to the ancient order
> of hypocrites, but not many. Old Jim Cushman was our
> favorite representative scamp. He used to vex his righteous
> soul over the admission of the unregenerate to prayer-meet-
> ings, and went off once shaking his head and muttering,
> "Too much goat shout wid de sheep." But he who objected
> to this profane admixture used to get our mess-funds far
> more hopelessly mixed with his own, when he went out to
> buy chickens. And I remember that, on being asked by our
> Major, in that semi-Ethiopian dialect into which we some-
> times slid, "How much wife you got, Jim?" the veteran
> replied with a sort of penitence for lost opportunities,
> "On'y but four, Sah!"

Although most readers of this passage will probably focus on the sketch of Jim and the mimicry of his speech, what stopped me was Jim's last name. Where did he get it? As the index of the genealogy shows clearly, by far the majority of Cushmans came from the northeast, most of them from Massachusetts and Maine. How did South Carolina get into the picture?

I found the answer in the sixth generation. My great-great-great-great-great-grandfather, Nathaniel Cushman, had nine children by his first wife, Sarah, and five more by his second wife, Temperance. The names of the first nine were Isaac, Sarah, Nathaniel, Consider, Simeon, William, Ambrose, Polycarpus, and Artemas; those of the next five Temperance, Rebecca, Abigail, Mercy, and Joab, who lived in Connecticut and is my great-great-great-great-grandfather. But under the name of Simeon, Joab's older half-brother, the genealogy notes laconically:

> Settled in Barnwell District, S. C., near the town of Aiken;
> m. there and had chil. Was a slaveholder.

Was a slaveholder? My ancestor? Well, your quadruple-great-grandfather's older half-brother is a pretty distant relation, isn't it? But the rationalization didn't work, and I felt something pecking at my impeccable Yankee credentials. Simeon had children in South Carolina, and his children had children in South Carolina. Did Jim belong to one of them? He must have.

Then again, perhaps he more than belonged. In a famous passage, which appears on the same page as the earlier one about opium, Mary Chesnut hands down a scorching indictment of slavery as a *"monstrous* system" that promotes miscegenation.

> —and every lady tells you who is the father of all the
> mulatto children in everybody's household, but those in
> her own she seems to think drop from the clouds, or pre-
> tends so to think.

Throughout *Army Life in a Black Regiment,* Higginson takes particular pride in asserting that because the First South Carolina "had not one mulatto in ten," his soldiers had dark skin. But even by his own reckoning, the regiment had somewhat fewer than eighty exceptions. Was Jim Cushman one of them? Did he and I both trace our ancestry to Nathaniel in the fifth generation of Cushmans descended from Robert the Puritan? Was Higginson's hypocritical scamp some number cousin several times removed and my ancestor?

Well, at least he fought for the North, my Yankee partisanship suggested lamely. But it was too late for that kind of reasoning now. Like Chappell's characters Harry and Lydie Beacham, I had wanted to learn something about the war from genealogical research, and suddenly I was learning plenty. With all those Cushmans in South Carolina, I must have Confederate ancestors, too. But if so, apparently they weren't South Carolinians. A. S. Salley, Jr., Secretary of the Historical Commission of South Carolina, compiled a three-volume work entitled *South Carolina Troops in Confederate Service* (1913–1930), and it doesn't include a single Cushman. Were there no men eligible for service? If there were, did they benefit from the Twenty Slave Law that entitled owners of twenty or more slaves (later fifteen) to stay home and manage them?

If I ever had a chance for the pleasure and satisfaction of compiling an accurate family history, that chance was fading fast. For every discovery I made, more questions, some of them now probably unanswerable, opened up. I needed order restored to my ramifying chaos. I needed exactly what Stephen Crane recoiled from, the dry, dusty, emotionless records that could tell me who did what where and when. I needed all 128 volumes of *The War of the Rebellion,* the official government records, the *OR.*

Among Civil War scholars it seems to be a point of professional honor to cite the *OR* whenever possible, much as a biblical scholar writing in English might cite an original bit of Hebrew or Greek to authenticate an argument or the research that buttressed it. And why not? The one hundred thirty-eight thousand pages of the *OR* include all the official documents—orders, letters, reports, memoranda, tables—that the Federal government started collecting in 1864, beginning with Union documents and adding Confederate ones after the war. Anyone who needs a visible, tangible image of the vastness of the Civil War, an image that no single book or film or battlefield or cemetery can give, has only to visit a large library that has the *OR* on its shelves and stand before them. When Lincoln closed his First Inaugural Address by invoking the "mystic chords of memory," a phrase that is itself so memorable partly because of the repetition and patterning of sounds within it, he wasn't thinking of anything as mundane as this monument of, and to, military bureaucracy; yet, well into the second century after the war, the writing on the white or gray or yellow pages of the *OR* provides us with some of the strongest chords of memory we still have, mystic or not.

But the *OR* or the *ORN,* the thirty-one-volume set for the Navy, isn't for everyone. If it were, scholars wouldn't consider it a mark of professional authenticity to cite it. For one thing, not everyone happens to have a large research library close at hand, and those who do may find that their libraries have the *OR* only on microfilm or in special collections from which one can request a mere volume or two at a time. For another, people who have come to require user-friendliness from their technology, electronic or otherwise, are quite likely to find the *OR* uncongenial and unaccommodating. Since it was printed in four parts or series, trying to proceed chronologically through the volumes will get one nowhere. Material on the Battle of the Wilderness, for example, appears in volumes 36, 40, and 51 of Series I and in volume 3 of Series IV. The first stop for anyone but a casual browser has to be the index volume. And finally, the apparently impersonal tone of most of the writing may not immediately satisfy people who prefer the more intimate letters and narratives of Katherine Couse, Mary Chesnut, or Samuel and Mercy Paine. I say "apparently impersonal" because after reading several reports, one can begin to recognize the individual nuances of tone and hear the significant differences between, say, Lee's consistently self-effacing use of the passive voice in his reports and Custer's consistently self-promoting use of the first-person pronoun in his. One can also learn to hear in a tersely understated phrase or formulation both loud enthusiasm, as when Longstreet describes a particular charge in the Wilderness as "executed with rare zeal and intelligence," or deafening censure, as when Meade comments witheringly on the role of the Ninth Corps in the Wilderness, "Burnside was unable to produce any impression."

But the *OR* is more than an image of enormousness; it is also an image of enormity. Every page in this hundred thirty-eight thousand-page paper trail leads to or from instances of men trying to kill each other, and the huge number of pages is not only an image but also the direct result of their successes and failures as killers, as I soon discovered. When I consulted the index volume, I found twelve Cushmans. Of these, two were civilians, one a clerk for the New York State Assembly and one a farmer on San Juan Island off the Oregon coast. Of the remaining ten, three were Confederates and seven Federals. Of the three Confederates, one was a captain in the First Tennessee Partisan Rangers, one a captain in the Thirtieth Louisiana, and one a musician in Company A, Second Florida. The musician, named only as H. C. Cushman, appears on a list of officers and men recommended by their regimental commanders after the Battle of Fair Oaks or Seven Pines, Virginia (May 31–June 1, 1862), for the "badge of honor to be awarded under general orders." The seven Federals belonged to the Third Iowa, Thirty-seventh Massachusetts, Ninety-fourth Ohio, Fourth Vermont, First Vermont Cavalry, Sixth Indiana, and the Fifty-third Illinois. Of these seven, the three from the east served in units that fought with the Army of the Potomac in the Wilderness. Of the ten soldiers, two were wounded—one at Chickamauga, one at Sayler's Creek—and two were killed.

The first, Oliver T. Cushman of the First Vermont Cavalry, is mentioned by his colonel in a report written at Culpeper Court House, Virginia, and dated August 3, 1862, six days before the Battle of Cedar Mountain. In *The Civil War Day by Day*, E. B. Long notes that on Saturday, August 2, "Elements of the Army of Virginia under John Pope advanced on Orange Court House and skirmished with Confederates." At that time a lieutenant in Company E, Oliver Cushman appears on a list of officers singled out after the skirmishing "on account of their gallant conduct, bravery, and exercise of sound judgment on this occasion." Not quite two years later, having survived the Wilderness, in which elements of the First Vermont Cavalry served as the advance skirmishers who on May 5 encountered the first Confederate horseman west of Craig's

Meeting House on the Catharpin Road, Oliver, now a captain, appears in a brief note written by Brigadier General J. H. Wilson on June 3, 1864, from Salem Chapel, or Church, west of Fredericksburg on the road to Chancellorsville.

> We have driven the enemy from the rifle-pits in this vicin-
> ity, having lost several of our most valuable officers—Lieu-
> tenant-Colonel Preston and Captain Cushman, [First] Ver-
> mont Cavalry, killed; Colonel Benjamin, Eighth New York,
> severely wounded.

The *OR* mentions the second ancestor killed, Albert W. Cushman, more often than it does any of the other Cushmans. Although one document refers to him as a private, the rest call him a captain, and he is the one who served with the First Tennessee Partisan Rangers. Using about ten pages scattered unchronologically throughout the *OR,* I managed to piece together the outlines of Albert Cushman's story, most of which has to do with prisoners and prisoner exchange. Cushman first appears in a letter dated January 5, 1863, written by the colonel of his regiment, R. V. Richardson, to the commander of the Federal post at Bolivar, Tennessee. In his letter Colonel Richardson proposes terms for an exchange of prisoners, offering to swap a surgeon and a second lieutenant captured from the Eightieth Ohio for his own surgeon and forage master. Anyone who thinks that official records have no emotion in them should listen closely to the tones behind Richardson's horse-trading language.

> In this exchange I give you the advantages in giving officers
> of superior rank for others of inferior rank, and in the
> instance of the forage master a commissioned officer for a
> private detailed to act as forage master, but I can afford to
> be generous to an enemy who violates the usages of civi-
> lized war and a solemn compact between belligerents.

Before reading this letter, I had thought of prisoner exchange as a mechanical, formulaic procedure: so many enlisted men for a sergeant, so many more for a lieutenant, and so on. But in Richardson's letter we hear the same kind of bargaining that goes on between boys trading baseball cards or between a car sales-man and a prospective buyer. The letter would be almost funny if it weren't about human beings. At any rate, in his negotiations Colonel Richardson names

Captain A. W. Cushman and several privates as "bearers of flag of truce and this dispatch."

Cushman's role as go-between for prisoners oddly foreshadows his own fate. In a report describing a skirmish near Covington, Tennessee, on March 8, 1863, Edward Prince, colonel of the Seventh Illinois Cavalry, details a clash between eight of his own men and twenty-six Confederates under the command of Captain Cushman: "The gallant little squad charged the rebels, severely wounding the captain in the arm." Presumably the severely wounded captain is Cushman, who the next day appears in the report of Colonel Benjamin H. Grierson, commander of the First Cavalry Brigade, Sixteenth Army Corps.

> We came upon him [the enemy] on Big Creek, 3 miles
> southeast of Covington, attacked and completely routed
> him, killing 22, wounding and capturing over 70, among
> whom were Captains Cobb and Cushman.

After appearances in Union regimental and brigade reports, Albert Cushman, now a prisoner, continues his climb up the chain of military command and appears next in the May 8, 1863, report of Brigadier General Alexander, commander of the Sixth Division, Sixteenth Army Corps.

> Thus another guerrilla company is destroyed, and I have
> now 4 noted guerrilla leaders here, Scales, Cotter, Cush-
> man, and Parks, all to be tried as highway robbers. Tomor-
> row our artist will combine the four in a picture.

Having played a role in securing the exchange of other prisoners, Cushman, now known to me as a noted guerrilla leader—too bad the *OR* doesn't include the artist's picture of him— becomes the subject of some hard bargaining by Brigadier General James R. Chalmers, who wrote on October 12, 1863, from his headquarters near Byhalia, Mississippi, to the commander of United States forces in Memphis.

> SIR: I am informed that Capt. A. W. Cushman, of Colonel
> Richardson's regiment Partisan Rangers, who was captured

by the U.S. Forces some time since has been confined in
prison, subjected to trial for a criminal offense, and treated
in other respects in a manner not consistent with the
usages of war. In the attack upon Colliersville on yesterday
I captured, among other prisoners, a captain and a lieutenant of the U.S. Forces, whom I shall hold as hostages for
Captain Cushman. They will be treated in the same manner, so far as may be possible, as he is treated, until I am
notified that he has been placed upon the footing of other
prisoners of war and placed upon the list for exchange.
When this is done I shall take pleasure in forwarding these
officers for exchange.

> I am, sir, very respectfully,
> your obedient servant,

The *OR* doesn't say whether or not this hard-nosed bargaining eased Cushman's lot, but it does show, in a letter written by the Confederate agent of
exchange in Richmond on January 18, 1865, that he spent time at the peniten-
tiary in Alton, Illinois. This letter, the one document that refers to Albert W.
Cushman as a private, is especially interesting because it reflects the continuation of prisoner exchanges nearly a year after Grant assumed overall command
in 1864, when such exchanges become much less common.

Albert Cushman was released from Alton or wherever he was being held as
of January 1865, but the next time he appears in the *OR*, his ties with the Confederacy sound quite shaky. In Special Order No. 22, dated at his headquarters
on March 22, 1865, Brigadier General William Hicks Jackson, who had
assumed command of all cavalry in Tennessee in February, charges Colonel
John F. Newsom of the Nineteenth Tennessee Cavalry with collecting "all men
absent from this command" and keeping "them in camp and under strict rule
and discipline." In these orders Jackson authorizes Newsom to "use the most
summary means and measures to break up all bands of robbers and guerrillas,
hanging the leaders of all such wherever found to have depredated upon our
people." Jackson then turns to specific instructions about specific people.

He [Newsom] will give notice to Colonel Swingley and
Captains Lucas and Cushman to return at once to this

command. On their failure to come out voluntarily he will
kill the latter, place the first two in irons, and forward them
to these headquarters and order all officers out.

Why did Albert Cushman deserve to be singled out for death? Did he
depredate more outrageously than his fellow guerrillas? Had he done something else to anger Jackson and, if so, did he do it before he was captured or
after he was released? The *OR* gives no answers and mentions Captain Albert
W. Cushman only one more time. On April 25, 1865—the day before Johnston
surrendered to Sherman and John Wilkes Booth was shot at Richard Garrett's
burning barn—Colonel Newsom reported to General Jackson the results of his
orders.

Captain Cushman has been killed. Swingler [*sic*] has disap-
peared and left no trail or token of his whereabouts, and
Captain Lucas escaped me. He ran when I tried to arrest. I
fired on him, but without any effect.

The passive voice conceals who killed Cushman, but the rest of this passage
strongly suggests that it was cavalrymen under Newsom's command, or other
Confederates.

Ten ancestors in the *OR*. Two killed. Twenty percent, which corresponds
roughly to the average of the war as a whole, if we take three million as an estimate for the total number of soldiers and six hundred thousand for the number
of dead. But since just under two-thirds of the dead died from disease, 20 percent killed in combat would be about three times the statistical average for the
war. Meanwhile, what about the fact that one of my dead fought for the North,
one for the South, and both were killed by Confederates? Does that finding
confirm any larger average or tendency or law? I can't think of any, unless it's
the law that reads: The more you learn, the less you know.

And there is still plenty to learn. Browsing in the library after my marathon
with the *OR*, I happened on the multivolume *Roster of Confederate Soldiers
1861–1865*, edited by Janet B. Hewett and published in 1996. Pulling down volume IV, I flipped to "Cushman" and found fifty-seven more names, at least ten
of which are probably duplicates. The remaining forty-five or so come from all
of the states of the Confederacy except North Carolina and about half of them

come from South Carolina alone. So my great-great-great-great-grandfather's half-brother's eighteenth-century migration from New England to South Carolina produced soldiers after all. Upon returning to the records compiled for the Historical Commission of South Carolina by A. S. Salley, Jr., I found that they cover only the first five South Carolina regiments, and no Cushman fought with them. Among my newly discovered Confederate ancestors I found infantrymen, cavalrymen, and artillerymen, as well as musicians, chaplains, a hospital steward, and someone from the signals corps. If the statistical average holds, eight or nine or ten of these men must have died in the war, from either combat or disease.

But which ones? And how? And if my New England origins produced so many Confederate ancestors, how many ancestors do I have on the Union army rolls and rosters? And what's 20 percent of that number? But enough. If learning more means knowing less, I'm not sure I can afford it right now. Having learned that two of my Confederate ancestors belonged to units that fought in the Battle of the Wilderness, the Sixth South Carolina and the Palmetto Sharpshooters, I know even less about what to think when I pass the green sign for the Wilderness, where Cushmans fought on opposite sides. In Fred Chappell's story "Ancestors," after the visit from Harry's first ancestor, the Beachams feel a bone-tiredness that they compare to the feeling of having lost the war. After my genealogical investigations I feel as though I've lost something, too. Simplicity.

FIVE

Reenactment

Y OU'RE INTERESTED in the Civil War. Would you please explain to me
what those people who reenact battles are all about? I get asked this
question a lot. Although I've never joined a reenacting unit, bought all
the authentic gear, and spent weekends driving long distances to help stage
famous battles, I have attended three or four nearby reenactments as a spectator, and I know both men and women who have committed themselves to Civil
War reenactment, some casually, some with an intense and all-consuming ded-
ication. No doubt, many reenactors will find my observations about their activities incomplete or unsatisfactory, but I hope they will at least find them sympathetic, since the observations come from someone who occupies the middle
ground between bemused skeptics and fanatical enthusiasts. Neither an academic historian nor an ardent reenactor, I have no particular stake in the mutual
suspicion and resentment that arise on occasion between professionals and
amateurs, although I think that suspicion and resentment are unfortunate and
probably unnecessary. After all, writing a narrative account of battle constitutes
a kind of reenactment. In fact, surrounded by traces and images of the Civil
War, anyone who thinks for any length of time about those traces and images
becomes a reenactor, too.

Although Civil War reenactment began to receive wider attention during
the 1980s, thanks to the 125th anniversary reenactments that began with First
Manassas–Bull Run in 1986 and to the use of large numbers of reenactors in
films, reenactment is neither new nor exclusively American. As others have
observed, reenacting is a form of theater, and the origins of reenacting coincide
with the origins of drama. In the western European tradition, a search for the

origins of drama leads eventually to Athens in the sixth century B.C. and the beginnings of tragedy. Various people have speculated about the prehistoric origins of tragedy, some associating it with ritual violence or sacrifice that symbolizes regeneration, but the truth is that we really don't know how tragedy began.

If we can't be certain about the connection between drama and religious ritual in ancient Greece, we can at least be certain of that connection in medieval Europe. The liturgy of the medieval church consists of reenactments of sacrifice, both daily in the Eucharist and annually in the observances of Palm Sunday, Good Friday, and Easter. In particular, historians of medieval drama usually point to the performance of the *Quem quaeritis* trope during services on Easter morning. A trope was a brief elaboration, a sort of skit, inserted into the service to help explain its meaning to people who could not read the Bible in Latin for themselves. The *Quem quaeritis* trope, records of which go back as far as the ninth century, called for four people to play parts, one as the angel at the sepulchre and the others as the three Marys. In English the *Quem quaeritis* (Latin for "Whom do you seek") goes this way:

Angel: Whom do you seek in the sepulchre, O Christians?
Marys: Jesus of Nazareth the Crucified, O Heavenly one.
Angel: He is not here; He is resurrected, as He foretold.

In this medieval context, reenactment served as both a ritual observance or commemoration, performed in the spirit of Jesus' command "Do this in remembrance of me," and a demonstration or teaching in which what is written down gets acted out for the benefit of people who don't read.

Connecting Civil War reenacting with religious ritual may make many defenders of the separation of church and state more than a little nervous, although with the widespread Christian revival in the Army of Northern Virginia during the winter before the Battle of the Wilderness, the connection may be more appropriate than many would like to admit. But even the most staunchly secular person cannot object to the simple observation that religious reenactments, like Civil War reenactments, serve two main functions, the first having to do with remembering and honoring, the second with teaching and demonstrating.

But there is a third function, too, one that going to church serves, and has always served, for those not particularly interested either in remembering or in being taught. Alexander Pope chided those who "to Church repair / Not for the doctrine, but the music there," and although many might respond quite sincerely that hearing religious music plays a crucial part in their worship, their legitimate response does not change the fact that for others churchgoing is primarily a form of entertainment. Likewise, in addition to their commemorative and instructional functions, battle reenactments provide many with sheer entertainment. In his social history of London (1984), for example, we learn from Roy Porter that Philip Astley, who was honorably discharged from the cavalry in 1768, "set up an Amphitheatre near Westminster Bridge, where a troupe of horses performed amazing feats, and dramatic reenactments were staged of news events like famous battles." As a veteran himself, Astley probably had at least some commemorative and instructional impulses, but it would be naive to think that his performing horses, or the reenactments they accompanied, had no importance as commercial entertainment. Then again, it isn't only battle reenactments that spectators have sought for entertainment. As many accounts of First Manassas–Bull Run make clear, civilian spectators have also sought out the original battles themselves, and not for commemorative or instructional purposes. Knowingly or not, people who go to reenactments of battles perform the roles of the civilian spectators who drove down from Washington to witness the fighting in July 1861.

Commemoration, instruction, entertainment. Under these three headings fall most of the reasons reenactors give for reenacting. Of course, there are probably as many individual reasons for reenacting Civil War battles as there were reasons to fight the originals. For every soldier who might have responded to the question, "Why are you fighting?" with the answer, "I'm fighting for states' rights" or "to preserve the Union" or "to abolish slavery," another soldier could have answered, "Because home is boring" or "Because I'm getting paid" or "Because I was drafted" or "Because all my friends are fighting" or "Because someone who has influence over me made me feel that I should." Similarly, some among the forty thousand reenactors must do what they do simply because it's what their friends do or because it's an interesting diversion from their jobs or because they are veterans and reenacting feels familiar. The two possible pronunciations of "recreation" suggest a connection between reenactment and fun that many would acknowledge.

But at least in their public statements, reenactors and their organizations tend to put commemoration first. On the Internet the Civil War Reenactors home page uses as its epigraph a sentence from the Gettysburg Address: "The world will little note, nor long remember what we say here, but it can never forget what they did here." The following text welcomes us to the Civil War Reenactors home page and explains, "This page is dedicated to the brave souls, North and South, who fought and died in the war between the states." Meanwhile, the home page of the National Civil War Association, which is based in northern California and shows that Civil War reenactment is hardly confined to the southeastern United States, turns to commemoration in the second paragraph.

> Members of the National Civil War Association (NCWA)
> seek to preserve the memory of the ideals of this period,
> the way of life for both soldier and civilian, and the lessons
> learned, through "living history," a re-creation of life in the
> War Years (1861–1865).

These two statements of purpose reflect two different versions of commemoration. Whereas the Civil War Reenactors home page focuses on remembering the dead, the National Civil War Association focuses on remembering ideals and lessons learned. The difference here reminds us how complicated memory, or the motivation to remember, is. Focusing on the dead makes the war personal and represents it as the sum of individual actions and sufferings whose larger implications or effects may not figure significantly in what is remembered. Focusing on ideals and lessons makes the war impersonal and abstracts from individual actions and sufferings larger implications and effects. These two kinds of commemoration, personal and impersonal, do not work altogether independently of one another, but they do reflect different attitudes toward the past. Personal commemoration involves remembering what, or who, has been lost; it may or may not involve some kind of consolation. Impersonal commemoration involves trying to turn loss into gain; it necessarily involves consolation.

In the Federal army, for which we have more statistics, fewer than one-third of the dead died in battle or from mortal wounds and, as I've observed, just under two-thirds died from disease. The remainder died from accidents, drowning, murder, execution (by Federals or Confederates), suicide, sunstroke, and unstated causes. If we add all these deaths together, we get, according to Long's *Civil War Day by Day*, 360,222. At this point we have a choice. Either we can say that we will remember and honor the 360,222 because they were people like us and for whatever reasons we can't forget them; or we can say that we will remember and honor the dead because they died for ideals we value and in their dying taught us lessons we need to keep in mind. In the first case, we affirm our resemblance to the dead. In the second, we affirm their difference from us, or at least from most of us. If we make the first choice, we can acknowledge that a particular boy from a particular farm may have been drafted into the army and died from dysentery or measles or friendly fire or execution for desertion and that there was nothing brave or heroic or purposeful about his death. It just happened, as it happens every day in ways that are not especially brave or heroic or purposeful. If we make the second choice, however, we cannot acknowledge this version of the boy's death. Instead, like Lincoln at Gettysburg, we must resolve that the unfortunate farm boy shall not have died in vain.

Neither kind of commemoration is necessarily better or worse than the other, but both kinds lead to the question, What is it people are reenacting when they reenact? The grammar of Lincoln's "shall not have died" tells all, because it implies that commemoration must be more than the mere inability to forget; it must reflect the decision to treat what cannot be forgotten as also worth remembering. Lincoln's "shall not have died" is an instance of the future perfect tense, a tense reserved for actions not yet completed, in the original sense of "perfected." The people who died between 1861 and 1865 have died, but no matter how long ago their deaths occurred, we the living complete those deaths with interpretation. If we say the dead died in vain, we complete them one way; if not in vain, another. When people reenact the Civil War, they complete the deaths of over six hundred thousand men with their implicit or explicit interpretations of those deaths. When people reenact the past, they finish it.

Or at least they try to finish it, since the past is not complete until it is forgotten. Any subsequent reenactment is another completion. Once we acknowledge the incompleteness of whatever we remember, we can begin to make some important observations about Civil War reenacting. The first has to do with the difference between what we cannot forget and what we choose to remember. When Sigmund Freud began working with World War I veterans, he discovered that many of them kept dreaming terrible dreams about episodes from the war, episodes they would obviously choose to forget if they could. This discovery led to *Beyond the Pleasure Principle* (1920) and the formulation of Freud's theory of the death drive. What matters for us here is that the veterans' nightmares confirm the difference between what cannot be forgotten and what deserves to be remembered. Even though Freud turned five the year the Civil War began, even though psychoanalysis emerged many years after Appomattox, and even though the term "shell shock" did not appear in medical literature until 1915, the Civil War had more than its share of events that people, both soldiers and civilians, wanted to forget but could not.

> Kind reader, right here my pen, and courage, and ability
> fail me. I shrink from butchery. Would to God I could tear
> the page from these memoirs and from my own memory. It
> is the blackest page in the history of the war of the Lost
> Cause. It was the bloodiest battle of modern times in any
> war. It was the finishing stroke to the independence of the
> Southern Confederacy. I was there. I saw it. My flesh trembles, and creeps, and crawls when I think of it today. My
> heart almost ceases to beat at the horrid recollection.
> Would to God that I had never witnessed such a scene!

This is Sam Watkins writing about his experiences in Hood's army at the Battle of Franklin, Tennessee (November 30, 1864). Anyone who has read his memoir, *"Co. Aytch": A Side Show of the Big Show* (first published serially in 1881–82), knows that Watkins doesn't usually indulge in overstatement. The physical feelings he describes—the trembling, creeping, crawling flesh and the disrupted heartbeat—sound like symptoms of what J. M. Da Costa called "soldiers' heart" in a study published in the *American Journal of the Medical Sciences* in 1871 and of what now goes by the name of posttraumatic stress disorder. But whatever the actual neurobiology of his reaction to memories of Franklin, Watkins makes clear that he reenacts the battle in his narrative because he cannot do otherwise.

> Would that I could turn the page. But I feel, though I did
> so, that page would still be there, teeming with its scenes of
> horror and blood.

Sam Watkins cannot forget the Battle of Franklin, and his narrative of the fighting there does not set out initially to commemorate the dead. Instead, commemoration comes afterward, as he tries to convert trauma that cannot be forgotten into what is worth remembering.

It lives in the memory of the poor old Rebel soldier who
went through that trying and terrible ordeal. We shed a tear
for the dead. They are buried and forgotten. But up yonder
. . . we will meet again and see those noble and brave spirits
who gave up their lives for their country's cause that night
at Franklin, Tennessee. A life given for one's country is
never lost.

In moving from unbearable memory to commemoration, Watkins's reenactment completes the past, at least for the reader of *"Co. Aytch."* Whether or not
the author ever again experienced the physical symptoms of trauma is another
matter.

No matter how completely they identify with their roles, contemporary
Civil War reenactors do not come away from reenactments with posttraumatic
stress disorder caused by their reenacting. Attractive as it might be to speculate
that Civil War reenacting constitutes posttraumatic stress disorder writ large, as
though reenactors were forced to repeat what the United States cannot forget,
such speculation strains credulity. If this explanation were correct, why would
it have taken reenactment 125 years to surge in popularity? In fact, the opposite
explanation makes much more sense: Civil War reenactment surged in popularity only after the war could be forgotten and what had been traumatic for millions no longer was. Watkins calls Franklin "the bloodiest battle of modern
times in any war," but in fact Sharpsburg-Antietam produced more American
casualties than any other single day in any war. For battle trauma it would be
hard to beat September 17, 1862, at least in the history of the United States, and
yet the reenactment for the 135th anniversary of the battle drew thousands of
participants and spectators, many of whom no doubt came to commemorate
but none of whom came because they couldn't forget the stresses of battle.
Commemorating the events in the Cornfield or at the Dunker Church or in
Bloody Lane or on Burnside's Bridge is a desirable way to spend the weekend
only if forgetting those events is a real possibility.

But what of the Southern bumper sticker that reads, "Forget, Hell!"? Does this
message imply commemoration? If so, does it imply the personal commemoration of remembering the individual dead, or the impersonal commemoration of
abstracting the dead into ideals and lessons? Does the person who displays this
bumper sticker do so because he or she cannot forget the trauma of war or

because he or she has resolved to think of the war as worth remembering? Although we don't know the reasons why a particular individual displays this message on a bumper, we can talk about the message the bumper sticker sends. The message behind the message becomes more obvious when compared to another bumper sticker on the same truck: "Lest we forget the Civil War; America's Holocaust." Both messages involve remembrance, but in tone and import they differ drastically. "Lest we forget the Civil War; America's Holocaust" urges personal remembrance of the dead, not as abstractions or ideals or lessons or heroes or models or exemplars or martyrs but as victims of systematic murder analogous to that practiced in Auschwitz or Buchenwald or Bergen-Belsen or Dachau. The rhetorical elevation of the archaism "lest" gives the message solemnity and dignity appropriate to the task of such remembrance.

Although the implied analogy between the six hundred thousand who died in the American Civil War and the six million who died in Nazi concentration camps has some serious flaws—how can we say that the death of a man who volunteers to try to kill other men is the same as the death of children murdered for their religious practices—the analogy is not completely false, as in the case of men brutalized and killed in Civil War prison camps, and it does suggest a corrective to the glib idealizing of the dead as brave or heroic or self-sacrificing. No one tries to soften the murder of babies in gas chambers by claiming that they gave their lives for noble beliefs in noble causes, and we should think twice, if not perpetually, about trying to sweeten all six hundred thousand Civil War deaths with the same rationalization. Yes, many men thought of themselves as willingly risking their lives for their principles, but many others thought of themselves as having little or no choice in placing their lives at the disposal of commanders whose unheroic miscalculations could extinguish them in minutes. All the lives stupidly wasted deserve a commemoration free of inappropriate sentimentality. If that commemoration involves reenactment of battle, then shouldn't the reenactment show the unwillingness to be wasted alongside the willingness to die for beliefs?

In the case of the message "Forget, Hell!," solemnity and dignity yield to irreverent vernacular, and the message behind this message has nothing to do with commemoration and everything to do with revenge, or at least with grudge bearing. Rhetorically, this message represents a response to an implied prior message, presumably an exhortation like "Forgive and forget." The refusal to forget does not involve the high resolution that the dead shall have died meaningfully but rather a refusal of the vanquished to be reconciled to the victor. For those who sympathize with the attitude implied by the "Forget, Hell!" bumper sticker, the reenacting of Civil War battles becomes complicated indeed.

Reenacting has always mixed remembering with reconciliation. The *New York Times* for July 4, 1913, for example, records that during the fiftieth anniversary of Gettysburg, elderly Confederate veterans who reenacted Pickett's Charge were met and embraced by their Union counterparts, both performing and revising the past: "But this time Hancock's men met Pickett's with outstretched arms instead of weapons, and there where Armistead broke through with his hat on his sword, shouting, 'Give them the cold steel, boys,' and died as he said it, his men and Webb's shook hands." Although that particular reenactment in 1913 included much that a contemporary reenactor would consider inauthentic—only "[t]wo of these men wore the uniforms they wore when they last met"—the former enemies' spontaneous expression of powerful feeling had an authenticity of its own, a moving beauty that it shares with Whitman's little poem "Reconciliation," which first appeared in *Sequel to Drum-Taps* (1865):

Word over all, beautiful as the sky,
Beautiful that war and all its deeds of carnage must in time be utterly
    lost,
That the hands of the sisters Death and Night incessantly softly wash
    again, and ever again, this soil'd world;
For my enemy is dead, a man divine as myself is dead,
I look where he lies white-faced and still in the coffin—I draw near,
Bend down and touch lightly with my lips the white face in the coffin.

Spectators at contemporary reenactments probably won't witness public displays of reconciliation like those at the fiftieth anniversary of Gettysburg, or private ones like Whitman's. But if they observe and reflect, they can't help but feel that the very idea of reenactment presupposes reconciliation. Whatever his or her sectional loyalties, the reenactor who performs a role at a public reenactment necessarily acknowledges, either implicitly or explicitly, the framing of that reenactment by shared assumptions about the importance of a common national history, assumptions that could not exist without some kind of reconciliation. Even more practically, if there were no reconciliation between enemies, or descendants of enemies, there would be no cooperation in the staging of the event.

But for all the reconciliation implied by reenactment, American Civil War reenactors perform their roles under a special kind of pressure, pressure we can understand more easily by comparing American reenactors with their British counterparts. Founded in 1968, the Sealed Knot is the British National Association of Reenactment Societies. As of 1994, it had fifty-eight hundred members in the United Kingdom and two hundred more overseas. These numbers may sound small compared to forty thousand reenactors in the United States, but the total population involved in reenacting is about ten thousandths of 1 percent in the U.K. and fifteen thousandths in the U.S. The Sealed Knot, which has fifty-four branches, including ones in Germany and the United States, specializes in reenactments of battles from the seventeenth-century English civil war. During three days in August 1996, for example, the Sealed Knot reenacted the Battle of Torrington on its 350th anniversary. A flyer for the reenactment gives a dramatic description of Torrington.

> It was Armageddon. The ground trembled, moving in
> waves. A blinding yellow and orange fireball thumped into
> the sky as a fist of hot air hurled men to the ground. Horses
> reared wildly, out of control, shrieking amidst the hail of
> masonry and the hiss as streamlined lumps of incandescent
> lead hit the wet thatch of the shivered cob habitations that
> surrounded what had been the church. It was judgement
> from God, or the last desperate act of desperate men.

Having set the stage accordingly, the three-day reenactment in North Devon culminated in the burning of a full-scale replica of the parish church, billed as "England's biggest bonfire," followed by fireworks.

While this particular British reenactment had spectacular features usually missing from American performances of Civil War battles, it lacked a dimension that the latter include, and that is the dimension of intensely felt partisanship. In the English Civil War, royalist Cavaliers fought against parliamentary Roundheads. Three hundred and fifty years later, the United Kingdom is a constitutional monarchy with both royalty and a parliament and no one walking around saying "Forget, Hell!" Whether because it happened two centuries earlier or because it did not result in the victory of one section of the country over another, the English Civil War does not stir up in many of the British the same tangled feelings that the American Civil War still stirs up in many citizens of the

United States. When members of the Sealed Knot reenact events in Torrington, their quest for authenticity is not complicated by lingering grudges.

The quest for authenticity in contemporary Civil War reenactment has many implications and raises many questions. In *Reliving the Civil War: A Reenactor's Handbook* (1996), R. Lee Hadden claims that the "authenticity movement" among Civil War reenactors got a big boost during the Bicentennial in 1976, when Revolutionary War reenactments reflected greater accuracy in uniforms and equipment. In Civil War reenactments before the Bicentennial, reenactors had only a vague notion of authenticity or what it entailed. In contemporary reenacting, by contrast, authenticity is so important that it has produced a kind of caste system among reenactors. At the top of the hierarchy stand the "hardcores," whom Hadden describes as "ultra-authentics, who would take authenticity to extremes, trying to attain as close to 100 percent accuracy as possible." So-called authentics occupy a middle ground, taking "great care in their uniform and accoutrements." Consigned to the bottom of the hierarchy are the "farbs," who use inauthentic equipment, such as modern eyeglasses, during reenactment.

In making authenticity a basic criterion, if not a fetish, Civil War reenacting diverges from the theatrical reenactments of both religion and drama. In the case of the *Quem quaeritis* trope, for example, the early records fail to show that anyone objected to the fact that males played the role of the three Marys at the sepulchre, and Elizabethan audiences did not complain about the inauthenticity of having boys play the female roles in Shakespeare's plays. Conversely, on the contemporary stage, the appearance of an actress in the role of Hamlet or King Lear or Richard II no longer surprises. In staging a Shakespeare play, a director who casts women as men or dresses actors in non-period costumes often receives praise for being innovative. But among Civil War reenactors such innovations constitute unforgivable trespasses, at least among hardcores and authentics. The undisputed presence of women disguised as men in the ranks of both armies during the Civil War has led to even more complication and controversy. To women who claim that these nineteenth-century precedents give them the right to perform as reenactors, many men respond that if a woman can pass as a man without detection, as women in the ranks did during the war, then she is truly authentic and can reenact. But if she cannot pass, then she is not authentic and should be excluded from an activity founded on the principle of authenticity. In response to this argument, a woman can always retort that neither army had many middle-aged TBGs, a reenactor abbreviation for "Tubby Bearded Guys," in it either. Despite the unavoidably comic aspects of this debate, it reveals the bad fit between civil liberties in the United States and the principle of authenticity in Civil War reenacting. In 1989, Laura Cook Burgess, a university administrator from North Carolina who reenacts as a Confederate soldier, won a lawsuit against Antietam National Battlefield Park. Her legal victory gives women the right to participate in public reenactment. One can imagine this same debate repeating itself along racial lines, when someone who cannot pass as a white Anglo-Saxon claims the right to reenact the part of a soldier in a unit of white Anglo-Saxons.

Even more troublesome in some ways than the gap between civil liberties and authenticity is the one between safety and authenticity. People who have accepted fake blood and stunt men for as long as they have been watching movies can easily accept that Civil War reenactors do not and should not shoot each other, no matter how fanatical their devotion to authenticity. Someone who has seen all the dead raised for a curtain call at the end of *Hamlet* or *King Lear* has developed the same ability to suspend disbelief that people call on at the end of Civil War reenactments during the "resurrection," reenactor slang for the moment when all the reenactors who have "taken hits" stand up and fall back in line with their units. As in the performances of most large drama departments and theater companies that employ a stage combat specialist, whose job it is not only to make the combat look believable but also to keep it safe for the combatants, codes and conventions govern the realism of wounding and death. For example, Hadden instructs new reenactors to lie still when they go down: "Don't lean on your elbow and watch the battle, shout at friends or the enemy, or do things wounded men would be unlikely to do."

Putting aside the oxymoron, safe combat, along with the limitations safety necessarily imposes on authenticity, we can return to consider how partisanship and lingering grudges complicate both authenticity and safety. On its home page the National Civil War Association states that to ensure the safety of both the public and the reenactors, the organization "has specific rules for the use of weapons during combat." The NCWA doesn't print these rules, but presumably they resemble closely the ones Hadden includes in his handbook. First among these rules is, "There should be no hand-to-hand fighting unless prearranged and scripted." Hadden gives specific instructions for what unit leaders should do if "the scenario gets totally out of hand" or when enemy units "are seriously misbehaving." The explanation for another rule, "Never try to touch or capture the enemy flag," reflects a similar recognition that real violence is a possibility: "An attempt to grab a flag will too often start a real fight."

If reenactors acknowledge the importance of safety, how can real fights break out and what do they mean? Well, couldn't we ask the same question of fights between athletes? Safety also matters to them, doesn't it? Yes, but there is at least one large difference between a fight that breaks out between, say, football players and one that breaks out between reenactors. Football players are trying to win a game the outcome of which has yet to be determined, but reenactors are re-creating a battle the outcome of which is already known. A football player who takes a swing at somebody because his team is losing and he feels frustrated is not hard to understand, but a reenactor who takes a swing at somebody during a re-creation of Pickett's Charge cannot defend himself with the same rationale. Even if historical research justifies the simulation of hand-to-hand fighting, it also makes the results of that fighting clear.

The eruption of a fistfight during a reenactment could have many causes, many of them trivial. One reenactor's carelessness damages another's regimental flag or other expensive piece of equipment. One reenactor taunts another with something meant, but not taken, in jest. Fights that arise from causes like these can and do happen in many contexts beyond reenacting. But the eruption of a fistfight or some other kind of serious misbehavior can also reflect the unpredictable consequences of the quest for authenticity. Acknowledging the personal importance of that quest, Hadden's description of the Civil War reenactor's epiphany suggests the possibilities for unpredictable behavior.

> There are moments when the reenactor loses track of the
> time period. At that moment he has gone beyond fooling
> others and is fooling himself. Reenactors live for moments
> like this. But this cannot be accomplished without authen-
> ticity.

Why do reenactors reenact? To commemorate, to teach, to entertain: these three reasons have served so far, but now they must make room for a fourth. Reenactors also reenact in order to lose track of time, to fool themselves, to experience a mystical moment when the seemingly impermeable boundary between the present and the past suddenly dissolves.

This mystical moment, this alteration in one's sense of what is real, sounds remarkably close to various descriptions of both theatrical and religious experience. Many actors live for exactly the same erasure of the distinction between themselves and the roles they play, and certain methods of acting promote this erasure. Likewise, going through the motions of religious ritual often leads people to an extraordinary sense of larger motions going through them. Hadden explains quite frankly that "many reenactors have a mystical bent toward the hobby," and stories of weird or supernatural events, such as seeing apparitions, are not uncommon among them. Among some reenactors, the mystical bent has even led to a belief that they are reincarnated Civil War soldiers. Hypnotherapist Barbara Lane has worked with several reenactors and published the results of her work in a book called *Echoes from the Battlefield: First-Person Accounts of Civil War Past Lives* (1996). As Lane explained to a reporter from the *Washington Post,* she became interested in reenactors when she attended an event at Fort Washington and found herself "haunted by the possibility that these weekend soldiers may actually have been replaying former lives."

It doesn't matter whether one believes in the possibility of past lives or chalks them up to the suggestibility of people who focus so much of their attention on the past. What does matter is the complicated function of authenticity in creating the moment that reenactors live for. Hadden anticipates some of the questions that an insistence on authenticity can raise.

> Authenticity can be a confusing concept for new reenactors. Some may feel that authenticity keeps you from wearing and doing what you want. This is not what authenticity is all about. Authenticity liberates you to do anything and be anyone in a simpler world that existed 130 years ago.

Not everyone will feel comfortable with the phrase "a simpler world," since it patronizes the past and does much of the simplifying it purports to describe. It's hard to see, for example, anything simple in the competing readings of the Constitution that emerge in the Lincoln-Douglas debates of 1858. But putting this quibble aside, we can use Hadden's explanation to return us to authenticity, unpredictability, and the eruption of violence in Civil War reenacting.

Authenticity does not restrict; it liberates. In the immediate context of his remarks, Hadden goes on to give as an example the possibility of a reenactor's choosing his or her clothing from among any of the fabrics available during the Civil War. Although this modest example may not raise any huge problems, the description of authenticity might. If Hadden represents correctly the prevailing attitude of reenactors—and since he has been a reenactor since 1979 and served in six units, Union and Confederate, there's no good reason to assume that he doesn't—then one way to understand that attitude is to examine the difference between script and improvisation. In the case of a Civil War battle, the script consists of all the available records of that battle: orders, dispatches, memoranda, reports, letters, diaries, newspaper articles, memoirs, histories, photographs, sketches, paintings. Reenactors in search of authenticity must saturate themselves with these records. Once saturated, they can commemorate or teach or entertain with a firm conviction that their re-creations of the past come as close to accuracy as we can ever get.

But what happens in the moment when, surrounded by accuracy, the reenactor loses track of time and the past becomes present? Suddenly the reenactor is no longer someone following a script based on multiple narratives of an event safely tucked away in the past, but a participant in an event unfolding in the present. To return to the comparison with a football player, the reenactors who, thanks to authenticity, lose track of time also lose their knowledge of the outcome of the battle exploding around them. In other words, they lose track of the conditions that determine what is or is not truly authentic. If reenactors manage to fool themselves into thinking that they are fighting during the nineteenth century, then they also manage to forget the present, the realm of studying the records that govern one's reenactment. At this moment the script evaporates, and improvisation necessarily takes over.

An example of this shift to improvisation, one now famous among reenactors, involves an anecdote from the filming of *Gettysburg*. At one point during a break, Martin Sheen rode on horseback past a large mass of Confederate reenactors, who spontaneously began cheering the image of Lee on Traveller. Their cheering did not appear in the script, but the cameras caught it anyway, and the scene subsequently appeared in the film. A close look at the scene shows that at first Sheen is surprised and confused, but then he settles into the role of Lee and responds to the outburst. This anecdote, told to me by a reenactor who worked in the film, demonstrates how authenticity can lead from the performance of what did happen at a particular moment to the performance of what could happen at any moment. Because they loved him, Lee's soldiers cheered him on many occasions, and reenactors whose authenticity can help them lose track of time and fool themselves into believing that Martin Sheen on horseback is Robert E. Lee on Traveller can perform their love of Lee with an authenticity not in any script.

Authenticity writes the script, but in its purest, most powerful form authenticity leads to improvisation. At one level this statement doesn't feel terribly profound. No matter how comprehensive and detailed the records, records do not specify what the individual reenactor must do in the same way that a director helps block out an actor's performance on stage. Consequently, reenactors must supply the missing details with improvisation. Should they kill or be killed? Hadden advises that "the more experienced reenactor should take the hit," but he adds, "Let your own honor be your guide." These rules of thumb obviously exist because reenactors need some way to limit the open-endedness of improvisation.

But at another level the recognition that authenticity leads to improvisation has some serious implications. In the case of "Forget, Hell!" Confederate reenactors, for example, the moment when they lose track of time and fool themselves is the moment that deeper impulses can come into play. A reenactor who can look at Sheen on horseback and see Lee on Traveller must also be capable of looking at a Union reenactor and seeing an enemy. That in their self-forgetfulness reenactors could vent authentic aggressiveness makes perfect sense. In fact, feeling aggressive toward the enemy would be one proof of authenticity. It's no surprise that on occasion authentic feelings of aggression actually get expressed. Another reenactor told me that, at moments, the re-creation of Gettysburg during the summer of 1997 got "downright physical." He also told me that many reenactments include an opportunity for participants to stage skirmishes with no predetermined outcome. These skirmishes tend to be private and are not open to the public. If he's telling me the truth, for many reenactors the final phase of living history turns out to be revising history. No longer performers recreating what happened, living historians act out what might have happened. In this final phase, authenticity of one kind undoes authenticity of another.

But what about the spectators? Why do they, or we, go to see battles reenacted? Do we want to commemorate or to be taught or to be entertained? In May 1996 I drove up the Constitution Route through Orange, Virginia, to witness a reenactment of the Battle of the Wilderness. The day I went, Sunday the nineteenth, was the second of a two-day event and turned out to be unseasonably hot, reaching the mid-nineties by two o'clock, the hour for reenacting what happened at the Widow Tapp's farm. I hadn't yet found Katherine Couse's letter or the meteorological records from the Washington observatory, so I didn't know for sure that the heat wave was not authentic, although I had a strong hunch that the conditions would have been more appropriate for a July performance of First Manassas–Bull Run or an August reenactment of the Battle of Cedar Mountain.

Of all the battles one could reenact, the one in the Wilderness has to be among the least accommodating. The same conditions that made Grant want to avoid a fight there, and frustrated Timothy O'Sullivan's hopes to photograph the new campaign, also make spectating difficult. Unlike Manassas or Sharpsburg or Gettysburg, the Wilderness has few open spaces, and the ones that do break up the dense woods tend to be modest clearings rather than sweeping expanses. In setting up the reenactment, the organizers had to stage events that happened in two of the open spaces, Saunders' Field, where fighting erupted on May 5, 1864, and Widow Tapp's farm, the site of important actions on May 6. Meanwhile, an event such as the dramatic race between George W. Getty's Second Division of the Union Sixth Corps and A. P. Hill's Confederate Third Corps offered no reasonable possibilities for reenactment because the May 5 race, for control of the crucial junction of the Brock and Orange Plank Roads, took place deep in the Wilderness, where there was little enough open space for the soldiers themselves and none at all for contemporary onlookers. As topography shaped events throughout the war, so it shapes reenactment of those events. In the case of reenactment, however, the demands of authenticity and the demands of "theater," which comes from the Greek for "seeing place," unavoidably collide.

The reenactment took place not on the actual battlefield but on a privately owned farm about fifteen miles south, near Clark's, also called Clark, Mountain, the vantage point from which Lee kept on eye on the Army of the Potomac during the winter and spring of 1864. Turning from the Constitution Route onto county road 628, I followed signs for the reenactment and soon found myself immobilized in a long line of cars. In retrospect I realize that a traffic jam along a narrow country road poses nothing like the challenges of getting a corps of twenty or thirty thousand men, along with artillery, wagons, and thousands of horses and mules, sorted out on, say, the Brock Road, on which Hancock had to about-face the Union Second Corps in order to return to Getty's aid at the intersection with the Orange Plank Road. But at the time I consoled myself by turning off my overheating engine and thinking the bottleneck an authentic representation of one of Meade's many headaches. Eventually, I crawled my way along a dirt track into a vast field that served as the mammoth parking lot for hundreds of cars, trucks, and trailers. Having bought a ticket at the gate for twelve dollars, I fell in with a long column of sweating civilians and began the two-mile hike to the spectator viewing area. In his chapter on "Health and Comfort," Hadden warns that heat and dehydration "are big problems in reenacting," and officials at the gate advised us to drink plenty of water during our long walk.

During the walk to the battlefield, we passed vehicles from local rescue squads and a phalanx of portable toilets before we came to the Federal camp. Those who had had enough walking could visit the camp—the Confederate counterpart lay on the other side of a pond—or Sutler's Row, where all kinds of souvenirs could be bought, or a seminar on "Women in the Civil War" or a book-signing with Gordon Rhea (pronounced "Ray"), whose study *The Battle of the Wilderness, May 5–6, 1864* won the Jules and Frances Landry Award for 1994. But none of these possibilities promised to help me lose track of time or to fool myself, so I swung past the pond and continued along a narrow dirt track into the welcome shade of cooler woods. It was along this track that the first signs of impending battle presented themselves in the form of Confederate soldiers warning us to get to the side because cavalry was coming through. In *The Red Badge of Courage,* Henry Fleming meets up with his mortally wounded friend, Jim Conklin, as they move toward the rear with a river of the maimed. During this grim march, Jim's greatest fear is that he will be run down in the narrow road by horsemen, and I have to admit that the prospect of getting mowed down by Confederate cavalry offered more authenticity than I wanted.

But that worry vanished when another fear snapped into its place, as guns began banging away somewhere up ahead. The firing came from a cavalry skirmish, scheduled just before the reenactment of the fighting at Widow Tapp's farm, and I felt like Henry Fleming approaching a battle he could hear but not see. Like the youth from New York state, I kept glancing at the people around me to catch the signs of fear on any other faces, but finding none, I pulled myself together with a reminder that only a simulation lay ahead.

Finally, our part of the civilian stream emptied from the woods into a broad field lined on two sides by hundreds of spectators. Having come so far, I resolved to continue along the side of the battlefield to the far end and the high ground. There I found a perspiring host, equipped with lawn chairs and water bottles, looking down at the battlefield while listening to loudspeaker commentary delivered by my friend Frank, whose grandfather fought for the Confederacy as a captain in Mosby's Rangers. From the back of a pickup truck Frank provided his narration while standing under the hot sun in the yellow-trimmed wool uniform of a Confederate cavalry captain.

Frank was explaining that in the field below we were watching the reenactment of two important moments in the Battle of the Wilderness. The first involved the near capture of Lee, Hill, and Jeb Stuart at Widow Tapp's farm. Resting in the shade of a tree as Henry Heth's division led Hill's corps along the Orange Plank Road toward the intersection with Brock Road, the three generals saw a line of Union skirmishers suddenly issue from the border of woods two hundred yards away. In his history, Rhea encapsulates the moment with the sentence, "Within pistol shot of the bluecoats, and for a moment breathlessly frozen in time, stood as rich a prize as a Yankee mind could imagine." Lee, Hill, and Stuart faced the skirmishers "helpless, unprotected, and ripe for plucking." But the Federals were surprised, too, and a Northern officer, "oblivious to his prime catch," ordered his troops back into the safety of the woods.

The second moment was that of James Longstreet's timely arrival from Gordonsville with his First Corps, which promptly smashed into the Union left flank and the Second Corps of Winfield Hancock, who later admitted to Longstreet, "You rolled me up like a wet blanket." Shortly after this success, Longstreet was wounded by fire from his own men, as Jackson had been at Chancellorsville nearly a year before to the day.

At least, I think these were the moments that Frank was explaining. I can't remember because as soon as four thousand rifles started firing—the promotional literature says four, but there may have been more—and eighteen or twenty cannons began booming, I got lost in sound.

> Of a sudden the guns on the slope roared out a message of
> warning. A spluttering sound had begun in the woods. It
> swelled with amazing speed to a profound clamor that
> involved the earth in noises. The splitting crashes swept
> along the lines until an interminable roar was developed.
> To those in the midst of it, it became a din fitted to the

universe. It was the whirring and thumping of gigantic
machinery, complications among the smaller stars. The
youth's ears were filled cups. They were incapable of hearing more.

Stephen Crane had never heard the sounds of battle when he wrote this passage, and neither had I when I read it. Is it an accurate description? How would
I know? Describing the sounds in Saunders' Field during the afternoon of May
5, 1864, Meade's chief of staff, Andrew Humphreys, later recalled that the noise
"approached the sublime." Nowadays the word "sublime" has nothing but pos-
itive connotations of magnificence and grandeur, but what I was hearing, the
biggest sustained sound waves ever to break against my auditory nerves,
brought on the terrified awe that Edmund Burke describes in his eighteenth-
century treatise on the sublime. My ears were filled cups incapable of holding
any more.

At least I felt so. This fearfully sublime sound came from a few cannons and
a mere four thousand rifles, approximately the number in two Civil War
brigades. In the early afternoon of May 5, as Humphreys listened, there were
more than seven or eight times that number engaged in Saunders' Field. Eight
times the decibels? My little Sunday afternoon reenactment amounted to nothing but a thin sliver of the real thing, and yet as the smoke cleared, as the cor-
dons around the battlefield came down and I began the long walk across it back
to my car, I had the sense that I had gotten what I came for. For some unmea-
sured bit of time, the sound and the smoke and the formations of men maneu-
vering toward each other across the field had fooled me. I lost track of time and
forgot the other spectators, the traffic jam, ticket gate, rescue squads, portable
toilets, sutlers' souvenirs, seminars, and book-signing. I forgot the contradictions and anachronisms and ironies of recreating the Battle of the Wilderness.
I forgot about commemoration and instruction and entertainment. I even forgot about authenticity. For a few seconds or minutes on an oppressively hot
afternoon in central Virginia, the smug, complacent detachment that buffers me
from May 1864 slipped just a little.

As we walked across the battlefield, littered with paper from cartridges,
spectators mingled with reenactors, some to ask questions, some to talk with
friends. I passed one small group gathered around a reenactor mounted on a
handsome brown horse. The spectators apparently knew the reenactor already,

and the group stood chatting and laughing. As I approached, the group split up, and the horseman turned in my direction. He had a beard on his face, a cigar in his mouth, and a blue uniform on his body. I thought about asking him some kind of question or making some kind of bland remark on the order of "I really enjoyed the reenactment." But then I noticed the three gold stars on each shoulder and realized that it was Grant looking down on me. Grant, who in his eastern debut lost or used or wasted 17,666 men before he retired to his tent and broke and wept. I said nothing. I haven't been to a reenactment since.

SIX

Eyewitness

EVEN THOUGH I haven't gone to a reenactment since the Battle of the Wilderness, I've continued to read. The Civil War generated and continues to generate a vast amount of writing; observers often call it the most written war or the most literate war. In the bibliography to *Battle Cry of Freedom,* James McPherson claims that as of 1988 there were over fifty thousand books and pamphlets on the war—about one for every reenactor. It would take someone reading three books a day nearly half a century to plow through all fifty thousand, but after fifty years so many new books would have appeared that he or she would still be hopelessly behind. Then there are all the newspapers and weeklies printed between 1861 and 1865, both in the United States and abroad. Finally, readers who still have their eyesight can spend it on the unpublished letters and diaries written by a significant portion of the 31,443,321 people recorded in the census of 1860.

A reader is a reenactor, especially if he or she is a reader of writings left by eyewitnesses whose observations, transcriptions, and responses have not been filtered through another person's reading. Someone who reads a good history witnesses a reenactment, but someone who reads an eyewitness, in a local historical society or a museum or a research library or an attic, re-creates a piece of the war. The moment when I opened Katherine Couse's letter felt something like the moment reenactors live for.

Katherine did more than keep her wits together during the Wilderness and Spotsylvania. She also managed to write her way through those nineteen days in May 1864. If shells were whizzing all around the house, I for one doubt seriously that I could hold a pen in my hand or would be tempted to try, and yet here she is, describing the day of the Bloody Angle, Spotsylvania, one of the worst in the four years of war.

> Thursday 12th. The fighting opens early this morning. The Rowe family came down just now, refugees old Mrs. Frazer and Mrs. Long have just come through the rain—coming for protection. I feel sorry for them. Oh! God there is now the most murderous battle raging the continuous roar of cannons the still more terrific musketry sounds awful indeed my feelings are intensely awful beyond description this fearful bloody struggle it is raining hard.

Even though we don't know exactly where Katherine's house stood, the Laurel Hill area lies no more than a mile or two from the Bloody Angle, a few miles closer than the closest part of the Wilderness battlefield. How did she stay focused on the page before her? Should we believe that in fact she kept writing as the fighting went on? If so, then her letter is a special document, since it transcribes events as they occur, unlike, for example, the memoirs of generals who recollect their campaigns several years after they fight them. In fact, Katherine's letter might serve to define one end of a spectrum of writing about the Wilderness, as it represents immediate, firsthand, first-person, present-tense observation of the battle. Toward the other end of the spectrum lie various other kinds of verbal representations of the fighting. These might range from the memoirs and histories of participants in the battle, which would fall closer to the middle of the spectrum, to recent re-creations of the battle in poetry or fiction, which would define the opposite end of the spectrum.

Or should we be suspicious of the present-tense immediacy of Katherine's letter? The manuscript, which belongs to the University of Virginia Special Collections, shows very few corrections and insertions. Either she managed to stay cool enough not only to write but to write without making any mistakes, or she recopied her diary-style letter from notes or an earlier draft. One doesn't have to be a cynic to wonder about the smooth continuity of Katherine's transcription, and the example of Mary Chesnut's diary, which C. Vann Woodward has shown to be a product of the 1880s based on a journal kept during the 1860s, should keep us from being too gullible about the authenticity of what we're reading.

But even if we cannot hope to establish the fact of authenticity, we can still acknowledge the powerful sound of authenticity, however it might have been created. Some might be content to call this sound the ring of truth, while others may insist on thinking of it as the product of various rhetorical devices and strategies, albeit sometimes unconscious ones.

Time of Battle
May 6th 1864

Dear Sister

    I will try to write a few lines to let you know how we are getting a long, we are giving the yank fits. I am still safe but had three men slightly wounded . . . I was also struck with a spent ball on the leg. I thought my leg was off it hurt but I did not leave the field . . . we have been doing some tall fighting for two days. I expect that about the time you were enjoying the weading [weeding?] we were pitching into the Yankeys. There is heavy skermishing going on we have already taken 18 or 20 pieces of artilry and a great many prisoners. old Grant hasn't got pemberton and Brag to fight he must do a great deal better if he wants to whip Lee. as the fight is not over yet I will close for the present and give you the full detail when it is over if I live

nothing more
good bye   your
Brother D B Huffman

Many soldiers' letters and diaries contain descriptions of battle hastily scribbled during moments of inaction. This one, written during the second day of the Wilderness to Annie Elizabeth "Bettie" Huffman by a Virginia soldier, contains some of the same elements as Katherine Couse's letter. D. B. Huffman is the same person as David B. Huffman, the captain of Company G, Mount Jackson Rifles, Thirty-third Virginia, who in the scenario imagined earlier gratefully received water from the five-year-old boy. Later in 1864, Huffman was wounded, captured, and imprisoned at Fort Delaware, from which he was released in June 1865. In this letter to his sister, the Virginia captain writes in the first person and often in the present tense. But here the present tense raises no suspicion, at least not in me, since it accompanies the shift from the writer's active involvement (narrated in the past tense) to observation (described in the present tense), a shift that makes the statement "There is heavy skermishing going on" feel persuasively authentic. It's not hard to imagine that after the earlier events he narrates (having three men slightly wounded and getting struck by a spent ball), Huffman uses a moment when he is not actually fighting to assure his sister that he still lives, a moment during which he can observe that men are still fighting on some other part of the field. In his letter, the present tense signals relief from the emotional and psychological intensities of involvement, relief that filters and mutes those intensities for both writer and reader.

But in Katherine's letter the present tense signals no such relief. When it comes, it comes to amplify emotional and psychological intensities, giving her narrative the nearly unbearable quality of relentless crescendo.

> Dr Howard came back just now. we took him some break-
> fast in the parlor. he belongs to Gen Grants staff. is a
> charming man. the whole air resounds with the continuous
> roars, the earth shakes Great God how more than awful—
> shells whizzing oh so fearfully my very soul almost dies
> within me.

Earlier I quoted part of a statement by Stephen Crane, recorded by his friend, the painter Corwin Linson. The statement reflects Crane's impatience with the narratives of *Battles and Leaders of the Civil War* (1884–1888), which he read in *Century* magazine: "'I wonder that *some* of these fellows don't tell how they *felt* in those scraps! They spout eternally of what they *did,* but they are as emotionless as rocks!'" Although Crane's exasperation reflects the restlessness of an especially gifted young novelist and anticipates some of his protagonist's sweepingly adolescent pronouncements ("'And I don't see any sense in fighting and fighting and fighting, yet always losing through some derned old lunkhead of a general'"), it also reflects both the curiosity of many civilians about the extraordinary realities of combat and the curiosity of the present about the past.

But for all his hunger to hear more about the feelings and emotions produced by the red animal, Crane himself describes what he imagines to be those feelings and emotions through the muting filters of the third person and the past tense. How would he have felt about Katherine Couse's letter, which expresses more raw feeling and emotion than all of the narratives in *Battles and Leaders* or than all of the official records compiled in the 128-volume *War of the*

Rebellion? Like Crane, as Linson describes him, many of us want something beyond the recounting of factual details, no matter how precisely rendered, some glimpse of personal reaction to those details to flesh them out and give them life. But when we get so much more than a glimpse, when we get the full blast of anguish, as in Katherine's "my very soul almost dies within me," are we satisfied? Somewhere between the 125th and the 150th anniversaries of the Wilderness, does the absence of irony or understatement in Katherine's written responses to the battle bring us closer to her experience or push us away?

Crane would have wanted someone still to be reading his novel more than a hundred years after its publication, but Katherine never intended her letter for me. Presumably the unidentified recipients of the letter would have had few, if any, of the questions and misgivings about its authenticity that I have. But I raise the questions and voice the misgivings not to dismiss the letter but rather to pinch myself to see if I'm dreaming when I read it. Anyone who has spent much time with even one volume of the *War of the Rebellion*, let alone all 128, or with the memoirs of many generals knows all too well what Linson means when he describes Crane's recoil from "the quality of dullness of the Civil War records." How can events so literally and figuratively earthshaking make for what many would consider such boring reading? Or to put it differently, how can the historical diverge so hugely from the aesthetic?

Well, some might say, people wrote differently in those days. We can't hold nineteenth-century writers to twentieth- or twenty-first-century standards. I can't agree. By the time the first general wrote his first report, Emerson, Hawthorne, Poe, Thoreau, Whitman, and Melville had written and published much of the writing that in many cases continues to shape our aesthetic standards. Well then, people who write historical records aren't thinking about aesthetic matters, and so we shouldn't think about those records aesthetically. Again, I can't agree. Although "aesthetic," "aesthete," "aesthetics," and "aestheticism" all have specific, often specialized, dictionary definitions that make these words and what they signify unattractive to many people (Whitman among them), the Greek verb from which these words descend simply means "to perceive," and historical writing no less than poems and novels is about perception: what the writer perceives, what the reader perceives the writer perceives, what the writer seems to want the reader to perceive, what the reader perceives about the way the writer writes, and so on. Admittedly, not every piece of writing, historical or otherwise, necessarily deserves to have its aesthetic qualities appraised and appreciated. Just because writing involves perception doesn't mean that a particular piece of writing automatically involves acute or interesting or memorable perception or that it produces acute or interesting or memorable perceptions in a reader. Still, believing that historical writing has no aesthetic quality simply because its primary function is to record or convey information is like believing that a house or school or church or public building has no aesthetic quality simply because its primary function is to give people a place to live or learn or worship or pay their taxes.

In *Memoranda during the War,* his record of nursing both Union and Confederate wounded, Whitman meditates persuasively on exactly this convergence of history and aesthetics in a passage that appears in a section titled "Soldiers and Talks," which he placed in the 1863 section of the book:

> I often have talks with them, occasionally quite long and
> interesting. One, for instance, will have been all through
> the Peninsula under McClellan—narrates to me the fights,
> marches, the strange, quick changes of that eventful cam-
> paign, and gives glimpses of many things untold in any offi-
> cial reports or books or journals. These, indeed, are the
> things that are genuine and precious. The man was there,
> has been out two years, has been through a dozen fights,
> the superfluous flesh of talking is long work'd off him, and
> now he gives me little but the hard meat and sinew . . .

In this description of his talks with soldiers, Whitman begins by thinking about what the soldiers tell him and moves to thinking about how they tell it, a move from history to aesthetics. In this particular passage, he's not specific about the actual subject matter of his conversations, but many other moments in the *Memoranda,* such as the account of atrocities at Upperville, make it quite clear that the soldiers supply him with crucial details about events he could never have witnessed but writes about at length nevertheless, as in the extended reenactment of the battle of Chancellorsville (May 1863), much of which Whitman stages in an entirely fabricated first-person voice:

> we hear Secesh yells—our men cheer loudly back, espe-
> cially if Hooker is in sight—hand to hand conflicts, each
> side stands up to it, brave, determin'd as demons, they
> often charge upon us—a thousand deeds are done worth to
> write newer greater poems on—and still the woods on fire.

The cheering of soldiers when their commander comes into sight is not a detail that would appear in "any official report," even one written by an especially egotistical commander like Hooker. Whitman could have found it in newspaper or magazine accounts of the battle, although such accounts tend to limit themselves to the kinds of details Linson parodies in his memoir of Crane: "Here was the wooded knoll, there rode the generals, elsewhere the formation of troops; one regiment did this, the enemy did something else." Then again, by the time he published the *Memoranda,* he also would have had other books on which to draw. Whitman may even have supplied the cheering from his own imagination. But whatever the actual source of the detail, it has the sound of something told to him by a soldier who was there.

Whitman's talks with soldiers must have yielded many such details about scenes he never witnessed, and those details, rendered, as Linson puts it, "down to the last belt and button," must have made the soldiers' narratives memorable for Whitman in the same way that the minute particulars of nursing make Whitman's *Memoranda* memorable for us. But for Whitman, as for Crane, mere details are not enough, even though they come from the participants themselves. Presumably, talking with wounded soldiers, both the dying and the convalescing, would have provided Whitman with more than his share of the personal reactions craved by Crane. But Whitman still looks for something more in his talks with soldiers, and that something resides in the style of the telling: "the superfluous flesh of talking is long work'd off him, and now he gives me little but the hard meat and sinew."

In his own writing Whitman himself often gives us much more than hard meat and sinew. Even Whitman's admirers, and I include myself among them, would have to admit that more than a little superfluous flesh often swells his lines, poems, and prose pieces. But if losing the superfluous flesh of talking is Whitman's image for simple, direct narrative that tends towards understatement rather than overstatement, then not only does that image shrewdly anticipate the twentieth-century taste for stylistic spareness gratified most notably by Hemingway, but it also describes some of the best moments in Whitman's own *Memoranda*:

> In one bed a young man, Marcus Small, Co. K, Seventh
> Maine—sick with dysentery and typhoid fever—pretty criti-
> cal, too—I talk with him often—he thinks he will die—
> looks like it indeed. I write a letter for him home to East
> Livermore, Maine—I let him talk to me a little, but not

much, advise him to keep very quiet—do most of the talking myself—stay quite a while with him, as he holds on to
my hand—talk to him in a cheering, but slow, low, and mea-
sured manner—talk about his furlough, and going home as
soon as he is able to travel.

No superfluous flesh here. The short, telegraphic sentences and phrases sketch
the scene with a few quick strokes, leaving unsaid what John Keats, speaking of
a line of Wordsworth's, called perfect pathos, the pathos of trying to cheer a
man who thinks he will die, and looks as though he will die, by talking about
his trip home, a trip that both speaker and listener know might well never happen. Whitman never tells us what happened to Marcus Small, who belonged to
the same regiment as Asa Candage, wounded in the Wilderness on May 6 and
the grandfather of a woman I know.

No, Katherine Couse never intended her letter for me, and cowering inside
the quaking house at Laurel Hill as the battle of the Wilderness exploded
around her, she probably gave little if any thought to the aesthetic qualities of
her recording. As for the suspicious neatness of her manuscript, perhaps she
recopied it or perhaps she was a person of unusual courage, one who wrote
steadily to steady herself as the world around her disintegrated. Besides, the letter contains more than enough other tokens of strain. In addition to the erratic
punctuation and capitalization, which wouldn't typify formal, leisurely composition by a woman educated enough to copy out quotations from Shakespeare's
Julius Caesar and *Two Gentlemen of Verona* on a leaf that accompanies the letter, Katherine's writing includes the mesmerizing repetition of the word
"awful" in "the still more terrific musketry sounds awful indeed my feelings are
intensely awful beyond description. . . . the earth shakes Great God how more
than awful," a repetition that someone editing her writing coolly after the fact
would be likely to change.

So I don't think I am dreaming. She was there in the Wilderness while it
happened, writing it down as it happened. When Whitman declares, "The man
was there," he implies that the mere fact of one's presence authenticates one's
narrative of that event. But it doesn't. The postwar years brought out many con-
flicting accounts of battles by men who were there but who disagreed about
matters of official record, such as who should get the credit for capturing a certain battery in Saunders' Field. Mere presence is not enough. Mere detail is not

enough. Mere use of the first person and the present tense is not enough, as Whitman's retelling of Chancellorsville makes embarrassingly clear. There has to be something more, something that lives in the file buried in the archives with the tens or hundreds of millions of other letters, diaries, and memoirs written by or to or about the millions of soldiers and sailors, something that explodes from the folder and makes the air roar.

> Near Spotselvania Court
> House, Va May 16th 1864

Dear Mother

I have just heard that there will be a chance to send letters home this morning, and I improve the oppernitunity to let you know that I am all right so far. We had a pretty hard battle on the 6th. I dont know what the battle is called but it was about 5 miles from Germania Ford on the Rapidan River.

This letter, written by Walt Whitman's brother George, is not unpublished, and I'm not reading it in George's handwriting. But I've singled out this passage because it helps me describe another aspect of the eyewitness end of the writing spectrum. Although George Whitman, a captain in the Fifty-first New York, First Brigade, Second Division, Ninth Corps, writes mostly in the past tense ten days after the unnamed battle he goes on to describe, he does use the present tense at one key moment: "I dont know what the battle is called." When George writes his mother, the fighting has ended, and so his letter does not have the powerful immediacy of Katherine Couse's account, but his ignorance of "what the battle is called" continues. Despite the passing of ten days, for George Whitman, as presumably for the other soldiers around him, the hardening of the present into written history has not yet begun. The present, or recent past, still has no name, and official records have not yet tagged and labeled it for future use by historians. This moment of prehistory is especially interesting because George's confession of his ignorance suggests that, unlike Katherine Couse, who gives no thought to the future christening of the chaos exploding around her, he knows that a name is forthcoming, along with the historical narratives a name entails. At this point in the *Civil War Letters of George Washington Whitman* (1975), editor Jerome M. Loving introduces a footnote to identify the unnamed battle as the Battle of the Wilderness and to explain that "The Wilderness was a wooded area near Fredericksburg, Virginia."

Readers who reenact bits and pieces of the war by reading eyewitness accounts have the opportunity to recover traces of a prehistoric moment when the past is still present. To seek this opportunity is not necessarily to succumb to a nostalgic fantasy of time travel or to delude oneself with the mirage of really being there. Instead, it is to try to strip off the layers of varnish that subsequent narratives paint over an event. Unlike the hardcore battle reenactor, would-be prehistorians live not for the moment when they lose track of time and fool themselves but for the moment when, having followed memoirs and histories back upstream, they get to the source, or as close to the source as they can get. For the would-be prehistorian a footnote identifying an unnamed battle is as disruptive and disconcerting as a farb's modern eyeglasses are to a hardcore reenactor.

> The civilian reader must not suppose when he reads
> accounts of military operations in which relative position of
> forces are defined, as in the foregoing passages, that these
> were matters of general knowledge to those engaged. Such
> statements are commonly made, even by those high in
> command, in the light of later disclosures, such as the
> enemy's official reports. It is seldom, indeed, that a subor-
> dinate officer knows anything about the disposition of the
> enemy's forces—except that it is unamiable—or precisely
> whom he is fighting. As to the rank and file, they can know
> nothing more of the matter than the arms they carry. They
> hardly know what troops are upon their own right or left
> the length of a regiment away. If it is a cloudy day they are
> ignorant even of the points of the compass. It may be said,
> generally, that a soldier's knowledge of what is going on
> about him is coterminous with his official relation to it and
> his personal connection with it; what is going on in front of
> him he does not know at all until he learns it afterward.

In this passage, which appears in his memoir "The Crime at Pickett's Mill" (1909), Ambrose Bierce accurately describes and explains George Whitman's ignorance of the name of the battle fought along the Rapidan during the first week of May 1864. A first lieutenant and Union General William B. Hazen's topographic engineer at the time of the fighting at Pickett's Mill, or Mills, Georgia (May 27, 1864), Bierce has given the civilian reader an account of disorientation particularly appropriate for a discussion of the Battle of the Wilderness, since the action at Pickett's Mill also took place in what E. B. Long calls "difficult and heavily wooded country."

Aside from the wry qualification "except that it is unamiable," Bierce's account of soldierly ignorance and disorientation sounds unusually free of his characteristic irony. More important, it gives us a good description of the prehistoric moment, for both a soldier engaged in actions he does not yet understand and a civilian reader confronted by an unedited, unfootnoted, sometimes illegible eyewitness account in a letter or diary. Like soldiers' knowledge, readers' knowledge of what is before them depends on the reports and narratives written after the eyewitness account. If those readers should be unaware of later reports and narratives, the eyewitness account remains an unsifted, unabsorbed, untamed piece of ongoing presence.

Here are entries for the same day from two different diaries, both in the University of Virginia Special Collections. Neither has been published or quoted in any history I have seen.

> April 1864
> Friday 6
> Heavy firing all along the lines to day very early in the
> morning. A stampede of portions of Heths & Wilcoxs
> Division occurred about 7 a.m., but were rallied by Genl
> Lee in person. He also rushed onto a charge heading one
> of Longstreets texas Brigades with hat in hand cheering on
> the men when they (the men) told him they would not fire
> a gun unless he went back which he did. Genl Longstreet
> very seriously wounded in the breast, but it is hoped not
> mortally. Went down to the battle field in the evening from
> which the yankeys had been repulsed. Saw a great many
> dead and wounded Yankeys and comparatively few Con-
> federates. While I was down there began firing quite sev-
> erly on right of plank road. Came back to Camp found a
> dead Confed Soldier in the rear of our camp named John
> Johnson Co. B 44 Regt NC, Kirklands Brigade. When Genl

got back at night said every thing was going on well for us.
Up to this time we have captured over 3000 Yanks. Remain
all night where we were last. To day one of the most
tremendous infantry fights of the war came off.

    (May 6th)
we was ordered out at 3 am in a hurrah not giving us time
get our coffe they marched us right to the front whare they
shoot prety carless we laid there till 11 am when our Brigade
was ordered in to make our mark our Regment charged over
three lines of our men and toke two lines of rifle pites from
the enemy but could not hold them for the reson that support did not folow up and we had to fall back. we lost heavy
in that charge lost our Cornel one Captain kiled one Capt
lost his leg and four Lieutenants woned the total loss of the
Regment is 11 kiled 84, woned 24 missing we charged three
times on the enemys works we captured in the first charge
one hundred prisoners it has been one of the most hard
fought Battles of the war the line of battle was over ten miles
long and hard fighting all along the line I saw 13,000 prisoners that was taken on the right in morning by some other
Corps the enemy was drove in every point to day it was a
sight to see the woned come back to the rear but it is the fate
of war night closed the tide of Blood

Two hands, two perspectives, two voices, no footnotes. Both men's handwriting is fairly legible, but I've had to guess at a couple of points. For example, until
I checked the *Roster of Confederate Soldiers,* I couldn't be sure about the first
name of Johnson in the entry of Diarist One (the dead soldier is one of forty-
one John H. Johnsons listed) or about the way Diarist Two forms what I take to
be the number three. Both men write in the past tense, reviewing Friday, May
6, 1864, after the fighting has ended, although for some reason Diarist One
begins writing "April 1864" above the entries starting with Thursday, May 5.
Perhaps the pressures of combat caused him to lose track of the calendar.
Diarist One is obviously more educated than Diarist Two, but the misspellings
of Diarist Two, like the invented spellings of a modern first grader, tell us a good
deal about how he heard and said words. Apparently, for example, he pro-

nounced the second syllable of "hurry," spelled "hurrah" in the first sentence, the way some people pronounce the last syllable of "Missouri." He may have come from the South or the Midwest.

Whereas Diarist Two makes no references to names that help identify his perspective, Diarist One is clearly a Confederate. One doesn't have to have read a single page of writing about the Civil War to be able to identify General Lee, at least no one who's inclined to spend a day scrutinizing Civil War diaries, and Diarist One gives himself away in the statement "we have captured over 3000 Yanks." Furthermore, his description of the relative numbers of casualties ("Saw a great many dead and wounded Yankeys and comparatively few Confederates") suggests partiality, at least to my ear, since someone whose side had lost many more men would be unlikely to take any pleasure in recording the difference using the elegant formula "comparatively few." By contrast Diarist Two states grimly, "we lost heavy" and leaves the enemy's losses unmentioned.

Meanwhile, Diarist Two is strangely anonymous and unplaceable. He never speaks of Confederates or Yankees, using instead the generic designation "the enemy." He also refers to no one above the rank of colonel, whereas Diarist One refers to generals freely but only one soldier of lower rank, who happens to be dead and lying near his camp. In addition, the perspective of Diarist Two is more limited and some of his information doubtful. He tells what happened to his brigade and regiment but excludes anything beyond the scope of his own witnessing. When he makes an attempt to describe something from a distance, he sounds no longer reliable, as when he claims that he saw thirteen thousand prisoners, a wildly inflated number. But I'm cheating a little, since I could only know that the number is inflated if I had some sense of the overall casualties for the battle. Using a photographic metaphor, we could describe Diarist Two as giving us a close-up with the foreground clear and the background out of focus, whereas Diarist One gives us both close-up and wide-angle shots.

But what of each man's relation to the events he describes? Diarist One seems to know more about the larger contours of action on May 6, but his account leaves his own role in that action unclear. Through the first half of his entry he tells us nothing that he couldn't have heard from someone else. Not until "Went down to the battle field in the evening" does he narrate his own actions, and the deliberate reference to the time of his visit suggests that he had not been to the battlefield earlier. He does not say, for example, "Went back down" or "Went down again." The next two sentences describe what he saw and heard, the former limited to the aftermath of fighting, the latter incorporating fighting still in progress. When he returns to camp, he receives information from a general, either directly or indirectly. When he puts the number of captured Union soldiers at a believable three thousand, he does not claim to have seen their capture. Instead, he reports a running total.

Diarist One seems to have spent May 6 behind the lines, where information is plentiful and actual fighting scarce. Conversely, Diarist Two spent the day not just in the lines but participating actively in defining them. The first half of his entry describes in detail what he was told to do and what he did. A confirmed empiricist, he concerns himself not so much with generalizations about the overall picture but with specifics that he can count (three lines, two lines, eleven killed, eight-four wounded, twenty-four missing, three times). Whereas Diarist One speaks as a receiver and synthesizer of information, Diarist Two speaks as a giver of information in the form of raw data.

For all their differences the two entries have two features in common. The first is that each diarist believes the battle is going well for his side. Diarist One reports the general's reassurance that "every thing was going well for us"; Diarist Two sums up that "the enemy was drove in every point to day." In passing along these favorable observations, both the information receiver and the information giver move beyond eyewitness into the realm of what they cannot know for sure. If the two diarists fight for the same army, their trusting statements corroborate each other; if for different armies, their statements reflect either the error of one or the relativity of perspective.

The second feature common to both entries is the diarists' use of superlatives to describe the fighting on May 6. Diarist One concludes his entry with the statement, "To day one of the most tremendous infantry fights of the war came off," and Diarist Two echoes him closely: "it has been one of the most hard fought Battles of the war." Admittedly, these statements wouldn't mean much if the people who wrote them were new recruits or conscripts, but the different perspectives of the two diarists give the coincidence of their judgment an undeniable weight.

Most historians who work with documents like these can't afford to devote so much written space to them. If they did, their one-, two-, or three-volume works would soon fill as many shelves as the OR. In Gordon Rhea's study, for example, which makes more use of manuscript material than any other book devoted exclusively to the Battle of the Wilderness, a letter or diary may have anything from a phrase to several sentences quoted from it, or it may only be cited in a footnote. Like Diarist One, Rhea focuses mostly on generals and the larger contours of action. For him a letter or diary is something to be distilled into evidence that supports the story he's telling, not something to be paused over and scrutinized and read closely for its own sake. Furthermore, all the letters and diaries that Rhea quotes must have been written by people who could have worked as university press copy editors, since their grammar, punctuation, and spelling far surpass anything I found in the letters and diaries of even the people who were obviously educated. Otherwise, Rhea must have silently corrected mistakes and edited the documents to produce the homogenized prose of his book. Although he doesn't mention Katherine Couse in his Wilderness book, I subsequently discovered that his 1997 study of the first few days at Spotsylvania does quote her twice and does silently correct her punctuation and spelling.

Rhea's procedures make perfect sense for the writing of a narrative synthesis, the kind of writing that most people associate with history. But for the prehistorian, the person who wants for whatever reason to explore and perhaps camp for a while by the headwaters of history, the power of writings left us by eyewitnesses lies not so much in their potential to give evidence but in their revelations of a disorganized, chaotic, confusing present not yet neatened into stories any more than our own ongoing lives are.

Who were the two diarists, and why did I pair them? Anyone who would prefer to savor prehistoric messiness should skip this paragraph and the two after it; anyone who wants the footnotes should read on. The first diarist is Hugh Thomas Nelson, who was born in 1845 and would have turned nineteen sometime during 1864. According to Philip Alexander Bruce's *History of Virginia* (1924), Nelson came from Albemarle County, Virginia, and served in the Confederate army "when a mere boy, during a part of the time being a courier for Gen. Robert E. Lee." Nelson's role as Lee's courier would explain his distance from actual combat, his preoccupation with generals, and his access to reliable information. The figure he gives for the number of Union soldiers captured turns out to be very close indeed. Long describes 3,383 Union soldiers as "missing," a category that apparently includes prisoners of war. Hugh Thomas Nelson survived the war and died in 1906.

Diarist Two is William Johnston, born December 9, 1839, in Rochester, New York, thus twenty-four years old on the second day of the Battle of the Wilderness. Johnston served with the Eighth Michigan, First Brigade, Third

Division, Ninth Corps. According to Rhea, on the morning of May 6, Ambrose Burnside ordered Colonel John F. Hartranft's brigade, which included Johnston's Michigan regiment, to proceed with another division through more than a mile of "'dense wood and an almost impenetrable undergrowth,'" which Johnston never mentions. In the afternoon, the Eighth Michigan took part in Burnside's assault just north of the Widow Tapp's farm. According to the troop movement maps prepared by Edwin Bearss in 1962, Hartranft eventually positioned his brigade approximately sixteen hundred feet—less than a third of a mile—from where Longstreet's Texas soldiers told Lee to go back to the rear. William Johnston also survived the war and died May 23, 1916.

In other words, somewhere in the seventy or seventy-five square miles of the Wilderness, Hugh Thomas Nelson and William Johnston may have stood within a few hundred yards of each other sometime during Friday, May 6, 1864. One man's perspective includes an incident now standard in narratives of the Battle of the Wilderness, the "Lee to the rear" incident, which the diarist himself may not even actually have witnessed, since according to Rhea only Lee's aide, Charles Venable, was present. The other man belonged to a regiment mentioned once in Rhea's book and not at all in the other recent studies of the battle. He witnessed plenty, but nothing he witnessed has found its way into modern narratives. His careful record doesn't pack much punch as evidence to cite in support of a larger story. As far as written history is concerned, his perspective barely exists, an absence some may not particularly regret, since Johnston's erroneous summary that "the enemy was drove in every point to day" shows how poorly his small picture fits in with the big one. Still, it is a picture, and although the historian may have little use for it, prehistorians cannot spare it.

Letters and diaries written from the Wilderness make the battle there real in a way that no other kind of writing can. But as the passage from "The Crime at Pickett's Mill" confirms, the prehistoric rawness of eyewitness accounts written during or just after the battle comes with a price, since the eyewitness perspective is necessarily a limited one. Throughout *"Co. Aytch"* Sam Watkins acknowledges the limitations of his perspective and explicitly refers his reader to "the histories" for details unavailable in his memory. At least one witness in the Wilderness also refers his reader elsewhere, refusing to describe the battle not because he can't but because he knows that his own account will not be as comprehensive as accounts available elsewhere.

I don't attempt to tell you news about the battle, because
you will learn fuller details from the papers. My darling
wife, God bless you! I hope soon to see you, and to rejoice
with you over a glorious victory to our arms.

These words come from a letter written by John Cowper Granberry, a chaplain
in the Confederate army, to his second wife, Ella. The letter is dated "Plank
Road, about 20 miles from Orange C. H. / Friday, May 6, 1864" and places
Granberry on the Confederate right, where "Ewell's battle could be heard very
distinctly, for the two roads are near; and Hill's wounded were going on being
carried by us to the rear." But despite his proximity to the dramatic arrival of
Longstreet, Granberry defers to the newspapers because, he thinks, they will
tell his darling wife more about what he has in front of him. In fact, if Ella
Granberry or her Northern counterpart turned to the papers for news of the
Wilderness, she would have found different details, though not necessarily
fuller ones.

SEVEN

Newspapers

I'VE NEVER counted them all, but common sense tells me that more words about the Battle of the Wilderness appeared in newspapers than anywhere else. Despite their sheer volume, however, common sense also tells me that most people who aren't professional historians of the Civil War know less about the words in newspapers than they do about the words of letters, diaries, memoirs, histories, or novels. When historical outsiders do encounter the words of newspapers, as in Ken Burns's documentary, those words exhibit themselves as quaint oddities that many find hard to take seriously. After all, newspapers exist to give us information, and since we now have so much better information from other sources, why bother with poring over wartime newspapers? How could anyone have fallen for the falsehoods they contained? This line of reasoning isn't so hard to understand, but for the prehistorian who hopes for a deeper sense of the wild unsettledness of the present before it becomes past, a present so often misled and misinformed, the wartime newspapers are crucial.

Reading those newspapers, I can't ever manage to forget completely that I know how the story comes out—not only the story of the Wilderness but also the story of the war as a whole—and so I'm not as completely at their mercy as the readers of May 1864 were. Thank goodness. But in my own time I've watched lots of big stories break, some of them painfully slowly, some of them falsely at first, and I think I prepare myself best for the wartime papers by trying to remember what it felt like to read the news of, say, 1968, beginning with the seizure by North Korea of the *Pueblo* and proceeding through the launching of the Tet offensive by the North Vietnamese, Lyndon Johnson's announcement that he wouldn't seek reelection, the assassinations of Martin Luther King, Jr., and Robert Kennedy, the Democratic convention in Chicago, and the election of Richard Nixon in November. When I can recall what it felt like to reel from the news of one day and wince in anticipation of the next, I'm ready for the Wilderness.

If Ella Granberry, wife of the Confederate chaplain who referred her to the newspapers for "fuller details," hoped for news of her husband and the battle around him, she probably would have been watching the Richmond papers closely. If she had picked up the *Examiner* for Thursday, May 5, 1864, she would have found, under the headline "Telegraphic" in the far right column on the first page, the foreshadowing of the battle that opened on the same day.

> Orange Court House, May 4—A body of the enemy's cavalry crossed at Ely's and Germanna Fords last night, and were reported this morning moving on Chancellorsville and Fredericksburg.
>
> The whole Yankee army is moving from Culpeper Court House towards Ely's and Germanna Fords, over which they have thrown pontoon bridges, and across which their infantry is reported to have been passing all day.
>
> Some slight skirmishing to-day with small arms is reported going on at these fords.
>
> The enemy withdrew their pickets on our front at the upper fords last night.
>
> Ample preparations are going on to meet the enemy, and the week can hardly close without a desperate general engagement.
>
> Our troops are eager and confident.
>
> Grant is reported to have a very large force.

Although she couldn't have been cheered much by the accurate prophecy of a "desperate" battle, Mrs. Granberry may have taken some comfort from the description of Confederate soldiers as "eager and confident." At least the news was coming to her relatively quickly, if not altogether accurately. In fact, only a part of the Army of the Potomac, Hancock's Second Corps, was "moving on

Chancellorsville," the rest passing several miles to the west, and none of Grant's force was aiming at Fredericksburg.

By contrast, Mrs. Granberry's Northern counterpart wouldn't have known even this much on May 5. Picking up, say, the *New York Times* for May 4, a reader would have found tucked away on page four a special dispatch written by Edward A. Paul on Tuesday, May 3, and forwarded from Washington.

> All is quiet with the Army of the Potomac to-day; everything is in readiness, however, for a movement at the proper moment. Our troops are in excellent spirits, and anxious to advance against the enemy under their new Commander-in-Chief. Gen. BURNSIDE's command is in a favorable position. The Fourteenth New-York Battery had a slight skirmish yesterday while going to the front. The men employed in the construction department, and all other supernumerary help, is being sent to the rear as fast as possible.
>
> Deserters from the enemy's ranks cross the Rapidan daily. All agree that LEE is making extensive preparations to meet Gen. GRANT there. People also profess to believe that Richmond is being evacuated.

It's hard to believe that Paul would indulge himself in a joke at such a critical moment. The campaign that many people, North and South, rightly believed would be the final one of the war was about to explode. During this presidential election year, when the North would go to the polls during civil war, victory for the Federal forces would virtually guarantee Lincoln's second term and the continuation of the Union, whereas another defeat in the East, or even an exhausting stalemate, could well convince a sufficient number of other Northerners to vote for McClellan and let the costly Confederacy go. And McClellan did not present Lincoln's only political challenge. Four weeks after Paul's dispatch, radicals in the President's own party met in Cleveland to nominate General John C. Frémont as their presidential candidate. In early May 1864 the political landscape looked as tangled and disorienting as the region south of the Rapidan.

But inappropriate and hence unlikely as any intentional joking on Paul's part might be, it's also hard to believe that any reader of the Northern newspapers wouldn't have heard the dark irony of Paul's opening summary, "All is quiet with the Army of the Potomac to-day." Ever since *Harper's Weekly* published Ethelind Eliot Beers's poem, first called "The Picket Guard," on November 30, 1861, the line "All quiet along the Potomac," which echoed McClellan's telegrams to the Secretary of War, served critics of Northern military policy as a satiric caption for images of generals who were indecisive, inactive, and inept. In *The Red Badge of Courage,* Stephen Crane revises the line and intensifies the irony just as Henry Fleming is about to go into action, now with his wounded head bandaged, on the second day of Chancellorsville:

> The youth wished to launch a joke—a quotation from
> newspapers. He desired to say, "All quiet on the Rappa-
> hannock," but the guns refused to permit even a comment
> upon their uproar. He never successfully concluded the
> sentence.

In its original context in Beers's poem, the line generates irony because a soldier is killed on a night that McClellan describes as "all quiet," an irony found also in the title *All Quiet on the Western Front,* the English translation of Erich Maria Remarque's *Im Westen nichts neues* (1929). Beers's poem explores the discrepancy between official reports and individual fates. Used subsequently to satirize the Army of the Potomac, the line produces irony by contrasting a quietness that marks the momentary absence of actual fighting with a quiet that marks the prolonged absence of initiative and determination. By the time it surfaces in Crane's novel, the irony has swollen into an image of ferocity, since quietness has been completely mauled by the red animal. In the mind of someone reading Paul's dispatch on May 4, the irony must have been approaching this third phase.

But Paul's description may have had a more practical aspect as well, since May 3, the day the Army of the Potomac broke up its winter camp, was anything but quiet in the region stretching from Culpeper Court House to Brandy Station, Virginia. As J. Cutler Andrews reminds us in *The North Reports the Civil War* (1955), Northern reporters had strict instructions not to write anything for publication until after the impending battle. Paul's bland and misleading summary may simply reflect the restrictions imposed on reporting by the War

Department. Those restrictions may also account for other strange features of his dispatch. Why, for example, would he single out Burnside's Ninth Corps for special mention? True, Burnside's corps included eight New York regiments, among them the Fourteenth Heavy Artillery, apparently involved in "a slight skirmish" on May 2. But if Paul wanted to satisfy the curiosity of the *Times* readership, he would have done better to mention Hancock's celebrated Second Corps, which had thirty New York regiments. Did Paul mention Burnside's corps because it had just come to Virginia from Annapolis? Was Paul traveling with this peripheral corps? Was the reference deliberately intended to distract attention from Hancock's, Warren's, and Sedgwick's corps? Or did the reference to Burnside carry the subtle implication, intended for both Northern and Southern eyes, that if even this undistinguished general was ready to fight, then the Army of the Potomac must be so well coordinated and well positioned that its enemies had real trouble before them?

Like the report in the *Richmond Examiner*, the *Times* dispatch paints a favorable picture for its readers. Predictably enough, both papers emphasize the thorough preparation and high morale of their respective armies. But in its final paragraph the *Times* carries the newsprint war one step further by referring first to deserters and second to the supposed evacuation of Richmond. Whereas the *Examiner* report includes nothing negative about the Union army, the *Times* report implies that desertion from the Confederate army is widespread enough to merit the adjective "daily." In fact, as Ella Lonn's *Desertion during the Civil War* (1928) shows, Union desertions totaled approximately two hundred thousand and Confederate approximately 104,000. Although one can soften this surprising difference by pointing out that the Confederate Army had many fewer soldiers, the rate of Union desertions is still unexpectedly high, peaking at 7,333 desertions a month in 1864. Furthermore, four of the six states that had the dubious distinction of leading in desertions are Eastern ones (Connecticut, New Hampshire, New Jersey, New York), so a large percentage of the desertions were occurring in the Army of the Potomac. As for the statement that "People also profess to believe that Richmond is being evacuated," it is an extravagant falsehood, scarcely excused by the disingenuous qualification, "profess to believe."

On the front page of the *Richmond Examiner* for Friday, May 6, 1864, the second day of battle and the one on which her husband wrote her about watching

Hill's wounded stream past him, Mrs. Granberry could have found the tele-graphic reports of the Press Associates at the top of the second column from the right. These reports consist of two dispatches. The final sentence of the first dispatch, "No cannonading has been heard here up to one o'clock today," establishes the time of the report, sent from Orange Court House on May 5. In fact, at just about 1:00 P.M. Griffin's division of Warren's Union Fifth Corps began its attack across Saunders' Field, led by the 140th New York. Heavy can-nonading did not precede the attack, and so none would have been heard twenty-three miles away in Orange Court House. But a reporter who had been at the scene would have heard heavy musket fire erupting before noon south of Saunders' Field. The dispatch contains no mention of this fighting and focuses instead on a Confederate scouting expedition into Culpeper Court House, recently abandoned by Warren's Fifth Corps: "The scouts report the country about Culpeper Court House covered with the debris of the enemy's camps, including clothing and blankets." The scouts also captured about a dozen stragglers.

If I imagine myself the wife of a Confederate chaplain, the most significant features of the first dispatch suddenly become two short paragraphs describing Grant's force and guessing at his plans.

> Grant's force has been variously estimated to be
> between one hundred and one hundred and eighty thou-
> sand men. The first number is most probably nearest the
> truth.
> From the fact that Grant took only four days' rations
> on leaving Culpeper, it is not improbable he will decline
> acting offensively, and will fall back to the heights of
> Fredericksburg.

Although the total number of men under Grant's command—about 120,000—falls within the estimate given by the dispatch, the passing image of a force one-third again as large as the one that actually crossed the Rapidan isn't comfort-ing. Still, for all its willingness to include an estimate that is admittedly not "most probably nearest the truth," the dispatch gets the numbers right. What it doesn't get even close to right is the moral to be drawn from the four—actually three, according to Grant's *Memoirs*—days' rations. To our ears, the elaborate double negative, "it is not improbable he will decline acting offensively," sounds nothing like the simple language of contemporary wire service reports, and while the substitution of elegantly phrased conjectures for hard facts may contradict our notion of what the news should be, we can hear in this unembarrassed guessing both a pathetic innocence about the relentless man who now heads the Army of the Potomac, and the wishful thinking of people too close to the action to be able to indulge themselves in the luxury of supposed objectivity.

Given the time of the first dispatch, one would think that the second, a short two paragraphs printed directly below it and also sent from Orange Court House on May 5, would tell us about the events of that Thursday. But it doesn't: "There was some skirmishing to-day, but no general engagement." The dispatch then turns to two sentences about the engagement of Rosser's cavalry brigade in a "spirited skirmish" and concludes, "The indications are that a fight cannot long be delayed." From this piece of erroneous reporting, which bears no marks of muzzling by Confederate authorities, I shift my attention to other items in the *Examiner*. In the next column to the right, for example, I can scan all the items that M. Cronly will be auctioning off on Wednesday, May 11, at his sales rooms in Wilmington, North Carolina, items that made up the cargoes of the steamships *Pet* and *Lucy* and included dry goods, shoes, "stationary," groceries, hardware, oils, drugs, and liquors, all presumably run through the Federal blockade. In *The Civil War Day by Day*, E. B. Long mentions that the *Pet*, a British ship, was captured near Wilmington on February 16, 1864, but three months later she was obviously back in business, bringing in such items as bales of flannel, silk handkerchiefs, bone buttons, cavalry boots, calfskin shoes, stitching twine, green tea, black tea, sugar, Jamaican coffee, "50 boxes adamantine candies," black pepper, starch, nails, whale oil, camphor, morphia, brandy, and rum.

Running my eyes farther down the front page—the *Examiner* consisted of two pages—I find advertisements for apple brandy, corn meal, lard, an "elegant carriage and harness," and a soap-boiler, and notices for new songs, such as "Pray, Maiden, Pray" and "I Remember the Hour when Sadly we Parted." Among these advertisements, I also find the following:

OVERESEER WANTS A SITUATION—An Overseer, of thirty years' experience, exempt from all military duty, desires situation. He understands thoroughly the cultivation of all the cereals and tobacco, as well as vegetables, flowers, shrubbery &c. He is perfectly capable of managing a large number of slaves, and taking care of a large estate.

Bordering this notice in the column to its right, the same one headed by the telegraph dispatches from Orange Court House, appears another kind of advertisement.

RUNAWAY—FIVE HUNDRED DOLLARS REWARD—Ran away from the subscriber on the 10th of March last, my negro man PEYTON. He is about five feet ten inches high, twenty-five years of age, black, large feet and hands, with prominent lips and eyes. Has, I think, a mark on his left arm, above the elbow, from disease[.] I will give a reward of three hundred dollars if taken in the county of Albemarle, or the above amount, if caught out of said county, and placed in some jail where I can secure him again.

A. P. Giles

Scottsville, Albemarle county, Va.

Then there are some of the most puzzling items in the *Examiner,* the excerpts from Northern newspapers. Because these excerpts usually appear without commentary, it's not always clear what their purpose is or how they should be read. Does one side print the other's stories to supplement the news with a broader picture? In its edition of May 4, in the column to the left of Edward Paul's dispatch, the *Times* candidly admits its dependence on Southern newspapers for just this reason.

Now that the public are so completely in the dark as to the military programme to be carried out in Virginia—now that they are not only ignorant as to plans, but even as to actual movements, so that it is impossible for them to get up their own plans, or even to speculate intelligently, we look with interest to the rebel journals for news of our army movements and for speculations as to the significance of these movements and what they portend.

Someone living in the path of Grant's army wouldn't have felt as deeply in the dark as most New Yorkers did, but most people in Richmond still depended on Northern papers for certain kinds of news, such as a report in the May 6 *Examiner* about several "important changes" taking place in the Federal Department of the South, with John P. Hatch replacing Quincy Adams Gillmore as commander there. This is a piece of information that the Northern papers supply to Southern readers quickly, reliably, and free of charge.

But how did John M. Daniel or the other editors of the *Examiner* want me to read the account of the burning of Madison Court House, Virginia, by Federal troops, an account reprinted from the *New York Herald* of May 3? Presumably they intended something more than the provision of otherwise unavailable information, and presumably most if not all of their readers would have responded with righteous indignation at the mistreatment of civilian property, a righteous indignation the editors probably intended them to feel. If this is the case, then would the editors have expected me to react differently to the brief report of the Fort Pillow affair (April 12, 1864), also reprinted from the *New York Herald*?

> Senator Wade and Mr. Gooch, the Sub-Committee on the
> Conduct of the War, who went to Fort Pillow to ascertain
> the facts as to the alleged massacre of coloured troops there
> have returned and report that the stories have not been
> exaggerated. That great cruelty was practiced by the rebel
> troops, after the surrender of the fort, there can be no
> doubt.

Mary Chesnut, another regular reader of the *Examiner,* seems to have received the story of the Fort Pillow massacre with skepticism. If other readers did the same, then they must have taken the reprinting of the story as an ironic gesture on the part of the editors, who reproduced the report as a shameless example of self-evident Yankee propaganda.

Moving through the Northern news requires that I execute nimble transitions from reading with simple curiosity to reading with righteous indignation, then from reading with righteous indignation to reading with a keen sense of irony. But when I come across an excerpt from a *New York Herald* editorial, I suddenly read with a feeling more complicated than simple curiosity, a feeling untinged by indignation or irony. Having urged the government to find employment for Lincoln's political opponents, George McClellan and John Frémont, the *Herald* comments that such a move would unify the North and "add immensely to the *morale* of our army." The editorial, or at least the excerpt reprinted in the *Examiner,* then closes with a sentence that rises beyond its immediate context to bring the spring of 1864 into prophetic focus: "This is the only way in which we can finish the war this summer; and if we do not finish the war this summer the war will finish us."

Although the *Richmond Examiner* of May 6 tells me nothing about the fighting in the Wilderness on May 5, at least I know approximately where Grant is, if not exactly where he's headed. By contrast, the *Times* gives me a very different, and badly confused, picture. In the May 5 edition dispatches from Washington appear on the front page, but these include only minor notes about "GEN. GRANT ON DISCIPLINE" ("official correspondence to be conducted through proper channels") and "GEN. GRANT ON TENTS FOR THE TROOPS" ("When troops refuse to accept shelter tents they will not be furnished with any"). Meanwhile, in the first column of page eight appear two items of much greater significance. The first is an order from Meade dated May 2 and directed to all soldiers "who refuse to do duty, on the ground that their term of service has expired."

> It will be made known to such men that their conduct
> being open mutiny they will be punished with death, with-
> out trial, unless they return to duty; and hereafter any sol-
> dier who refuses to do duty on a similar plea will instantly
> be shot, without any form of trial whatever. The honor of
> the service and the necessities of the hour admit of no
> other disposition of such cases.

But it is the second item, a report that somewhere along the Orange and Alexandria Railroad Confederate guerrillas have attacked black troops serving in Burnside's Ninth Corps, that causes more trouble. Although the *Times* of May 5 prints a report from the *Washington Star* asserting that, contrary to rumor, no black troops were killed or wounded, other papers show no such restraint. As Andrews narrates in *The North Reports on the Civil War,* "On May 5, several New York newspapers issued extras announcing that Burnside's corps had been badly beaten and practically wiped out." Anyone agitated by these erroneous reports would have awakened to find the *Times* of May 6 announcing in large headlines that the Army of the Potomac had crossed the Rapidan without opposition. Since the following reports make no mention of Burnside's supposed repulse at Thoroughfare Gap, it appears either that the *Times* did not participate in the hysteria of rumor or that it was doing a more responsible job of censoring itself according to War Department instructions. But accurate as the *Times* headlines are, the first dispatch, sent from Washington, slides from fact into speculation.

> If LEE intends to make a stand this side of Richmond, it is possible he may be met near the old battle-ground of Chancellorsville, but it is the general impression that he has fallen back from his position on the Rapidan to Richmond, in order to protect that City from the formidable force now marching upon it from the rear, and which is as likely to strike on one side of the James River as the other.

This dispatch is unsigned, but whoever wrote it says nothing about how he gathered "the general impression" that Lee had retreated to Richmond. The limitations imposed on the Northern press by the War Department do not account for the printing of this impression, since it does nothing to fool the Confederates and everything to mislead the Northern public. Working my way down the first column of the front page, I find three subsequent dispatches, none of which addresses the fate of Burnside's Ninth Corps. The "Second Dispatch" paraphrases a message from Grant stating that "forty-eight hours would determine whether he was to have battle on the Rapidan, or whether under the works around Richmond." Grant's dispatch, written May 4, will prove an accurate forecast, but it does nothing to foster the general impression that Lee has retreated to Richmond. Then in "Another Dispatch," dated 2:00 P.M. on May 5 and based on an extra issued in Washington, the writer, having implicitly acknowledged the limitations placed on reporting, reports the Rapidan crossing accurately but soon clouds the report with his mistaken beliefs.

> We feel authorized to state, since it can't now afford information to the enemy, that the Army of the Potomac had advanced toward Richmond, and the struggle for the possession of the rebel capital is begun.

> Our army moved on Tuesday night, and has now
> crossed the Rapidan. The crossing was made at Jacob's,
> Culpepper [*sic*], Germanna, and United States Fords, and
> was effected without serious opposition.

So far, so good. But then comes the misleading statement, "LEE has been com-
pelled to fall back from the strong position where he has held us at bay all Winter." Having read this sentence, I hope I can be forgiven for imagining that the
mighty Army of the Potomac has forced Lee back from the Rapidan, when in
fact he has merely withdrawn his pickets from the fords and is marching the
Army of Northern Virginia toward Grant along the Orange Turnpike and the
Orange Plank Road.

But it's the closing paragraph of "Another Dispatch" that mixes fact with
speculation and reflects how little the Northern press and public knew about
Grant's new policy of focusing on Lee rather than Richmond, a policy com-
municated to Meade in a confidential letter dated April 9, 1864, one year to the
day before the surrender at Appomattox: "Wherever Lee goes, there you will
go also."

> It is the opinion of some that he [Lee] will fight at Chan-
> cellorsville. Every hour may now bring us news of battle,
> but we are inclined to the belief that it will be a foot race
> for Richmond. The rebel capital will undoubtedly be
> flanked and invested should LEE'S army occupy its
> defences, and the country may reasonably hope that this
> time Richmond will fall.

Having read plenty of war news, I accept the expressions of conjecture and
belief as features of wartime reporting even in the *Times,* which, according to
Andrews, by the outbreak of war had already established itself as "one of the
greatest newspapers of America" because of "its excellent news service, which
even then devoted special attention to foreign affairs, its stable editorial policy,
and its general sobriety of manner." As a somewhat experienced reader, I've
come across the journalistic formula "profess to believe" in more than one
place. But how do I know when to believe in belief? Is it when I believe in the
people who believe, or when I have no other choice?

With the *Times* of May 7 come two reports, one of them true, the other false. Happily, the true report states succinctly, "There is no truth, whatever, in reports of the repulse of BURNSIDE at Thoroughfare Gap," explaining instead that "BURNSIDE'S reserves, which follow the main army, are now across the Rappahannock." Relieved by this news, I almost let my guard down just enough to accept the second report.

> There is little doubt but that LEE is falling back from the
> Rapidan upon Richmond, having been driven to this by
> the flank movement of Gen. GRANT. The race will now be
> for Richmond.

Faced both with the muzzle imposed on them by the War Department and with the dark ignorance confessed by the *Times* on May 4, the Northern newspapers have to decide what to print. As the May 5 dispatch from Washington shows clearly ("We feel authorized to state, since it can't now afford information to the enemy"), the *Times* is following the spirit of the news blackout. If the newspaper has information about the Battle of the Wilderness that could help the Confederates, it has to withhold it. If it has no information, the newspaper can possibly justify its dependence on conjecture, impression, and professed beliefs. But what is most puzzling is the presentation of falsehood as confirmed fact. Here is "Another Dispatch," dated Washington, Friday, May 6, and printed by the *Times* in the column to the right of the headlines.

> Information has been received that our army has
> passed safely through the "Wilderness," but nothing fur-
> ther is known this morning of the onward movement.
> Rumors prevail of fighting, but they are founded on
> mere conjecture, as it is known that up to 7 o'clock on
> Wednesday none had taken place.
> There are troops remaining on this side of the Rapi-
> dan, but it would not be proper to state their exact loca-
> tion. These include some, if not all the colored soldiers.

Sorting out the tangle of threads in this dispatch presents several challenges. First of all, who could have given information about what hadn't happened? No one traveling with the Army of the Potomac, especially in the rear, could have believed that it had passed through the Wilderness as of May 5. The single exception could be someone positioned near the head of Hancock's Second Corps, which had arrived west of Todd's Tavern, near the outskirts of the Wilderness, when its rear was still barely out of Chancellorsville and the order came to turn around and march north, back into the Wilderness, to protect the Brock Road intersection from Hill's advancing Third Corps. But how could such a person, located among the southernmost elements of the Army of the Potomac, get back to send a dispatch to Washington without crossing behind an army heavily engaged in combat?

Then there is the somewhat contemptuous dismissal of conjecture, which was sufficient for dispatches on the preceding days but suddenly is found wanting. For some reason, the writer feels justified in basing his dismissal of rumor on information that, by May 6, is two days old. Of course, the awful irony here is that in this case the rumors and conjectures are true, whereas the information that has been received is false. Finally, the dispatch appears to consolidate its authority by revealing a knowledge of troops still on the north side of the Rapidan and withholding information about their location because of the War Department restrictions. But that authority is meager and qualified.

When I try to put myself in the place of a New Yorker in May 1864, I feel bewildered. From the perspective of an era obsessed with transmitting and receiving information instantaneously, the Northern newspapers of early May 1864 look like the impenetrable thickets of the Wilderness. That the news comes so slowly is hard enough, but that it also comes so hopelessly confused is altogether unnerving. It's not simply a matter of unknotting the true from the false; it's a matter of trying to distinguish among all kinds of truths, half-truths, withheld truths, rumors that could be truths, believed truths, and wishful thinking. When a newspaper admits that it's in the dark, that it's looking to the enemy's newspapers for information, that it can't print all of what it does know because it's not allowed to, then what am I to believe? But perhaps wartime readers didn't feel this way at all. Perhaps I, a reader of newspapers that employ fact checkers and print corrections daily and can be sued for printing damaging falsehoods, am projecting my computer-age expectations onto a readership that didn't read newspapers that way.

Perhaps. But I don't think so. Or even if I am projecting, many of those readers would have shared at least some of my expectations. What would a reader of 1864 have expected from a newspaper? One answer comes from Mark Twain's *Roughing It* (1872). After the brief, inglorious stint in the Confederate army that he later described in "The Private History of a Campaign That Failed" (1902), Samuel Clemens, who was not yet Mark Twain, traveled to Nevada in 1861. From 1862 until 1864 he worked as a reporter for the Virginia City *Territorial Enterprise* under the supervision of Joseph T. Goodman, editor and proprietor. When he joined the *Enterprise* the same month as Second Manassas–Bull Run, the young Clemens asked Goodman "for some instructions with regard to my duties." Goodman's answer, even through the filter of humorous recollection, clinches the point.

> "Never say 'We learn' so-and-so, or 'It is reported,' or 'It is
> rumored,' or 'We understand' so-and-so, but go to headquar-
> ters and get the absolute facts, and then speak out and say 'It
> is so-and-so.' Otherwise, people will not put confidence in
> your news. Unassailable certainty is the thing that gives a
> newspaper the firmest and most valuable reputation."

Mark Twain's account of the flush days of Nevada silver mining during the Civil War does many things, one of which is to string together a series of tall tales in order to probe the complexities of truth and falsehood. At one level, *Roughing It* unwinds a comic fable about credibility and credulity, and at many points the narrative flaunts its own untrustworthiness. But no matter how heavily Twain may have tinged Goodman's instructions with irony, those instructions reflect the existence and value of a journalistic principle called "unassailable certainty." Unassailable certainty may be hard, if not impossible, to come by, and, when apparently achieved, it may be only an illusion at best. But Goodman's instructions, recalled by a man who left his reporting job to go farther west during the same month that the Battle of the Wilderness was fought, demonstrate that newspaper readers of the 1860s expected the news to consist of confirmed facts just as I do now, however naive I may be.

In other words, to excuse the use of beliefs, impressions, conjectures, speculations, and rumors by arguing that these were conventional features of nineteenth-century journalism is to patronize the past. True, I would never expect the *New York Times* of today to admit that it relied heavily on other papers for news, let alone for mere speculation. But to conclude simply that journalism has come a long, long way since the Civil War is to miss one very important point. Of course journalism has changed since, and partly because of, the war. As the *Times* itself observed on its fiftieth anniversary in a passage quoted by

Andrews, the Civil War taught New York newspapers "the surpassing value of individual, competitive, triumphant enterprise in getting early and exclusive news" and "the possibility of building up large circulations by striving unceasingly to meet a popular demand from prompt and adequate reports" (September 25, 1901). But to interpret the unreliability of reports from the Wilderness in May 1864 as evidence of immaturity in the history of journalism is to fail to see and feel the crisis of the hour. It's not that the *Times* didn't know what unassailable certainty was or what prompt and adequate reports were; it's that the Wilderness swallowed up certainty and made a shambles of both promptness and adequacy. In the first week of May 1864, the *Times* sounds as confused and bewildered as any of its readers could have felt.

Meanwhile, May 7 brought Richmond readers something much different. The headlines in the first column of the *Examiner,* preceded by an eerie error in dating, "Saturday Morning, ...May 6, 1864" (Saturday was the seventh), fulfill the prophecy of the May 4 dispatch.

THE WAR NEWS—DESPERATE BATTLE BETWEEN THE TWO ARMIES IN VIRGINIA—THE YANKEES BEATEN— CAPTURE OF A LARGE NUMBER OF PRISONERS AND ARTILLERY—THE ENEMY IN JAMES RIVER—LARGE REINFORCEMENTS COMING UP—ONE OF THEIR GUN- BOATS BLOWN UP—SKIRMISHING AT PORT WALTHALL, ETC.

The following report opens with a long paragraph not about the "desperate battle" but about the "noble alacrity" with which troops and citizens of Richmond responded to the news of "the Yankees ascending the James river with a large fleet." News of the Wilderness comes in a second paragraph headed "THE FIRST NEWS OF THE MORNING—A GREAT VICTORY BY OUR ARMY IN NORTHERN VIRGINIA."

The morning opened with a cloudless sky, and the news commenced to come in gloriously. Just as the city was rushing to arms to meet the movement of the Yankees in the James river, the rumour came that our army in Northern Virginia had won a great victory. This news was swiftly

confirmed by the following official dispatch from General
LEE, which was received about nine o'clock, and was soon
posted on the bulletin boards of the different newspaper
offices.

From a Confederate point of view, the news couldn't have been better, and
Richmonders could have reveled in it as long as they didn't read Lee's dispatch
too closely or too skeptically. In the *Examiner* the dispatch is dated May 6,
1864, but in Clifford Dowdey's edition of *The Wartime Papers of Robert E. Lee*
(1961), it's dated 11:00 P.M. on May 5. With the information provided by the
Examiner, we can track the flow of news, which left Lee during the last hour of
Thursday, arrived at the newspaper office twenty-two hours later on Friday, and
appeared before the public Saturday morning. In the dispatch, Lee reports that
the enemy crossed the Rapidan "yesterday," that Ewell and Hill "moved to
oppose him" on the Orange Turnpike and the Plank Road respectively, that
Ewell "repulsed" the attack made on him, that Hill "successfully resisted
repeated and desperate assaults," and that Rosser's cavalry drove back a large
force of cavalry and artillery. Before he reports the death of General J. M. Jones
and the wounding of General Leroy A. Stafford, Lee then summarizes the
action of May 5, in the typography of the *Examiner,* "By the blessing of God
we *maintained our position against every effort* until night, when the contest
closed."

In their exultation readers may or may not have thought about the typography used by the *Examiner,* but had they considered it, they might have realized that the emphasis was probably not Lee's. In his *Wartime Papers* this
telegram, along with all others, appears in all capital letters with no emphasis.
If Lee had chosen to emphasize one part of the sentence more than the other,
it's far more likely he would have chosen "*By the blessing of God.*" In view of the
emphasis placed by the *Examiner,* readers may have wondered how the newspaper drew the conclusion that Lee's telegram confirmed that the Army of
Northern Virginia had won "a great victory" on May 5. Maintaining one's position "against every effort" is not the same as driving the invader back across the
Rapidan. Perhaps the willingness to stretch from holding one's own to glorious
triumph over the enemy reflects the fondness for the sensational that helped
make Daniel's *Examiner,* according to the Richmond correspondent of the
Charleston *Courier,* whom Andrews quotes in *The South Reports the Civil War*
(1970), "one of the most readable and attractive newspapers in the South" (Feb-

ruary 12, 1862). At any rate, if the *Examiner* did construe Lee's restrained dispatch more favorably than the actual report warranted, it was not alone: "The
effect of the news was most inspiriting to our troops, and they took their line of
march [to meet the enemy coming up the James] amidst huzzas and cheers all
along the streets."

But the battle isn't over yet, and as I work my way across the front page
from left to right, I watch the news arriving. In the second column, under the
heading "THE BATTLE RENEWED YESTERDAY," I discover that ignorance
about the events of May 6 does not diminish the celebration of May 5.

> It was not known up to a late hour yesterday whether the
> battle had been renewed by the armies along the Rapid
> Ann. There were various rumours on this point, but the
> matter was put to rest by a dispatch received about three
> o'clock, stating that fighting had been renewed at daylight
> yesterday, and was raging along the whole lines. Accounts
> received up to five o'clock reported that everything was
> progressing satisfactorily, but intimated that a most desper-
> ate battle was being fought. We will give what later news we
> receive, keeping our columns open to the latest moment.

The last sentence reflects not only the importance of the events unfolding
twenty or twenty-five miles from Orange Court House but also the pressures
the *Examiner* faced as it prepared its edition for Saturday, May 7. Since the
paper wouldn't publish on Sunday, May 8, it had to extend its resources in
every way to cover the untimely gap in its reporting. In the third column, a paragraph headed "THE LATEST FROM OUR ARMIES IN VIRGINIA" works to fashion belief into news before the paper signs off.

> We could get nothing official from the War Department last
> night, but we think, from the information we have from
> other reliable sources, we may safely assure our readers
> that our army has won a great and signal victory over the
> enemy, capturing large numbers of prisoners and driving
> him at every point: at least, this was so up to nine o'clock
> yesterday morning. It was reported here that the battle
> rested for the day, but other accounts state, and correctly

we believe, that the battle was renewed and raged all day—
our forces driving the enemy at all points.

In the jumble of time references spread across the front page of the *Examiner,* "last night" appears to mean the night of May 6, implying that this latest report is being written in the early hours of May 7, and "nine o'clock yesterday morning" refers to the morning of May 6. If the *Examiner* had reliable information through 9:00 A.M. on May 6, it actually knew a fair amount, since by that hour much had already happened. On the Confederate left, along the Orange Turnpike, Ewell's soldiers had attacked Sedgwick's Sixth Corps at 4:45 A.M. with the sunrise, and on the Union left, along the Orange Plank Road, Hancock's soldiers had attacked Hill's Third Corps. The latter assault overwhelmed the Confederate right, caused the stampede of Heth's and Wilcox's divisions that Hugh Nelson describes in his diary, and set the stage for Longstreet's dramatic arrival from Gordonsville and the famous "Lee to the rear" incident that Nelson also narrates. The adverse effects of Longstreet's counterattack appear in Union dispatches to headquarters as early as 6:20 A.M., and by 8:00 A.M. the fighting on the Orange Plank Road was already subsiding.

But the *Examiner* hadn't finished yet. When it pledged to keep its columns open to the last minute early on the morning of Saturday, May 7, it meant what it said. Moving to the sixth and presumably the last column to be set in type, I find even later news, for that column contains four dispatches telegraphed by the Press Associates from Orange Court House on May 6. The first two narrate the events of Thursday, May 5, repeating and supplementing the details of Lee's earlier dispatch, although the first dispatch—which describes Ewell's corps as fighting the Union Fifth Corps, "including Syke's regulars," a unit led by George Sykes, not Syke, at First Manassas–Bull Run—shows no awareness that Sykes, who had commanded the Fifth Corps at Gettysburg and during the Mine Run operations until Grant arrived in the East, was subsequently relieved and replaced by Warren, the guardian of Little Round Top. The Battle of the Wilderness found Sykes far away, serving in the Department of Kansas.

With the arrival of the third dispatch, the *Examiner* had information about May 6 that took its readers up to midday. By that time Longstreet's aide, Lieutenant Colonel Gilbert Moxley Sorrel, had led through the unfinished railroad cut the successful flanking maneuver that caught Hancock by surprise and rolled him up, as he later put it, like a wet blanket. Sorrel's attack began about

11:00 A.M., and within the next hour and a half, Longstreet had been shot by the
Twelfth Virginia, General Micah Jenkins of South Carolina had been killed by
the same friendly fire, and Union General James Wadsworth had been mortally
wounded. Here is the version the third dispatch gave the *Examiner:*

> The attack by the enemy this morning was very violent.
> They were repulsed in every instance. A strong effort was
> made to turn our right. We drove them on our left, but they
> were stubborn until Longstreet finally forced them to give
> way. General Longstreet received a severe wound in the
> shoulder. General Paul Jennings was mortally wounded.
> The fighting was principally with musketry, the ground
> being unsuitable to artillery.
>   Colonel Brown, of the Virginia artillery, was killed.
>   The battle was fought near the Wilderness. The enemy
> have been pushed back to Chancellorsville. Everything
> looks well. A full account will be sent to morrow.
>   The Yankee General Wadsworth was killed.
>   Seventeen hundred prisoners have been received here.

In its fourth sentence the dispatch doesn't make clear that "they were stub-
born" on the Confederate right, not left, nor does it mention that Longstreet
was shot by his own men. It also garbles Micah Jenkins into Paul Jennings (the
Roster of Confederate Soldiers lists no Paul Jennings), and announces the death
of Wadsworth two days before it actually took place. At no time during the battle did the Army of Northern Virginia push the Army of the Potomac back to
Chancellorsville. But for all its inaccuracies, this dispatch does something that
no earlier one had done; it gives the battle a place and a name: "The battle was
fought near the Wilderness."

With this name to orient me, I can skim over the fourth dispatch from
Orange Court House, headed "FURTHER PARTICULARS," which contains no
later news and few fresh details, except that Confederate General Henry
"Rock" Benning was wounded and that the "Richmond Ambulance Committee arrived here this morning." This last detail, along with two items in the
fourth column, is sufficient to recall attention from the glorious victory to the
pressing work that follows it.

BANDAGES FOR THE WOUNDED—To-day will witness,
doubtless, the arrival in Richmond of many hundreds of
our suffering wounded from the battle-fields, and it is the
privilege as well as the duty, of the citizens and others to
provide as many alleviating appliances as possible. Surgeon
J. B. Read, in charge of General Hospital No. 4, Tenth
street between Clay and Leigh, requests that the ladies
send to the hospital, early this morning, as many clean
linen rags, for bandages, as they can provide. Attention to
this appeal is earnestly enjoined upon all who have the
linen to spare. The stock on hand in the hospitals is quite
limited now, and as No. 4 hospital is central, the bandages
can be distributed to the others if a surplus is found.

The second item, headed "SEABROOK RECEIVING HOSPITAL,"
announces the readiness of accommodations for between six and seven hundred wounded men from "the sanguinary battles now progressing in Northern
Virginia." Twenty-two cavalryman, wounded on May 5, have already arrived.
"Their wounds were mostly serious, requiring amputation." With that news,
I've had enough and can put down the newspaper, welcoming Sunday, May 8,
when the *Examiner* rested.

But the *New York Times* published on Sunday, May 8, the first day of the fighting at Spotsylvania, and the Sunday edition cost four cents rather than the usual
three for weekdays. Having been reassured by the edition of May 7 that Burnside's Ninth Corps had crossed the Rappahannock unharmed and that the general impression pointed to Lee's falling back on Richmond, I notice the large
boldface words "THE BATTLE" at the top of the first column. I also see at once
the large map covering the top half of the third, fourth, and fifth columns, a map
of Virginia from Fredericksburg south to the North Carolina line and from
Gordonsville east to the Chesapeake Bay, which I use to orient myself as I work
my way through the six columns of military news. As I read, I discover that the
Times has printed different reports of the fighting and openly comments on
their credibility. Reading all the news only serves as prologue to deciding what
news to believe.

In a few short headlines, I learn much of what Southern readers learned
one day earlier.

THE BATTLE. / IMPORTANT NEWS FROM VIRGINIA. / A
Great Battle Begun on Thursday. / Lee Confronts Grant
with His Whole Army. / Severe Engagement Between Han-
cock and Longstreet. / HEAVY LOSS ON BOTH SIDES. /
The Fifth Corps also Partly Engaged. / The Battle
Renewed on Friday Morning. / Gen. Burnside's Corps on
the Ground for Support. / STUART'S CAVALRY ROUTED
BY SHERIDAN. / The Troops Enthusiastic to a High
Degree.

After promising "FULL PARTICULARS FROM OUR SPECIAL CORRESPON-
DENT," the report, dated "Washington, May 7," tells little that is true beyond
the fact that the loss was heavy on both sides. On Thursday, Lee did not make
"a tremendous and violent attack to pierce" the Union center because he did
not want to bring on a general engagement until Longstreet arrived from Gordonsville; Sheridan did not rout Stuart's cavalry; and the commander of the
Second Corps was Hancock, as named in the headline, not Hitchcock, as a
proofreading lapse later in the report suggests. The possible contribution of the
Times to anyone's comprehension of events in central Virginia comes not with
the accuracy of its own reporting but with the intelligent cautions it administers
elsewhere.

Following its own report, the paper prints a lengthy dispatch from the *New
York Tribune,* dated Friday, May 6, at 9:00 P.M. and sent from Union Mills, Virginia, about twenty miles from Washington. Although unsigned, this dispatch
results from the legendary trip of young Henry Wing, who rode, swam, and
walked in order to bring the first news from the Wilderness to Washington,
where, the story goes, he received a kiss from Lincoln. In his dispatch Wing
notes that he left the battlefield at 5:00 A.M. on May 6, just as "heavy firing"
became audible on the Union right. The young reporter gets much of the picture correct, although he locates the three Confederate corps incorrectly, placing Hill on the Union right with Ewell and Longstreet on the Union left on
Thursday, the day before he actually arrived. The dispatch concludes that there
"ought to be no doubt that there has been a grand victory," a conclusion the
Times addresses elsewhere. But by comparison with the next report, reprinted
from the *Washington Republican,* the *Tribune* report presents a model of
accuracy.

The *Republican* report, in column two, has the Battle of the Wilderness raging for three days, not two, with hostilities opening on Wednesday, May 4. Of all the Union corps the *Republican* mentions only Burnside's, swelling its ranks by 50 percent—from twenty to thirty thousand soldiers—and conjecturing that "Unless LEE received reinforcements equal to BURNSIDE'S corps, the battle of Friday must have proven terribly disastrous to him." Then, giving the three-day news blackout an original and optimistic twist, the *Republican* concludes that the "fact that we have received no news of yesterday's fighting leads to the belief that LEE is endeavoring to get away to Richmond, and GRANT is in pursuit." But the exaggerations and inaccuracies of the *Republican* report do not make up the most significant aspect of its appearance in the *Times*. Most significant is the decision by the *Times* to print such a report at all, since that decision reveals the predicament of a sober, responsible newspaper faced with the inscrutability of the Wilderness. It doesn't want to spread sensational rumors, but in the face of its own ignorance it can't afford to dismiss any story, even this one. An editorial note inserted in brackets after the *Republican* report shows the discomfort it causes the *Times* editors.

> The above dispatch is so extravagant in its statements, and
> corresponds so poorly with other and more reliable
> advices, that it is doubtless entitled to very little credit.
> —ED. TIMES

Having sounded this caution, the *Times* devotes most of the rest of the second column not to reporting but to helping its readers analyze and interpret the many reports now coming in. Like the May 8 *New York Herald* (the *Tribune,* which had printed Wing's story on May 7, did not publish on Sundays), the *Times* prints a press dispatch from Washington, a dispatch that takes its cue from the *Washington Star,* which rejected a report by the Independent Telegraph Line that Grant already had achieved a great victory, admitting that the Lincoln administration had received no "information of more decisive results than that furnished by the *Tribune* dispatch." The dispatch meditates with wise and clear-eyed eloquence on the agonizing uncertainty of events in Virginia.

> During the day many inquiries were made of officers of
> the Government, but without the satisfaction naturally
> desirable on the part of those who have imppatient [*sic*]
> desires for early and complete success, and who forget that
> the work must be necessarily stubborn, heavy and persis-

tent on both sides, owing to the great importance to each of
the result.

The fragmentary information received from time to
time shows nothing decisive, but serves to contradict many
rumors and speculations concerning the whereabouts and
designs of the rebels which were so confidently asserted.

In newspaper writing, both during the Civil War and today, so much is
ephemeral, perishable, obsolete in a matter of hours. Since newspapers exist to
deliver timely information, and information is only timely when it is an advance
on old news, we don't expect newspapers to sustain us with abiding wisdom.
But forced to concede the absence of timely information about the Wilderness,
the *New York Times* of Sunday, May 8, 1864, instructed its readers in more than
how to cope with the excruciating gaps in the reporting of the battle; it told
them, by implication, how to read the war itself. In an extraordinary paragraph,
headed "Giving the Battle-News" and located at the bottom of the second column on page four, the *Times* first inveighs against "utterers of fabricated news"
and then describes the wartime challenge facing its readers.

So long as the war continues there will not only be a class
of vampires found glutting in the life-blood of the country,
but there will be professional pimps to cater to their lust. It
is part of the national sacrifice to endure this affliction, in
addition to the prime evil of the war itself.

How does one live with no news, especially when the appetite for reports
of violence is so powerful that it invites pornographic stimulation by false or
distorted news? How does one live with uncertainty, the uncertainty, in a
phrase from the same column, of "painfully meager" details, when there is
always a brand of false or distorted certainty for sale? Although the *Times*
doesn't use this language, in its reactions to rumors from the Wilderness it
urges on its readers the patience to live with doubt, mystery, and uncertainty
without grasping after the first convenient or attractive explanation that comes
along. Someone hoping for accurate news from the Wilderness in 1864, like
someone hoping for even partial comprehension of the Civil War a century or
two later, must endure the affliction of living, in the language of the press dispatch, without the satisfaction naturally desirable on the part of those who have
impatient desires for early and complete success.

Combing the rest of the Sunday edition, I find among other things another Richmond paper, the *Enquirer,* mocking the *Times* for laboring under "unveraciousness" in its reporting of the "so-called" massacre at Fort Pillow; news of the reception of Garibaldi in London; an item about the draft in New York; an item about the pay of black soldiers; an advertisement for treatment of hypochondriacs and hysterics by Dr. Jones in 9th Street near Broadway; an advertisement for Barnum's American Museum; an advertisement for the Duplex Elliptic Spring Skirts, the "New Skirt for 1864"; notice of a new poem by Robert Browning in the current *Atlantic;* a notice about government pensions for widows, mothers, children, and sisters of deceased soldiers and seamen; a story about a counterfeit hundred-dollar greenback; and a story about the recent decline in recruits from New York for Hancock's Second Corps. I also discover, at last, that "the locality of the battle-ground is in the densest part of that wild tract known as 'the Wilderness,' and only a short distance from the Chancellorsville battle-ground, even if the conflict does not rage over a portion of the same field." But nothing I find convinces me that the *Times* errs in concluding from the shrouded beginnings of the Wilderness campaign "that there is no miraculous interposition to be looked for in this war."

On the morning of Monday, May 9, the day Union General John Sedgwick was killed by a Confederate sharpshooter at Spotsylvania, both Northerners and Southerners would have shared the happiness of triumph, as they woke to the news that their respective armies had won a great victory. After the silence of Sunday, the *Richmond Examiner* resumed its suspended narrative.

> Up to the hour of going to press with our Saturday morning's paper nothing was known of the result of the battle of Friday, and hence the public mind was left, for the time, in a most painful suspense. But this anxiety was relieved early Saturday morning by the following official dispatch from General LEE, announcing that our army had repulsed the enemy at every point, and driven him to the cover of his entrenchments.

The *Examiner* prints dispatches sent to the Secretary of War by Lee on both May 6 and May 7, the first of which reports of the enemy that, in the typography of the Richmond paper, *"Every advance on his part,* thanks to a merciful God, *has been repulsed,"* but neither one of which contains the details of "a complete victory," if "complete victory" entails forcing the Army of the Potomac to retreat, as it did after Chancellorsville. Nevertheless the paper concludes "that GRANT had been whipped" and, in the words of the headlines, was "IN RETREAT ON FREDERICKSBURGH."

Meanwhile, the *Times* for the same day opens its first column on the front page with joyful headlines.

> GLORIOUS NEWS / Defeat and Retreat of Lee's Army. / TWO DAYS
> BATTLE IN VIRGINIA / Lieut.-General Grant Against Gen. Lee. / The
> Struggle of Thursday and of Friday in the Wilderness. / IMMENSE
> REBEL LOSSES. / Lee Leaves His Killed and Wounded in Our Hands.
> / Our Loss Twelve Thousand.

The following report consists of two "SPECIAL DISPATCHES TO THE N.Y. TIMES" sent from Washington. The first, based on news received in Washington up to seven o'clock on Saturday evening, comments that the fighting of Thursday and Friday "was very severe" but adds that the "rebels were reported retreating yesterday morning," that is, the morning of Saturday, May 7. The second dispatch, written "from headquarters at Wilderness Tavern, Friday, May 6th," reports that "the Army of the Potomac has added another to its list of murderous conflicts." This report contains inaccuracies—it places Hancock's "iron old Second Corps" on the Union right, for example—but it gives a keener sense of the topography than any other report so far.

> Although the nature of the ground has been of a terrible
> character, most of it being so thickly wooded as to render
> movements all but impossible, and to conceal entirely the
> operations of the enemy, yet he has been signally repulsed
> in all his attacks, and nothing but the nature of the battle-
> field has prevented it from being a crushing defeat.

Not surprisingly, the two newspapers agree on relative casualties no more closely than they do on the victor and the vanquished. In the *Examiner*, Lee's first dispatch reports, "Our loss in killed is not large, but we have many wounded, most of them slightly, artillery being little used on either side." To this encouraging picture the newspaper adds a sharp contrast with the accurate summary, "The enemy's loss is very large," a statement that may have softened the effect of the previous sentence on Southern readers: "As in the case of STONEWALL JACKSON, Generals LONGSTREET and JENKINS were shot through mistake, by our own men."

In the *Times,* the May 6 dispatch written at Wilderness Tavern concludes, "The loss on both sides has been very heavy, but at this hour of hasty writing, I cannot even give an estimate." The dispatch based on news received in Washington up to seven o'clock on the evening of May 7 gives an unusually accurate estimate of Union losses: "The number of wounded is reported at about ten thousand; the killed at two thousand." In fact, according to Long, the wounded numbered 12,037 and the dead 2,246. The dispatch makes no mention of the 3,383 missing, most of them captured, and its representation of Confederate losses, while a predictable accompaniment to the report of Union victory, contains no truth at all: "The loss of the enemy exceeds this."

But the *Richmond Examiner* and the *New York Times* do agree on one feature of the fighting in the Wilderness. The latter, with customary reserve, calls it "very severe," and the former, less reserved and readier to brandish superlatives, gets something about the battle exactly right, even as it mistakes the local retreats on the Union left or right for a full retreat of the Army of the Potomac.

> All accounts say the carnage was terrible. The Yankees
> fought with more desperation than ever before during the
> war. . . . But our men proved too much for the Yankees, and
> after a desperate struggle—such, probably as was never
> before known in this war—the Yankees gave way and were
> soon in full retreat. . . . It is plain that the Yankees have suf-
> fered terribly in this battle, and that GRANT'S army has
> been badly worsted.

If I had been a Southerner reading this last sentence, I think I would have had mixed feelings, the gratitude for victory complicated by the acknowledgment of new desperation in the fighting. But whatever my feelings, I couldn't have lingered over the sentence about Grant's army being "badly worsted," as the next line, "REPORTED FIGHT NEAR SPOTSYLVANIA COURT HOUSE," shows that desperate fighting in the Wilderness has concluded nothing. Also,

the adjacent column contains the first batch of news dreaded by every woman
with someone to lose in the Army of Northern Virginia.

> OUR WOUNDED OFFICERS.—The following are the names
> of our wounded officers who had been received at the offi-
> cers' hospital, (Baptist Institute,) Tenth street, up to last
> evening. We are informed by the surgeon in charge that
> very few of the wounds are serious, and not more than five
> or six are looked upon as dangerous or likely to result in
> amputation, and fewer still in death.
>   Lieutenant R M Hood, Thirty-first Georgia, wounded
> in thigh; Lieutenant P Byron, Tenth Louisiana, in arm;
> Captain J D Graham, Seventh South Carolina, arm; Lieu-
> tenant H L Farley, Third South Carolina, cheek; Lieu-
> tenant T S Norman, Fifth South Carolina, chin . . .

And so on down a column otherwise unbroken by spaces or indentations.
These first few men fought in the First and Second Corps, under Longstreet
and Ewell, but farther down the list appears "Lieutenant J J Hicks, Second Mississippi, shoulder." Hicks fought with Heth's Division of Hill's Third Corps.
Was he one of the wounded men whom Ella Granberry's husband saw going to
the rear early on May 6?

I don't find such a list in the *Times* until the edition of Tuesday, May 10,
which opens the first column of the front page with the headlines:

> VICTORY! / "ON TO RICHMOND." / Lee's Defeat and Retreat Fully
> Confirmed.

Searching the lists, I see more than just wounded and more than just officers.

> Among the killed are the following: Lieut.-Col. Burt, Third
> Maine; Maj. Gray, Fourth Maine; T. J. Whittemore, do.; M.
> Sweeny, Seventeenth Maine; T. Toole, do.; T. M. McIntyre,
> do.; Sergt. Baker, do., Wm. Sibley. John Paerson. Sergt.
> Fanhour, Lieut. Doe. The Seventeenth Maine entered the
> fight with 450 men, and lost about 200.

These men all belonged to Birney's Third Division of Hancock's Second Corps, which confronted Heth's Division of Hill's Third Corps near the Brock Road the afternoon of Thursday, May 5. But this fact is more than most readers could have known on May 10, 1864.

On May 6 Chaplain Granberry excused himself from attempting to give his wife "news about the battle" by telling her that she would learn "fuller details in the papers"; yet the papers didn't contain such details as which regiments faced each other in the woods of the Wilderness. Only with the later publication of memoirs and official reports could civilians have begun to sort out the mess in the Wilderness, and they would never have finished, since the sorting out still goes on. Still, for all that the newspapers could never tell, no matter how courageous their reporters or responsible their editors, anyone who read the *New York Times* on May 8, 1864, could have found a statement that told him or her the truth about "rumors of defeat and brilliant victories" in the Wilderness.

> The thoughtful, however, came to the conclusion that a single encounter would not determine the contest, and a series of battles may have to be fought before there can be any decisive result.

No newspaper could speak more accurately. May 10 brought a general attack at Spotsylvania. Two weeks later came the Battle of the North Anna. One week after that Cold Harbor. In two more the attack on Petersburg, and after that, siege. By then, who won or lost the Wilderness, according to the newspapers, couldn't have mattered less to anybody reading them.

EIGHT

Weeklies

T WO OR THREE years after the Appomattox centennial, my family settled into an evening routine. Right after dinner, or sometimes with dinner on trays if we were running late, we'd gather in front of the television for the CBS Evening News with Walter Cronkite. During 1967 and 1968
much of the news, both domestic and international, made swallowing dinner a
little difficult. In particular, I remember Cronkite's recitation of the weekly
casualty figures from Vietnam. In the background over his shoulder we'd see
images of two flags, the American and the North Vietnamese, along with numbers that the most trusted man in America read out in the same level tone he
used for the Dow Jones industrial average, a tone we'd heard slip only once on
camera, a few years before when he gave us the bad news from Dallas. I was in
sixth or seventh grade in 1968, and I didn't know anyone fighting in Vietnam,
but I understood simple arithmetic well enough to know that, since each week
the total invariably showed the North Vietnamese losing more soldiers, it was
only a matter of time until we won.

To me Vietnam—the war of helicopters, rice paddies, and napalm—meant
our black-and-white television, just as the Civil War—the war of trains, corn
fields, and Minie balls—meant black-and-white photographs. I still can't think
about the Tet offensive or the siege at Khe Sahn without Walter Cronkite, any
more than I can think about Sharpsburg-Antietam or Gettysburg without
Alexander Gardner's team. But this analogy, true as it is for me, doesn't tell the
whole truth, since I was also getting images of Vietnam—vivid color images—
from somewhere else. Vietnam meant television at home only on weeknights.
During the days, however, at every newsstand, in every checkout line, in every

waiting room, Vietnam meant *Life, Time,* and *Newsweek,* just as for hundreds of thousands of people living through May 1864 the Civil War meant *Leslie's* and *Harper's Weekly.*

In May 1864 the Battle of the Wilderness didn't mean photographs to anyone because Timothy O'Sullivan didn't take any, except for three stereo views of the Rapidan crossing on May 4, first issued to the public about six weeks afterwards. Even if O'Sullivan had taken photographs of the Wilderness after the battle, and even if he had returned to Washington or New York and organized a public exhibition of those photographs, they wouldn't have reached as many people as the drawings in the two most famous weeklies. Perhaps O'Sullivan could have reached a wider audience by selling his views of the Wilderness to companies such as the War Photograph and Exhibition Company of Hartford, Connecticut, which produced three-dimensional stereoscopic photographs for owners of stereoscopes to view at home. But even if he'd chosen this option, by May 1864 the Northern market for views of more bodies couldn't compare with the market for the Journal of Civilization, as *Harper's Weekly* subtitled itself, a journal in which people not necessarily looking for them would have seen visual images of the Wilderness mixed in with the other artifacts of contemporary civilization.

Five years after Louis Daguerre announced his photographic discovery to the world in 1837, the first number of the *Illustrated London News* introduced to the English-speaking world a powerful combination of verbal images in writing and visual images in black-and-white wood engravings enhanced by the new electrotype technology, which made possible full-page pictures. By the time war broke out in 1861, the United States had two prominent illustrated weeklies of its own, *Frank Leslie's Illustrated Newspaper,* started in 1855, and *Harper's Weekly Magazine,* started in 1857. Both appeared on Saturday, like their London model, and both were printed in New York. A few pages shorter than the *London News,* both *Leslie's* and *Harper's Weekly* usually consisted of sixteen large (about eleven-by-sixteen-inch) pages. By late May 1864, subscriptions to *Leslie's* sold for four dollars a year, to *Harper's Weekly* three, and the two weeklies were keen competitors.

The weeklies enjoyed wide circulation. By the early 1860s *Harper's Weekly* had over one hundred thousand subscribers, many of whom lived in the South. With the outbreak of war, the *Magnolia Weekly* and the *Southern Illustrated News* started up in Richmond to try to fill the void left for Southern subscribers to Northern weeklies. Although Mary Chesnut doesn't mention the Northern weeklies specifically (when she speaks of *Harper's*, she refers to the monthly magazine, not the weekly newspaper), her November 1861 lament for the loss of other periodicals reflects the feelings of many Southern readers.

> Last January I sent for all the English reviews. *Blackwood's*,
> &c&c—*Atlantic, Harper's, Cornhill*, &c. Threw away my
> subscription money. Everything stopped with Fort Sumter.
> How I miss that way of looking out into the world! The
> war has cost me that. How much more?

Southern replacements couldn't compete with their Northern counter-parts in length, number of illustrations, or reliability. For example, the *Southern Illustrated News*, which published its first issue on September 13, 1862, and its last on September 3, 1865, suspended publication for three issues (May 21, May 28, and June 4, 1864) by order of the Governor of Virginia, William "Extra Billy" Smith, who "imagining that the time had come when Richmond was no longer safe, made a grand haul upon every man capable of bearing arms, shut-ting up the shops, closing the weekly newspaper offices entirely, and keeping the hands employed in the daily offices in readiness to march at a moment's notice" (*Southern Illustrated News*, June 11, 1864). This gap, like the blank in O'Sullivan's photographic record, serves as another image of the fighting that began in the Wilderness. Meanwhile, the *Magnolia Weekly*, which ran until April 1, 1865, contained no illustrations other than its weekly logo at the top of the front page.

When I look through issues of the two Southern weeklies, I find yet another image of the lopsided distribution of material resources between North and South. Subtitled "A Homejournal of Literature & General News," the *Magnolia Weekly* consisted each week of large pages the size of those used by the *London News* and the Northern weeklies, but there were only eight of those pages, about a third of the usual number in an issue of the *London News*. Pub-lished Saturday evening in Richmond at the corner of Cary and 10th Streets, the *Magnolia Weekly* cost twenty Confederate dollars a year, the same price as the *Southern Illustrated News*, published nearby at the corner of Cary and Vir-ginia Streets on Saturday afternoon. Unlike its pictureless rival, the *Southern Illustrated News*, which also consisted of eight delicate pages, printed an aver-age of three or four drawings in each issue, none of which ever covered a full page. The first drawing, usually a portrait of a general, appeared on the front page. One or two drawings of non-military subjects followed in the subsequent pages, and often a political cartoon attacked the North on the last page. In 1864, the year the *Southern Illustrated News* published the most issues, a subscriber might have seen between 150 and two hundred drawings. By contrast, a subscriber to *Harper's Weekly* would have seen over seven hundred drawings the same year, many of them full-page and several of them covering two pages.

What did the Southern weeklies contain, if not visual images of the war? The *Magnolia Weekly* for May 7, 1864, the day of skirmishing between the Battle of the Wilderness and Spotsylvania, opens with three pages of Dickens's *Tale of Two Cities* (1859), serialization of which began March 12, 1864. Then come two poems and several short prose pieces, all written for the *Magnolia Weekly* and not reprinted from elsewhere. But the item that hits me hardest is not a literary one. It appears under the modest heading "President Davis."

> The late bereavement of the President, in the melancholy
> death of his little son, will be met with the sympathies of
> our people, who will condole with him in this that, to the
> heavy cares of State is allied the sorrow of domestic afflic-
> tion. Upon the dawn of the glorious consummation of our
> independence, to which our noble President has steadfastly
> guided us, it is hard indeed that, for him, the shadow of a
> great loss should fall . . .

The *Magnolia Weekly* inclines toward brave phrases such as "the glorious consummation of our independence," and a feisty tone characterizes the writing under "Notes on the War," which every week appears under the masthead in the first column of page four.

> It is possible that, before our distant readers shall have
> received this number of our paper, the great and final battle
> of the war will have been fought. . . . It is necessary that the
> coming campaign should be decisive in its nature—so deci-
> sive as to send gold out of the reach of Chase's secretarial
> vision, and to encourage the peace-men of the United
> States in the formation of an organized resistance to the
> despotism of the war-party of the North. One great defeat
> will do this.

Having set the stage for the conclusive battle that turned out to be the inconclusive Battle of the Wilderness, first news of which arrived in Richmond the night before, the *Magnolia Weekly* returns to literary matters, such as a notice, among two columns of advertisements on the back page, for *Macaria,* the "Great Romance" by the "Madame de Stael of the South," Miss Augusta Evans of Mobile: "It is a Southern book, relating to the woful incidents of the time, but without rival in interest and artistic beauty." A copy of *Macaria* sold for five dollars.

Although it had drawings, the *Southern Illustrated News* printed nothing to rival Dickens during the spring of 1864, not even a Dickens novel published five years before. Instead, this weekly filled its columns with poems, stories, and nonfiction usually written exclusively for it. In the edition of April 23, 1864, for example, the writing included part four of "The Cartridge Papers" by Shrapnel; part six of "The Exile in France"; and the first three chapters of "The Rivals: A Chickahominy Story" by M. J. H. A small illustration for this last story provides one of four drawings in the issue. Under a sketch of two young white gentleman and an elderly black man dressed like a butler, the caption reads "'Now, Mars Walter,' replied Thomas reprovingly." Meanwhile, the front page prints a portrait of Major General Cadmus Wilcox, whose division would break two weeks later in the stampede caused by Hancock's attack the morning of May 6, and the back page a two-panel cartoon entitled "An Expedition in Pursuit of Live Stock." In the first panel, "A Flank Movement Planned," two soldiers sneak up on the object of their quest. In the second, "Failure of the Expedition," their quarry escapes. The livestock pursued is a frog.

But if neither the literary offerings nor the sketches of the *Southern Illustrated News* contained much of lasting significance, the regular column titled "The Times," also printed in the first column of page four under the masthead, furnished fiery editorializing.

> The quotas to the [Union] army of the delinquent States,
> are being made up as well as practicable, out of imported
> foreigners and stolen negroes, the Yankee people being, to
> a great extent, tired of fighting, though willing to carry on
> the war if they can get somebody else to fight for them; and
> to this end they cry for emancipation and the promotion of
> immigration, and the enlistment of negroes. . . . The next
> great battles in Virginia will be participated in by the blacks

from Fortress Monroe and Norfolk, and like their coerced
fellows at Port Hudson and Fort Wagner, the hardest and
hottest work will be given them to do. It will be their espe-
cial duty to stop Southern bullets, and impede the progress
of Southern shot and shell. Together with the Yankee, Irish
and Dutch, they will share magnificently in the harvest of
death for 1864.

Contemplating the appearance of black soldiers in the Army of the Potomac
and anticipating their participation in what would become the Wilderness campaign, readers of the *Southern Illustrated News* may have turned away from the
weekly with their patriotic ardor fired, but they wouldn't have come close to
replacing what they lost when they lost contact with its Northern counterparts.
Except for the stray copy of *Leslie's* or *Harper's Weekly* that somehow got
through, gratification of appetites for a weekly journal depended heavily on
issues of the *Illustrated London News* that penetrated the Federal blockade.
With luck, a Southern reader might also see one of 350 or 400 copies of the
Index, Henry Hotze's Confederate propaganda newspaper printed weekly in
London, but the *Index* contained no illustrations and focused so intently on
winning British recognition of the Confederacy that it had little space left to
cover the rest of civilization.

During the spring of 1864, simple geography prevented the *London News*
from furnishing its readers with timely news of the fighting south of the Rapidan. But none of the weeklies specialized in timeliness. Although the first
report of Grant's spring campaign didn't appear in the *London News* until May
21, it didn't appear any earlier in either *Leslie's* or *Harper's Weekly*, despite the
advantage the latter enjoyed by publishing on the western side of the Atlantic
Ocean. Instead of timeliness, then, readers would have looked to the abundantly illustrated London journal for periodic summaries of what it called "the
war in America" and for visual images of that war. In the edition of April 2, 1864,
for example, the *London News* reproduced a half-page picture with the caption
"The War in America: Winter Quarters of the Left Wing of the Confederate
Army on the Rapidan." The drawing presents a broad landscape sweeping
from a few bare trees and stumps in the foreground to a mass of tents in the
middle distance and then across open fields and woods to the Blue Ridge
Mountains rising against the horizon. As drawings of the war go, this one by the
London News "Special Artist and Correspondent," not identified but probably

Frank Vizetelly, is not particularly memorable. But the text that appears on the following page provides a revealing glimpse of a larger context.

> There curled the blue smoke from the tent of Robert E.
> Lee, whose hand I had just shaken, and whose friendship I
> am proud to own; there were the quarters of the gallant
> Stuart, whose guest I had been for the past few days, and
> whose hospitality in the field I had enjoyed for many
> months. Yes; every soldier of the army of Northern Virginia
> was a comrade; we had marched many weary miles
> together, and I had shared in their dangers.

As he takes his sorrowful leave of his Confederate comrades, the special artist notes that "Across the Rapidan, which flows beyond the nearer crest of hills, lay the enemy, only waiting probably for the first approach of spring to renew the awful drama that has spread desolation over many a once smiling acre of Virginia soil." He then concludes his meditations by telling his readers that if they have not "benefited as they might have done by my experiences, it is the fault of the rigorous blockade which has intercepted much destined for your pages." An editorial note explains that the special artist is now back in London, and illustrations he brought with him will appear "from time to time in this Journal."

Illustrations of the war in America subsequently do appear "from time to time" in the *London News*, but much more space goes to pictures of the war in Denmark, fought between the Danish and the Prussians, to celebrations of Shakespeare's tricentennial (April 23, 1864), and to the construction of the embankment along the Thames. One drawing that does stand out appears in the January 21, 1865, edition and shows Mosby's men on horseback in the mountains, a deeply romantic image perfect for readers of Sir Walter Scott inclined to project their fantasies onto the Confederacy.

But for all the mutual attraction between England and the Confederacy, editorial commentary on the war in the *London News* approaches a detached neutrality obviously missing from Northern and Southern weeklies closer to the war. In the issue of May 28, 1864, which contains a full, and largely accurate, narrative of the Battle of the Wilderness, the first column of the front page is devoted to "The War in America."

"The War in America: Winter Quarters of the Left Wing of the Confederate Army on the Rapidan." *Illustrated London News,* April 2, 1864. Courtesy of Special Collections, Alderman Library, University of Virginia.

Those political seers whose ken enables them at a glance to comprehend the exact position of American affairs inform us, with an air of authority, that the campaign which has just commenced in Virginia is to be the last of the war between the Federal and Confederate parties. The events of the first few days of the renewal of hostilities alone would suffice to sanctify a fervent wish on the part of all thinking men that the prediction may be verified. If the dispute between these belligerent brethren is to be settled by competitive slaughter, most assuredly a great deal has been already done toward its solution. Making every allowance for a natural, and still more an American, tendency to exaggeration, the numbers of slain in these last battles on the road to Richmond are such as to lead to a belief that the exhaustion of both parties is a question of a very precisely given time. Nothing has more struck the general mind of Europe in the contemplation of the civil war in America than the vastness of the hosts which have been brought together in the shock of battle.

Driving by the green Wilderness sign every day, I'm haunted by the proximity of a place where the Red Horse of Revelation 6:4 galloped wildly: "its rider was permitted to take peace from the earth, so that men should slay one another." But in my hauntedness, it's easy for me to become so preoccupied with the local that I forget to take the long view. Reading the *London News* reminds me that the convulsions in second-growth woods just up the road also shook observers thousands of miles away. Those observers, whatever their partisanship, could see the fighting of May 1864 in a way that I can't or usually don't, much as they can see my Americanness in a way that I can't or usually don't. One can read thousands of pages written by participants or eyewitnesses, along with thousands more based on the writings of participants and eyewitnesses, and not find any description of the Wilderness campaign as concisely accurate as the phrase "competitive slaughter." Free from mystical faith in Lee or anxious reliance on Grant, unimpressed by extenuating debates about the Constitution or the expansion of slavery into the territories or abolition or Northern aggression, the *London News* describes the Wilderness, and the war, in the same way I think about news of two tribes or two factions trying to exterminate each other several time zones away. I don't understand all the complexities behind the killing; I just wish it would stop. In the cool, stately prose of the *London News,* the English shudder makes me shudder.

But the twenty-four-page May 28, 1864, edition of the *London News,* which contains a half-page drawing of the Confederate cruiser *Georgia,* a half-page illustration of three women modeling the "Paris Fashions for June," illustrations of "Restorative Treatment for the Apparently Drowned," and a chess column, also represents the war in America in another way, a way that anyone who depended solely on the weeklies for knowledge of the Wilderness campaign would understand all too well.

> The mode in which the news of the events of the American
> war has reached this country has always been akin to that
> by which the writers of serial stories contrive to stop short
> in each number at a sensational point in order to keep
> interest alive until the issue of the next chapters.

Even people who could read a major metropolitan newspaper every day in Richmond or Charleston, New York or Washington, could recognize this image of the Civil War as a serialized story to be read in installments. Without television or radio news broadcasting twenty-four hours a day, North Americans had the war ladled out to them in evenly spaced portions, just as Europeans did. Those North Americans who had no access to daily papers featuring telegraphed reports had to wait for the weeklies, anticipating the latest war news along with the next section of stories or novels, such as *A Tale of Two Cities.*

On May 21, 1864, the price of a yearly subscription to *Frank Leslie's Illustrated Newspaper* rose from $3.50 to $4.00, an increase implicitly explained in a note on the second page of the May 21 issue.

> We need scarcely call the attention of our readers
> to our new and trim dress. The paper this week is
> printed entirely from new type, and cannot fail to
> please by its general beauty and interest, independent

Mosby's Men, *Illustrated London News,* January 21, 1865. Courtesy of Special
Collections, Alderman Library, University of Virginia.

of its surpassing pictorial illustrations.

It is but another proof that the proprietor will spare no expense to retain the position which his Illustrated Paper has so long and justly held.

After this bit of self-congratulatory advertisement, the next item in the column defends the authenticity of the sketches in *Leslie's* against an attack by the executive committee of the New York Historical Society, an attack charging "that the illustrated newspapers are full of sketches purporting to be pictures of important scenes, but the testimony of parties engaged shows that these representations, when they are not taken from photographs, are not always reliable." As William Frassanito's work has shown, Civil War photographs themselves "are not always reliable." What's more, the reliability of photographs has nothing to do with representations of battle by artists who sketched for *Leslie's*, since photography couldn't capture the action of combat anyway. But leaving these debates aside, we can move on to the rebuttal, hearing in it both an opportunity for more advertisement and a recitation of a journalistic creed.

Our Artists are with every important army; and not a movement of consequence in this, we trust, decisive campaign of the war shall take place without our receiving from our corps of Artists full, accurate and vigorous sketches, which we shall, as far as our limits allow, present to our readers, engraved in our best style. Our only difficulty will be to make the best selection; the sketches will be too numerous and valuable to give us even a temptation to invent.

In the campaign of 1864, as in the those of the three preceding years, FRANK LESLIE'S ILLUSTRATED NEWSPA-PER will contain the most prompt, truthful, graphic illustrations of the war, from the valley of Virginia, from the Peninsula, from Tennessee, from Charleston, from North Carolina, the Mississippi, Louisiana or Texas.

This list of places doesn't include the area on both sides of the Rapidan, but the next item, titled "Summary of the Week," reports the Battle of the Wilderness, now two weeks after its conclusion. Although it credits no source, the summary in *Leslie's* depends heavily on the May 6 dispatch sent by Henry Wing from Union Mills, Virginia, and it follows that dispatch verbatim in its description of the events of Thursday, May 5.

But *Leslie's* brags about its pictures, not its news reporting, and I find the first pictures from the Wilderness in the next issue, May 28. This issue contains sixteen drawings and a cartoon. Six of the drawings represent the war, the first of them, on the front page, depicting Grant and Meade standing together beside a tree, in consultation on the knoll across the Orange Turnpike from the Lacy House. Although the large illustration shows the taller Meade leaning sociably toward Grant, his left arm supporting him against the tree Grant has his back to, I can't help thinking that in fact the sketch unwittingly presents an image of the split command that hobbled the Union army during the Battle of the Wilderness. Elsewhere in this issue, one drawing shows a view of "The Campaign on the James River," another gives a panoramic view of the Battle of Spotsylvania Court House on May 10, and the remaining three present different glimpses of the Wilderness. Of these three, one is by J. Becker and two by Edwin Forbes.

The Becker drawing, labeled "The War in Virginia—Double Line of Breastworks Thrown Up on the Night of May 6, in the Wilderness, by the 5th Army Corps—The 14th New York Awaiting the Enemy," follows a small paragraph of explanation on an earlier page.

> The battles have not been in open field, as our readers
> know. The armies fought in dense woods, and used them
> for defence. At night trees were felled, and formed with
> earth into temporary breastworks. If time permitted a dou-
> ble line was made, as shown in the case illustrated by our
> engraving. Here our men would make a stand against the
> enemy, whose approach was heralded only by their pres-
> ence.

Readers of histories of the Battle of the Wilderness won't find the Fourteenth New York, which figures prominently in Thomas Dyja's novel *Play for a Kingdom* (1997), listed among other regiments of the Fifth Corps in the Order of Battle. According to C. E. Dornbusch's *Military Bibliography of the Civil War* (1961–62), the Fourteenth, originally from Brooklyn, became the Eighty-fourth

Grant and Meade in consultation in the Wilderness. *Frank Leslie's Illustrated Newspaper,* May 28, 1864. Collection of the Author.

New York, part of James Rice's Second Brigade of Wadsworth's Fourth Division in the Wilderness, on December 7, 1861. Having started the battle fighting under Warren south of Saunders' Field, on the Union right, Rice's brigade finished the battle under Hancock along the Brock Road, on the Union left. Becker's drawing, which I haven't seen reprinted in any history, shows about two dozen of the New Yorkers encamped behind breastworks. Immediately beyond the works, a corridor has been cleared to provide a treeless field of fire.

Beyond the corridor broods the Wilderness itself, a dark, menacing, other-worldly place. Becker's trees are thin, bare, and relatively branchless, so that they crowd toward the breastworks, tents, and soldiers like a host of stark, skeletal phantoms, in no way resembling the lovely, leafy background of Homer's *Skirmish in the Wilderness*. One month after Becker made his drawing, the members of the original Fourteenth who survived Grant's move into Virginia were mustered out.

Then there are the pictures by Edwin Forbes, whose sketches of the Wilderness give us some of the most vivid images we have. Forbes had been working for *Leslie's* since 1861, the year he turned twenty-two, and three years later he makes an appearance in the May 12 entry of Katherine Couse's unpublished letter.

> Mr Forbes—the artist scetcher for Frank Leslies calls in out
> of the rain, his right arm is helpless he scetches with his left
> hand, has not the use of all his fingers on that hand

J. Becker, "The War in Virginia—Double Line of Breastworks. . . ." *Frank Leslie's Illustrated Newspaper*, May 28, 1864. Collection of the Author.

Katherine doesn't say what happened to him, or when it happened, but the May 28 and June 4 editions of *Leslie's* contain a total of three sketches identified as Forbes's. Some of the others he made in the Wilderness appeared subsequently in his folio volume *Life Studies of the Great Army* (1876).

Sorting out the chronology and referents of Forbes's sketches gives me some problems, since in its captions *Leslie's* is not always accurate, as in the case of Forbes's full-page sketch, "The War in Virginia—Sketch on the Line of the 2nd Corps at the Battle of the Wilderness, May 10—Waiting for the Enemy," published in the June 4 edition. By May 10, Hancock was at Spotsylvania, nearly ten miles away from the Brock Road where the sketch was made. It seems that the editors at *Leslie's* either misread or misinterpreted the date Forbes put on the sketch, now in the Library of Congress, taking it as the date of battle rather than the date of composition. (Actually, it looks to me as though Forbes has written "May 11th.") Nevertheless, Forbes gave *Leslie's* readers, and continues to give us, both long-distance and close-up images of the Wilderness that project distinct impressions of its menacing uncanniness.

The two Forbes sketches published in the May 28 edition of *Leslie's* help set the scene. The first shows "Meade's Army Crossing the Rapidan, May 5," a caption that corresponds to Forbes's own on the original in the Library of Congress. On May 5, Burnside's Ninth Corps crossed the river, and Forbes has sketched Burnside's crossing from above the northern bank of the Rapidan, whereas O'Sullivan's photograph taken the day before looks from the southern. The particular power of Forbes's perspective lies in its use of the Wilderness itself as a background. In the foreground soldiers and wagons file down to the river, which they cross on two pontoon bridges. In the middle distance large numbers of soldiers have assembled in formations that fill a cleared space. But in the distance billows of smoke rise from a wall of dark woods. The battle is already in progress, with fighting in Saunders' Field and near the Brock Road intersection, and its effects loom over the sketch like the eruption of a volcano.

Forbes's other sketch in the May 28 edition typifies the wide-angle panoramas offered by *Leslie's* during the Wilderness and Spotsylvania but not by *Harper's Weekly*. Forbes's panorama, which covers the top halves of the two center pages while Becker's panorama of Spotsylvania covers the bottom, looks from just north of the Wilderness Tavern south toward the Lacy House in the distance. In the foreground soldiers, identified as stragglers in Forbes's handwritten caption on the Library of Congress sketch, look across wagons that fill

Edwin Forbes, "Meade's Army Crossing the Rapidan, May 5." *Frank Leslie's Illustrated Newspaper,* May 28, 1864. Collection of the Author.

the roads in the middle distance toward the wooded horizon from which smoke billows in three separate areas. The largest cloud of smoke hovers over the left, or east, side of the sketch, where Hancock and Burnside are fighting. On the Library of Congress sketch, Forbes has written the word "smoke" against the middle cloud, which hangs over the vicinity of the Widow Tapp farm or, beyond it, Parker's Store or, beyond it, the Catharpin Road, where cavalry fought on May 5. The right-hand cloud covers the action in and on either side of Saunders' Field. For the smoke to be so prominent in all three areas at once, Forbes must have been sketching during the afternoon of May 5, unless he wanted to give us a time-lapse image that condenses the action of two days into a single moment.

From these distant views Forbes moves closer to the action in the June 4 *Leslie's*. This issue contains the full-page engraving of Hancock's Second Corps "Waiting for the Enemy," not on May 10, as the caption claims, but more likely on May 6. This picture consists of several planes. In the foreground, a few men talk in small groups. One holds out a cup of something to another. In the next plane, defined by the waist-high breastworks that gently recede as the low wall runs from left to right, two dozen soldiers lounge in various attitudes. Some play cards; some sit against the breastworks, talking; a few stand leaning against the wooden wall; one man's legs protrude from a low tent or blanket he has rigged up to shade himself during a nap. In the middle of this plane, and in the center of the sketch, stand a lone cannon and cannoneer. In the next plane, where the ground consists of small low stumps, eight men work clearing away trees. Some wield axes; one carries a long trimmed trunk. Next come the woods themselves, a mixture of deciduous trees and evergreens, but all with leaves or needles. Above the woods, slightly to the right of center, hangs another cloud of smoke, presumably from Saunders' Field.

On the one hand, this engraving offers a relaxed, familiar, domestic image of war, as do so many of Forbes's other sketches, especially in *Life Studies of the Great Army*. In fact, the relaxed ease of these Second Corps men makes soldiering look much more attractive than it does in the sketches of camp life in which relaxation has fermented into monotony, boredom, dreariness, and dereliction. But on the other hand, it's also a terrible, terrifying picture precisely

Edwin Forbes, panoramic view of the Battle of the Wilderness. *Frank Leslie's Illustrated Newspaper,* May 28, 1864. Collection of the Author.

because it's not about the routines of camp life. The background of dark woods
and smoke keep the prospect of competitive slaughter fresh in my mind. The
picture shows no wounded or dead men, but the incongruity of nonchalance,
embodied in most of the men, and vigilant anticipation, embodied by the cannoneer, makes the image unsettling. The relaxed soldiers will soon be fighting
fiercely.

Apparently, Forbes himself found the incongruity powerful enough to
return to, since he included a similar scene, entitled "The Lull in the Fight," in
Life Studies of the Great Army. In this engraving, the woods have receded somewhat, and a narrow road runs from the foreground, through the breastworks,
into the distant trees. The men in the foreground now include several captured
Confederates being marched to the rear, a drummer boy, and a black man holding the tether of mule. Two cannons and the flag of the United States protrude
above the breastworks. From this engraving, or from the sketch on which it is
based, Forbes also produced a twelve-by-twenty-six-inch oil painting that he
exhibited at the National Academy in New York and the Boston Athenaeum. In

Edwin Forbes, "Waiting for the Enemy." *Frank Leslie's Illustrated Newspaper,* June 4, 1864. Courtesy of the Library of Virginia.

Edwin Forbes, "The Lull in the Fight." *Life Studies of the Great War* (1876). Courtesy of Special Collections, Alderman Library, University of Virginia.

this painting, the woods have advanced once again, but Forbes has left them indistinct, so that the leafy Wilderness now looms as though through fog, a ghostly realm.

Some people consider "The Lull in the Fight" Forbes's best sketch, but I would nominate two other views of the Wilderness, neither of which appeared in *Leslie's* and both of which number among the forty copperplate etchings sold by subscription in the portfolio-sized (nineteen-by-twenty-four-inch) *Life Studies of the Great Army,* the original prints of which Sherman subsequently bought and placed in his office in the War Department in Washington. The first, "A Night March," is the sixteenth plate.

Forbes doesn't identify the action represented, but Gordon Rhea describes a night march during the first hours of May 6, as Custer's brigade followed orders to shift toward Brock Road, a march that apparently included both infantry and artillery, as represented in Forbes's engraving. Alternatively, Forbes may have made his sketch the night of May 7, as the Army of the Potomac marched toward Spotsylvania. Whatever the referent, the engraving represents the Wilderness as a demonic, infernal landscape in which giant trees, fully leafed, dwarf the men who ride or march. In the left foreground, a single pine tree has been set on fire to serve as a huge torch, illuminating some men and turning others into black silhouettes as it casts shadows toward the viewer. To the right of the roadway, toward the middle of the picture, a cloud of white smoke rises from burning underbrush.

The second engraving, "Through the Wilderness," is the third plate and

shows six horses hauling a loaded caisson and a rifled Parrot gun, with the distinctive heavy band around its breech, through thick mud that cakes the spokes and rims of the large wheels. The battery toils away from me from lower right to upper left, as three men ride the horses closest to me and two more trudge along beside the mud-encumbered wheels. The Wilderness fills most of the space above the diagonally slanting road, especially to the right, the fully leafed trees crowding the muddy road. Ahead of the battery, another is barely visible. In the left foreground lies a dead horse, one of the sixty thousand horses and mules that accompanied the Army of the Potomac into the Wilderness. Images of death are rare in *Life Studies*—I find only two plates that show human dead— so this single horse, apparently killed by the strain of towing so much weight through the mud, must stand in for all the deaths not pictured elsewhere. Once again, the context of the engraving is unclear to me, since the weather during

Edwin Forbes, "A Night March." *Life Studies of the Great War* (1876). Courtesy of
Special Collections, Alderman Library, University of Virginia.

Edwin Forbes, "Through the Wilderness." *Life Studies of the Great War* (1876).
Courtesy of Special Collections, Alderman Library, University of Virginia.

the Battle of the Wilderness included no rain. But the title of the plate points to
May 1864, since during the campaign the previous year, the Army of the
Potomac failed to get through the Wilderness. Forbes could have been thinking
of a scene he witnessed during Spotsylvania, which included plenty of rain and
mud (after she describes Forbes on May 12, Katherine Couse comments that
"the house is perfectly mudy and hogish"). But he may also have had more figurative meaning in mind. Just as the badly mired battery has had its progress
through the Wilderness stymied by mud, so the Army of the Potomac, eager to
hurry through the tactically uncongenial region, allowed itself to get bogged
down there. Forbes's title is ironic, since his picture is not so much about getting through the Wilderness as about getting stuck there.

Forbes's *Life Studies* won a gold medal at the Centennial Exposition in
Philadelphia in 1876, and his justly celebrated works helped many visualize the
Battle of the Wilderness both during and after the war. But Forbes's counter-
part at *Harper's Weekly*, London-born Alfred Waud, also gave the weekly read-

ership several images from the Wilderness, at least one of which is now among the most famous and widely reprinted. Born in 1828, Waud came to the United States during the 1850s and soon joined the staff of *Harper's Weekly*. By May 1864, readers of the weekly would have been especially familiar with his prolific sketching. In the May 7 issue, for example, Waud's full-page illustration bears the caption "Negroes Escaping Out of Slavery" and accompanies text by the artist that begins, "Coming in from the reconnaissance many negroes joined us." The text goes on to describe how the escapees, including one party "said to contain eighteen, principally pickaninnies," rode the "spare and captured horses." Waud's image, which shows several dozen men, women, and children riding and walking at night through the rain, would have had added significance for anyone who had seen the previous issue of April 30, since that issue included a full-page engraving of "The Massacre at Fort Pillow," a graphic and sensational picture of black soldiers and their white officers being shot, clubbed, bayonetted, and knifed. In the context of subsequent Northern outrage, Waud's image of slaves determined "to follow the Yanks" may well have helped strengthen Northern resolve as Grant opened the spring campaign.

But the *Harper's Weekly* of May 7 doesn't mention that campaign, except for a single sentence under "Army and Navy Items": "The recent order of General GRANT banishing sutlers from the army rids it of over twenty-eight hundred supernumeraries." Meanwhile, the same page devotes a long paragraph to announcing the serialization of Dickens's latest novel, *Our Mutual Friend* (1864–65), in *Harper's Magazine,* beginning with the June number. The paragraph goes on to quibble pedantically over Dickens's title, calling it "ungrammatical and inelegant," since the phrase "mutual friend" should not be applied to the third person, and offering the correction "Our Common Friend." Elsewhere in the issue, which includes representations of the war in Louisiana and North Carolina, appears the eighteenth chapter of George Augustus Sala's novel *Quite Alone,* "Printed from the Manuscript and early Proof-sheets purchased by the Proprietors of 'Harper's Weekly,'" and an illustration showing the laying of the cornerstone for the monument in Central Park commemorating Shakespeare's tercentenary. Northern Anglophiles could hardly ask for more.

The next issue, May 14, opens with a column titled "The Situation," in which the editors situate Grant's spring campaign in an international context, asserting that in Europe "the question of general war will be decided by the success of our campaigns," as success or failure will determine the likelihood of

French interference on behalf of the Confederacy. The only illustration of Grant's momentous campaign is a half-page engraving "made from a photograph furnished us by our artist, A. R. Waud," which shows a workshop at Army of the Potomac headquarters and provides the *Harper's Weekly* readership with a glimpse of the work required to maintain the massive army behind the lines, the same kind of glimpse I find throughout Alexander Gardner's *Photographic Sketch Book of the War* (1866).

The issue of May 21 contains no drawings by Waud or sketches from the Wilderness, although it does include a map of eastern Virginia and opens with a celebration of Grant's "victory," moralizing that although the "chapter of our history which opened on the 3d of May is not ended as these words are written," the result of fighting south of the Rapidan "is of such augury that we have the right to hope for a success which should bring every true American to his knees in religious gratitude." On the facing page, which precedes a full-page illustration entitled "Grand Musical Festival in Philadelphia in Aid of the Sanitary Commission," the description of fighting under "The Military Situation" gives an optimistic narrative, in which Warren "handsomely" drives the enemy on May 5 in Saunders' Field and Longstreet's flanking of Hancock receives no mention. Meanwhile, the most compelling illustrations in this issue sit on the two center pages above the caption "Rebel Atrocities." In a series of scenes arranged around a central drawing, they show, in counterclockwise order, "Genl. Forrest Shooting a Free Mulatto," Belle Isle Prison in Richmond, Paducah, Fort Wagner, Fort Pillow, Milliken's Bend, and "Negro Teamsters Tied to Trees and Shot." The central drawing casts Jefferson Davis as Satan, horned, winged, and cloven-hoofed, surrounded by other demons. Its caption reads "The Traitors in Council." By May 21, Edward Ferrero's division of black troops, which had guarded Germanna Ford during the Wilderness, had, in soldier's slang, seen the elephant of combat at Spotsylvania. Illustrations such as "Rebel Atrocities" aimed to convince the *Harper's Weekly* readership that by the opening of the 1864 campaign the interests of white and black had become inseparable.

The issue of May 28, which features a portrait of the dashing Hancock on its front page, contains the first visual images from the Wilderness. There are three images altogether, and all three are uncredited. The first, a full-page illustration facing a full-page portrait of Grant, shows "Bartlett's Brigade of Warren's Corps Charging the Enemy." Whereas the illustrations in *Leslie's* for the same date provide the topographic context of combat, offering a panoramic view of the Wilderness from the Wilderness Tavern and an image of the leafless woods brooding malevolently behind soldiers waiting for the enemy, the first *Harper's Weekly* illustration represents soldiers going into actual combat. Apparently set in Saunders' Field, the engraving looks over two long, well-formed lines of Union soldiers trotting up a slight rise towards a single unbroken line of Confederate soldiers—they'd have to be Ewell's—backed by leafy trees. As an idealized image of infantry advancing across a clear field, with long unbroken lines perfectly organized, the engraving reminds me of descriptions of Pickett's Charge more than it does any descriptions of chaotic fighting in Saunders' Field. Mounted officers lead the charge, obvious targets for every Confederate rifle, and in the right foreground a mounted officer, just to the rear of the infantry, jumps his horse across a small trench, which somehow has not upset the unified ranks of soldiers trotting in step. Low clouds of smoke rising from the waiting Confederates show that firing has begun, but the advancing Union lines have suffered no casualties.

The illustration in the May 28 issue that I admire most is the second, which covers the two center pages and shows exhausted soldiers of the Union Fifth Corps, identified by the crosses on their hats, "Sleeping on Their Arms," presumably in the vicinity of Saunders' Field the night of May 5. The trees are confined to the upper left quadrant of this engraving and don't convey the awful tangles surrounding the field, but the details of the sleeping bodies flung down on the ground in every position suggest careful, close observation and the absence of any idealized order or neatness. A single sentry, his bayonetted rifle held vertically against his right shoulder, defines the central vertical axis of the picture. Behind him to the right and left, eight or nine other sentries rise at various distances above the clumps of sleeping soldiers. At his feet men sit and slump and curl and huddle, some with blankets, some without, their rifles and canteens and knapsacks protruding or littering the ground. Beyond the literal immediacy of May 5, the engraving presents a powerful image of deep war-weariness that many readers of *Harper's Weekly* would have recognized all too well in the spring of 1864.

The third May 28 illustration is one I've seen before but never in its original context, where it faces an engraving of three women modeling "Paris Fashions for May, 1864," an engraving that also appeared in the April 30 *Illustrated London News*. The half-page illustration represents Hancock's Corps crossing the Rapidan at Ely's Ford on May 4 and shows the soldiers marching or riding from left to right toward the three women, the first of whom wears a mazarine

"Bartlett's Brigade of Warren's Corps Charging the Enemy." *Harper's Weekly,* May 28, 1864. Courtesy of Special Collections, Alderman Library, University of Virginia.

"Sleeping on Their Arms." *Harper's Weekly,* May 28, 1864. Courtesy of
Special Collections, Alderman Library, University of Virginia.

Hancock's Corps crossing the Rapidan at Ely's Ford. *Harper's Weekly*, May 28, 1864.
Courtesy of Special Collections, Alderman Library, University of Virginia.

blue dress for a wedding party, "with three black velvet lozenges, edged with
narrow black guipure"; the second a silver-gray evening dress for a young lady,
"richly trimmed, as shown in the engraving, with blue silk stripes and narrow
edging"; and the third an iron-gray walking dress, "provided with a fluted skirt,
surmounted by four rows of passementerie." In visual representations of the
Wilderness, the Rapidan crossing constitutes a subgenre of its own, but neither
Forbes's sketch of the Ninth Corps crossing the next day upriver or the O'Sullivan photographs at Germanna Ford show as clearly as the context of the
Harper's Weekly sketch that by 1864 the opening of the spring campaign had
become another annual event to be anticipated along with the latest Paris
fashions.

    After two issues in which his work either doesn't appear or is not credited
to him by name, the *Harper's Weekly* of June 4, 1864, with a portrait of Sherman
on the front page, belongs to Alfred Waud and contains the two most powerful
images of combat conditions in the Wilderness I found in either of the leading
weeklies. Altogether Waud has five illustrations in this issue, but three represent

"Paris Fashions for May, 1864." *Harper's Weekly,* May 28, 1864. Courtesy of Special Collections, Alderman Library, University of Virginia.

scenes from Spotsylvania. Of the other two, one covers a full page and shows "Major-General Wadsworth Fighting in the Wilderness." Accompanying text explains that the "sketch gives a good idea of the almost impenetrable nature of the Wilderness, and of the disadvantages under which our soldiers fought." The sketch represents Wadsworth's troops, Fourth Division, Fifth Corps, firing away from the viewer towards the left, two dead or wounded soldiers lying squarely in the foreground, and a bank of white smoke rolling up before the firing line. Some of the soldiers aim rifles, some raise ramrods, one sits wounded against a tree, another falls as if just hit, and to the right one man with a face that is the whitest object in the engraving turns from the battle toward the viewer and the rear. Here and there officers with swords stand behind the soldiers, looking on. But although the foreground, middle distance, and background all contain trees, one or two of them rather large for second-growth woods, actually the woods pictured here are not impenetrable. The sketch shows the Wilderness as a lightly forested region, with trees unleafed and almost no undergrowth, except for a few bushes in the lower right. In fact, the woods are

Alfred Waud, "Major-General Wadsworth Fighting in the Wilderness." *Harper's Weekly*, June 4, 1864. Courtesy of Special Collections, Alderman Library, University of Virginia.

so open that two other lines of infantry parallel to Wadsworth's, one in the middle distance and one in the background, are clearly visible hundreds of yards away. If the Wilderness had resembled the terrain in Waud's sketch, no one could have gotten lost in it.

Waud must have drawn on his imagination for this sketch, since in truly impenetrable woods he couldn't have gotten close enough to witness the scene and still be safe. Likewise, Edwin Forbes must have imagined a very similar sketch that *Leslie's* didn't publish and Forbes didn't include in *Life Studies.* Housed in the Library of Congress, it bears the handwritten caption, "The 6th Corps / Battle of the Wilderness fighting in the woods." Forbes's caption doesn't give enough information to locate the scene precisely, but Sedgwick's Sixth Corps fought on the extreme right, closest to Germanna Ford, over some of the worst ground in the area. Like Waud's sketch, Forbes's shows the backs of infantrymen firing towards the left, a few dead and wounded in the foreground. But unlike Waud's sketch, Forbes's shows the woods as much thicker and leafier. Beyond the firing line, the trees recede into light sketching, suggesting their unbroken continuation. Nothing is visible in the distance. If Forbes submitted this sketch to the editors at *Leslie's* at the same time as the others published by the weekly, it's hard to understand their decision not to engrave it. It can't be that they thought it would be too shocking, since in the June 11 number they published Forbes's two-page illustration of vicious fighting at Yellow Tavern, where Jeb Stuart was killed. I can't help wondering if Forbes made his sketch, which he didn't date, after he saw Waud's, having admired his rival's image of combat but not his picture of the Wilderness.

But Waud could well have witnessed the scene that led to his most harrowing—and most famous—image from May 5 and 6. Laid out on the top half of the page facing "Major-General Wadsworth Fighting in the Wilderness," it bears the caption "Army of the Potomac—Our Wounded Escaping from the Fires in the Wilderness" and precedes Waud's own explanatory note on the following page.

> The fires in the woods, caused by the explosion of shells,
> and the fires made for cooking, spreading around, caused
> some terrible suffering. It is not supposed that many lives
> were lost in this terrible manner; but there were some poor
> fellows, whose wounds had disabled them, who perished
> in the dreadful flame. Some were carried off by the ambu-

Alfred Waud, "Army of the Potomac—Our Wounded Escaping from the Fires in the Wilderness." *Harper's Weekly*, June 4, 1864. Courtesy of Special Collections, Alderman Library, University of Virginia.

    lance corps, others in blankets suspended to four muskets,
    and more by the aid of sticks, muskets, or even by crawling.
    The fire advanced on all sides through the tall grass, and,
    taking the dry pines, raged up to their tops.

The Battle of the Wilderness is not the only battle in which woods burned. In his memoir "What I Saw of Shiloh" (1909), Ambrose Bierce records that an Illinois regiment, which when surrounded refused to surrender, had been swept by fire in a deep ravine. After his own regiment had been relieved, Bierce "obtained leave to go down into the valley of death and gratify a reprehensible curiosity."

    Along a line which was not that of extreme depression, but
    was at every point significantly equidistant from the heights
    on either hand, lay the bodies half buried in ashes; some in
    the unlovely looseness of attitude denoting sudden death

by the bullet, but by far the greater number in postures of
agony that told of the tormenting flame. Their clothing was
half burnt away—their hair and beard entirely; the rain had
come too late to save their nails. Some were swollen to
double girth; others shriveled to manikins. According to
the degrees of exposure, their faces were bloated and black
or yellow and shrunken. The contraction of muscles which
had given them claws for hands had cursed each counte-
nance with a hideous grin. Faugh! I cannot catalogue the
charms of these gallant gentlemen who got what they
enlisted for.

His cruel sarcasm intensifying the horror of this passage, Bierce knows full well
that his reprehensible curiosity will be ours, too, and such curiosity accounts in
part for the effectiveness of Waud's illustration, a large version of which covers
a wall in the Chancellorsville Visitors' Center. Other battles may have had burning woods, but no other battle has so deeply associated itself with images of a
pastoral inferno. In the same way that amputation quickly became, and continues to be, the defining image of the Civil War, so the burning woods and fields
became and continue to be the defining image of the Battle of the Wilderness.

Waud's picture shows four soldiers, two of them in the baggy pantaloons
of Zouaves, carrying a bulging blanket suspended from four muskets. They
move from right to left, as flames leap up behind them. Around their feet lie
other wounded men, and in the upper left quadrant stand a few trees. But it is
not entirely accurate to say, as I did, that a large reproduction of Waud's drawing covers a wall in the Chancellorsville Visitors' Center, because Waud's original sketch, also in the Library of Congress, differs from the *Harper's Weekly*
engraving in one significant respect. In Waud's original sketch, which includes
the handwritten caption "Wounded escaping from the burning woods of the
Wilderness," the four soldiers carrying the wounded man hidden in the bulging
blanket, an image of all the casualties hidden from noncombatants, form a distinct pattern. The front soldier closest to the viewer and the rear soldier farthest
from the viewer both stare straight ahead, whereas the other two soldiers look
anxiously back over their left shoulders at the pursuing flames. Waud's arrange-
ment gives the sketch a neat symmetry at the same time that it suggests a larger
Janus-like awareness of what lies ahead and behind as of May 1864.

But whoever engraved Waud's sketch for *Harper's Weekly* made one change, destroying the original symmetry and creating a more complicated image in the process. In the *Harper's Weekly* engraving, which is what is reproduced on the wall of the Chancellorsville Visitors' Center (a smaller version of Waud's original hangs in the corridor of exhibits), the forwardmost soldier no longer looks straight ahead but rather out of the picture directly at the viewer. His fixed stare, peering from the page against a backdrop of flame, feels to me like the visual equivalent of Bierce's expletive "Faugh!" Such a stare should be enough to hold for a moment even the gaze of someone flipping casually through the weekly in search of the twenty-fourth chapter of Sala's *Quite Alone.* But even if it isn't enough, it's sufficient—once I've skimmed the features and arrived safely at the columns of advertisements in the back pages, the notices for Burnett's dandruff-killing Cocoaine or Beautiful False Moustaches from C. W. Philo or Madame Demorest's Mirror of Fashions or the U.S. Artificial Leg Depots or Benjamin's Rupture Cure Truss or American Steel Collars—to make me contemplate with momentary uncertainty an ad for Brandreth's Pills, which asks in bold type, "Have you an Affection of the Heart?"

NINE

Acoustic Shadow

I N HIS *Civil War Wordbook* (1994), which defines various sayings, phrases, expletives, and slang terms arising from or pertaining to the war, Darryl Lyman describes acoustic shadow as a "phenomenon in which the sounds of battle cannot be heard by people nearby, but are clearly audible many miles away." Also known as "silent battle," an acoustic shadow results from "a variety of factors, such as thick woods and unusual atmospheric conditions." Although the Wilderness would seem to have provided more than enough thick woods to muffle sound, no letter or diary or memoir or history I've read has mentioned that acoustic shadows developed during the battle. In fact, eyewitnesses who comment on the sound, from Katherine Couse to Meade's chief of staff, Andrew Humphreys, agree that it was overwhelming.

But the Battle of the Wilderness, for all the noise it made and for all the writing it spawned, did produce at least one pocket of silence, one very deep pocket. No matter how much I read or how hard I listen, I cannot hear the voices of private soldiers in either the First Brigade, commanded by Colonel Joshua K. Sigfried, or the Second Brigade, commanded by Colonel Henry G. Thomas, of Brigadier General Edward Ferrero's Fourth Division of Ambrose Burnside's Ninth Corps. These private soldiers were black.

Admittedly, the soldiers of the Nineteenth, Twenty-third, Twenty-seventh, Thirtieth, Thirty-ninth, and Forty-third United States Colored Troops, along with a detachment from the Thirtieth Connecticut, guarded Germanna Ford and did no fighting in the Wilderness. Faced with a mountain of documents to shape into a coherent narrative of mostly incoherent fighting, what historian could afford to devote valuable space to discussing the undocumented thoughts and feelings of untried soldiers farthest from the fighting? In *The Wilderness Campaign* (1960), Edward Steere mentions Ferrero's division six times in over four hundred pages. Gordon Rhea refers to the black troops four times in about the same number, and one of those references includes the image of Ferrero's soldiers cheering as they passed Lincoln's reviewing stand during a march through Washington on April 25, 1864. The revised and enlarged edition of Robert Garth Scott's *Into the Wilderness with the Army of the Potomac* (1992), a book half as long as the other two, names Ferrero three times. Shelby Foote discusses Ferrero's division in connection with the Battle of the Crater at Petersburg (July 30, 1864) but doesn't mention the black soldiers during his narrative of the Wilderness.

And what is there to mention? History depends on documents, and where there are no, or few, documents, there can be little or no history. If there were a diary or collection of letters left by a black soldier who arrived at Germanna Ford on May 6, having marched forty miles from Manassas Junction since May 4, historians would have worn deep tracks through it by now. If there were even a good memoir left by one of Ferrero's white officers, a Virginia counterpart of Higginson's *Army Life in a Black Regiment,* we might hear at least echoes of the soldiers' voices. One small source I found is the diary of Colonel Albert Rogall, company commander in the Twenty-seventh U.S. Colored Troops, which came from Ohio. Edited by Frank Levstik and published in *Polish American Studies* (1970), the diary contains this short entry for May 6:

> The report of cannons plain. The fight begun at 3½ o'clock
> in the morning. Beautiful day and more beautiful country.
> Curious that this people would consent to fight. Whole day
> a heavy battle. We advanced, sore feet, men hardly could
> walk, yet forward and forward was the command. In the
> evening and at night the fight going on. At 11 o'clock at
> night marching orders—marching whole night. Crossed
> Rapidan.

"Curious that this people would consent to fight." A Polish nobleman who, as Florien Albert Rogall de Salmonski, arrived in America in 1851, Rogall doesn't make clear whom he means by "this people." Since it isn't at all curious that black people would consent to fight, he apparently means the American people considered as a whole, a reading strengthened by two subsequent comments, the first on May 8, the second May 9:

> Beautiful day all Sunday, beautiful, lovely country, free peo-
> ple, happy before—now in deadly struggle for notion sake
> of some scoundrely preachers.

> Strange that one people having enjoyed the happiness and
> blessings of all kind for so long time should fight with such
> bitterness, but it is civil war.

Although Rogall's diary gives us insights such as these—as well as details like "the smell of putrified bodies of dead men laying unburied since last four days" (May 8), "Dead bodies sticking their feet, hands, broken skulls, etc." on the ground where the Union Eleventh Corps collapsed at Chancellorsville the year before (May 12), and attacks on his soldiers by guerrillas (May 15 and 19) during Spotsylvania—it doesn't give us much insight into the thoughts and feelings of the soldiers he commanded. In fact, Rogall's representations of his own troops have a nasty, unsympathetic edge to them.

> All niggers are thieves. Poor rebel wives and widows, the
> cruel consequences of a war, make me feel sorry. (May 30)

> Men and officers became scared, fired in every direction till
> the cattle passed, then all was over and our army cattle
> showed more sense than soldiers of the 4th Div., 9th Army
> Corps. (June 15)

> The niggers are pushed forward though I am certain they
> will never do on account of being too green troops. (June 19)

In Special Collections at the University of Virginia I did find a muster roll and payroll signed by Rogall for Company G of the Twenty-seventh, a document that told me the names of many of his soldiers, as well as what happened to some of them in the Wilderness. For example, I learned that Henry Young, Brady Oscar, and Haywood Franklin were left sick in Chancellorsville on May

15, 1864. Otherwise, however, all I could learn was that the inspector and mustering officer, Charles I. Knight, rated the soldiers' discipline "good," instruction "wanting," and military appearance "fair."

For more sympathetic and comprehensive representation, I turned hopefully to *The Black Military Experience* (1982), part of the massive *Freedom: A Documentary History of Emancipation, 1861–1867,* edited by Ira Berlin and others, but it includes next to nothing about the experience of black soldiers in the Wilderness, although it did introduce me to Simon Prisby, a soldier from Pennsylvania who in a letter of July 20, 1865, complained to Secretary of War Stanton about harsh treatment in the all-black Twenty-fifth Corps, created December 3, 1864. In the course of his complaint, Prisby compared his postwar situation with more favorable treatment under Burnside in the Ninth Corps.

> When we joined the 9th A[rmy]. C[orps]. at annoppolis
> M. D. in 64, Gen. Burnside Rode through our Camp and
> told us that he wanted us to Be Good Soldiers for he had
> Some Work for us to Do last Summer While we was in his
> Corps, there was not a man Struck With a Sword.

If Prisby's testimony is accurate, then at least we know that on May 6, 1864, the soldiers arriving at Germanna Ford may have complained about their sore feet and the forty-mile march from Manassas but not about unfairly severe enforcement of discipline.

To the little we can glean from these sources we can add bits and pieces from wartime newspapers and weeklies. In a dispatch dated May 3 at Fredericksburg, for example, readers of the *Richmond Examiner* for May 4, 1864, would have learned that "Burnside's whole corps, excepting the negro brigade, has passed to the front, crossing the river at Rappahannock station yesterday." Although Burnside's corps contained two black infantry brigades, not one, the dispatch correctly describes the subordinate role those brigades would play in the upcoming campaign, after "relieving the white troops" who had been guarding the Orange and Alexandria Railroad so that those troops could proceed to the front. The next day, May 5, readers of the *New York Times* could have read that the black troops at Manassas "were attacked by a small party of guerrillas, who suddenly pounced upon them, but the negroes drove them off without sustaining any loss." Finally, in the *New York Herald* of May 10, James Fitzpatrick, having had "the misfortune to be captured by a portion of Stuart's cavalry, who deprived [him] of his notes of the recent battles," closed his description of May 6 with the statement, "Up to the time I left the field the colored troops had not taken part in the battle," although other regiments of the Ninth Corps, many "under fire for the first time," acquitted themselves "in a most creditable manner, some of them standing to the work like veteran regiments."

The scarcity of documents makes the acoustic shadow thick enough. Since Simon Prisby or another black soldier in Ferrero's division didn't write letters home to a Pennsylvania newspaper as Corporal James Henry Gooding of the Fifty-fourth Massachusetts did to the *New Bedford Mercury,* the shadow remains unlightened. But what thickens the shadow even more is that when images of black soldiers in the Wilderness do appear, they are images of silence. Anyone who looked at the front page of *Leslie's* for June 4, 1864, for example, would have seen a large illustration showing a black soldier standing beside two white officers. The black soldier, drawn in profile, has a rifle on his left shoulder and stands to the right of the picture. The two white officers, one of whom looks steadily at the black soldier, carry no weapons and occupy the center of the illustration. The caption reads "AN INCIDENT IN THE BATTLE OF THE WILDERNESS—THE REBEL GENERALS BRADLEY JOHNSON AND E. STUART TAKEN TO THE REAR BY NEGRO CAVALRY, MAY 12" and contains multiple misspellings and inaccuracies. Major General Edward "Allegheny" Johnson and Brigadier General George H. "Maryland" Steuart were both captured on May 12 at the Bloody Angle during the Battle of Spotsylvania, not the Wilderness. But on June 4, 1864, few Northern readers could have spotted the inaccuracies, and it's probable that most would have seen the profiled cavalryman as the first image of black soldiers published by *Leslie's* after the Battle of the Wilderness rather than as an image of silence.

Besides, pictures don't talk anyway, so one shouldn't read too much into a visual image of a black soldier with his mouth shut. After all, the white officers have their mouths shut, too. But what about the image of another black cavalryman, this one in Robert Penn Warren's novel *Wilderness* (1961)? After dark on April 30, 1864, two of Warren's characters come upon a hospital tent where a surgeon is tending to a black cavalryman wounded during an encounter at one of the Rapidan fords. As the surgeon works, a white lieutenant, also wounded, keeps babbling pathetically about how the black cavalryman, who saved his life and got hit while doing so, is going to die just to spite him. In narrating the episode, the lieutenant recounts how the cavalryman, whom he refers to throughout as "that black son-of-a-bitch," "never said a word when he was hit" and adds, "He hadn't even grunted." A page later, Warren refers again to the cavalryman's silence, now transformed into a larger, more emblematic stoicism: "He had never taken his gaze from the man on the table who was silent as stone and from whom the blood would not stop coming."

Silent as stone. The prayers of Pygmalion brought his statue to life, but another description, this one by someone who actually saw Ferrero's troops at Germanna Ford, turns life into stone.

> He [the horse] bore me speedily along a densely wood-
> bordered road, spotted by cast-away blankets and deserted
> now, save that here and there lay prone a sick or completely
> exhausted Negro soldier of Ferrero's over-marched colored
> division. They were not ordinary stragglers, and I remem-
> ber no more pleading objects. Most of them had lately been
> slaves, and across the years their hollow cheeks and plain-
> tive sympathy-imploring eyes are still the lonesome road-
> side's bas-reliefs.

This passage from the 1910 memoir of Morris Schaff, an ordnance officer who served on Warren's staff during the battle, deepens the silence of black soldiers in the Wilderness by representing them not as quiet men who suffer stoically but as sculpted figures raised just slightly above the background surface of the landscape.

Of course, images by whites of silent blacks are nothing new, and even though recent fictional appearances of black soldiers in Thomas Dyja's *Play for a Kingdom* and Donald McCaig's *Jacob's Ladder* (1998) help me imagine what Ferrero's soldiers might have said, images of silence predominate. In an entry dated April 13, 1861, the day after the firing on Fort Sumter, Mary Chesnut wonders why her slaves "make no sign" that they hear "the awful row that is going on in the bay" or understand its implications. She then asks, "Are they stolidly stupid or wiser than we are, silent and strong, biding their time?"

Straining to hear something, anything, through the acoustic shadow in the Wilderness, I wonder whether I can't hear anything because not enough black soldiers could write and not enough white ones cared to record what they said

or because, silent and strong, the black soldiers of Ferrero's division were biding their time. When their time came, soon after the Wilderness, they put their
voices on record with three words heard loud and clear by white men on both
sides, three words that serve as shorthand for much of what they must have
talked about on the long march from Manassas or during the long wait at Germanna Ford, three words they didn't have to write down to make themselves
heard: *Remember Fort Pillow.*

TEN

Memoirs

EADING THOUSANDS of pages of Civil War memoirs might not help anyone penetrate the acoustic shadow that muffles the voices of black soldiers, but it could teach him or her plenty, not only about the war but also about the state of letters in late nineteenth- and early-twentieth-century America. Beginning soon after the war—Jubal Early's *Memoir of the Last Year of the War for Independence* first appeared as a pamphlet published in Canada late in 1866—the flash flood of personal reminiscences washed the country for a good sixty years, lasting at least until the publication of John Gibbon's *Personal Recollections of the Civil War* (1928). To help put these sixty years in the perspective of literary history, we need only remember that they span the careers of both Mark Twain and Henry James, the publication of T. S. Eliot's *Waste Land,* and the early novels of William Faulkner, Ernest Hemingway, and F. Scott Fitzgerald. In other words, during the convulsive stretch that literary histories describe as running from the emergence of realism to the flourishing of high modernism, a stretch that included the Spanish-American War and World War I, Americans steadily wrote and read personal narratives of the Civil War.

Not all of these narratives reached wide audiences, and few will be read during the twenty-first century, except by people especially interested in the Civil War. Two exceptions could prove to be the memoirs of Sherman (1875) and Grant (1885–86), both of which, with their publication in the Library of America series, enter the new century carrying passports stamped "literature." Thanks to the publicity it received from Ken Burns's documentary, Sam Watkins's *"Co. Aytch"* (1881–82) may also enjoy a healthy shelf life for some time yet. Meanwhile, some new memoir may be discovered and published at any-time, and the 150th anniversary celebrations between 2011 and 2015 undoubt-edly will generate yet another wave of interest, perhaps causing a few more non-specialists to sample the writings of Edward Porter Alexander, Benjamin Butler, Joshua Lawrence Chamberlain, Abner Doubleday, John B. Gordon, John Bell Hood, Oliver Otis Howard, David Hunter, Joseph Johnston, James Longstreet, George McClellan, John S. Mosby, Philip Sheridan, Lew Wallace, and others. In sampling what appears to be the genre of generals (Mosby was a colonel), some may even discover that in fact neither generals nor men have a monopoly on the Civil War memoir. Examples by Louisa May Alcott, Belle Boyd, Sara Emma Edmundson, Rose O'Neal Greenhow, Mary Livermore, Susie King Tay-lor, and Loreta Janeta Velazquez represent wartime roles and experiences that include laundering, nursing, spying, and passing as male soldiers in the ranks.

But for the sixty years directly following the war, generals' memoirs received the most attention. For one thing, publishers were much more willing to invest in narratives by men whose names the war had made famous. In our own time, this purely commercial instinct helps explain in part the canonization of Sherman and Grant by the Library of America. Whatever the literary merits of the memoirs themselves, and those merits are not always unambiguous, most educated Americans can recognize the names of these two Union generals, one of whom went on to become president and the other of whom probably could have if he had wanted to. Some might argue that Sherman and Grant appear in the Library of America because the North won the war, and literature necessar-ily reflects the tastes of the victors. True perhaps, but that argument is a little too easy in this case, since Lee never wrote his own memoirs and Jackson died before he could have. My guess is that if either of those Confederate generals had written a narrative as readable as Sherman's or Grant's, the ongoing national romance with the South would have ensured even greater sales for the vanquished than for the victors.

Another reason for the dominance of generals' memoirs may be that nine-teenth- and early-twentieth-century readers were less likely than we are today to believe that the story of a private soldier might be just as compelling as that of an officer, or more so. General officers, after all, had the big picture and could describe the movements of large armies authoritatively, whereas private soldiers and their line officers knew only what they saw in front of them, as Ambrose Bierce showed so convincingly in the passage from "The Crime at Pickett's Mill." Never mind that Sam Watkins, for all the stylistic excesses he sometimes permits himself, has ten pages on the battle of the Dead Angle at Kennesaw Mountain (June 27, 1864) that convey the massive horror of that encounter much more fully than Sherman's half paragraph, which includes the indigestible understatement, "By 11.30 the assault was in fact over, and had failed." Never mind that Morris Schaff's virtually unknown memoir *The Battle of the Wilderness* (1910) runs circles around Phil Sheridan's account of the battle, which confines itself to Sheridan's disagreements with Meade about the proper role of the cavalry and an uninspired description of the uninspired part played by that cavalry on May 5 and 6, 1864. Sheridan was a general and Schaff a lieutenant (albeit one attached to Warren's staff), and so Sheridan's picture must come closer to omniscience.

The implicit assumption that a Civil War memoir gets better the closer it approximates omniscience raises some complex questions about the genre and helps account for some of its conventions, quirks, and characteristic features. In his glossary of literary terms, M. H. Abrams usefully distinguishes between autobiography, in which emphasis falls on the author's developing self, and memoir, in which emphasis falls on people the author has known and events the author has witnessed. Of course, this distinction doesn't always hold fast. Grant's memoirs, for example, begin with his ancestry, birth, and boyhood, then follow him through West Point and the Mexican War, before turning to the Civil War. Even though this early development occupies only about one-sixth of his narrative, Grant clearly uses it to frame his self-presentation. In fact, in view of what every reader knows is coming, it's hard not to hear the great first sentence of the memoir as prophetic: "My family is American, and has been for generations, in all its branches, direct and collateral." The very antithesis of Melville's "Call me Ishmael," which establishes the narrator of *Moby-Dick* as a wandering outcast, Grant's opening sentence, which amounts to "Call me American," identifies the narrator with a nation that is more than the sum of its parts, not merely with a particular state among a collection of states. That one can imagine Lee's memoir beginning, "My family is Virginian, and has been for generations, in all its branches, direct and collateral," throws into sharper relief Grant's relentless Unionism.

If we accept as a starting point the description of memoirs as narratives in which authors describe people they have known and events they have witnessed, we can begin to understand some of the paradoxes and contradictions inherent in the genre of the Civil War memoir. Since by definition memoirs, unlike histories, supposedly confine themselves to the limitations of one point of view—the word "memoir" establishes personal memory as the legitimate source of the narrative—readers of memoirs should value them not for an approximation of omniscience in relation to an intricate maze of complex events but for the expression of powerful memories of those events, however incomplete, inaccurate, and limited those memories may be. In a post-Freudian world, some readers may even feel that memoirs become more interesting and significant the farther they stray from objective omniscience into the vagaries and idiosyncracies of recollections shaped by impulses the author doesn't try to correct or censor. Certainly at least one pre-Freudian, Stephen Crane, felt strongly that Civil War memoirs would have benefitted greatly from the inclusion of more emotion recollected in tranquility.

But writers, publishers, and readers of Civil War memoirs valued, and probably in most cases continue to value, those memoirs not for their individualized expressions of personal memory but for the contribution those memoirs make to the establishment of an official record and the writing of history. In his chapter on the Battle of the Wilderness, for example, Longstreet reveals his self-consciousness as a memoirist whose narration is not an end in itself but a contribution to a larger project.

> As the purpose of this writing is to convey ideas of personal observations and experience, it will be confined, as far as practicable, to campaigns or parts of them with which I was directly or indirectly connected. So, when participants and partisans have passed away, I shall have contributed my share towards putting the historian in possession of evidence which he can weigh with that of other actors in the great drama.

For the moment let's take Longstreet at his word and assume that this disinterested purpose—to enable historians to write more fully informed histories—motivates not just the writing of his memoir but also the reading of that memoir by others. Actually, Civil War memoirists wrote for different reasons. Grant, for example, badly needed the money Mark Twain offered him, and many memoirists wrote to justify their own actions or to settle old scores, especially with men who had already written other memoirs, so that the genre tended to perpetuate itself as memoirs bred more memoirs. Then there are the old soldiers who couldn't just fade away quietly and wanted instead to recapture some of the public attention they enjoyed during the war. Obviously, a particular writer could write for all these motives, as well as many others.

Longstreet's assumption that the memoirist serves the historian, not to mention the historian's willing acceptance of that assumption, placed and places constraints on both the writing and the reading of Civil War memoirs. Some might argue that we can't help reading the memoirs of public figures who played significant parts in significant events much differently from the way we read the memoirs of private citizens, and their argument has validity. But the question is, is reading a memoir for its contribution to the historical record the only way to read it? For that matter, is writing a memoir for its historical contribution the only way to write it? If the answer to each of these questions is yes, then literate Americans who aren't particularly interested in Civil War history can't be expected to have much use for the sixty years' worth of memoirs that close the nineteenth century and open the twentieth. But if the answer is no, then there's a chance that during the twenty-first century a few people may be tempted to sift through this huge body of work in order to discover some of the gems it contains.

Before turning to consideration of three other memoirs, let's look briefly at the case of John B. Gordon's *Reminiscences of the Civil War,* published in New York by Scribner's in 1903. At the Battle of the Wilderness, Gordon (1832–1904) was a brigadier general commanding a brigade in Early's Division of Ewell's Second Corps, and during Spotsylvania (May 14, 1864) he was promoted to major general, Early having succeeded Ewell as corps commander after a fall from his horse at the Bloody Angle left Ewell unfit for further field service. Gordon's memoir, which provides an early example of a Confederate referring to the war by its Northern name (after the war Gordon served in the United States Senate), embodies many of the characteristics that typify the genre. As one would expect of a set of personal reminiscences, it confines itself to one point of view, a point of view still warm with "the impetuous ardor of youth" that Douglas Southall Freeman, in his biography of Lee (1934–35) attributes to the not yet thirty-two-year-old general in the Wilderness. Gordon spends the twenty-seven pages of his narrative of May 5 and 6, 1864, talking almost exclusively about himself, first in relation to the way he saved the day south of the Orange Turnpike on May 5 and then in relation to his flank attack on the Union right north of the Orange Turnpike on May 6. Some may find the exaggerations and egotism of Gordon's account too much to take, but the heady exuberance and unabashed pride in what he takes to be his stupendous accomplishments are so ingenuous that, if one can forget for a moment that he is describing events in which thousands of men killed and wounded each other, his enthusiasm can become infectious.

> In such a crisis, when moments count for hours, when the
> fate of a command hangs upon instantaneous decision, the
> responsibility of the commander is almost overwhelming;
> but the very extremity of the danger electrifies his brain to
> abnormal activity. In such peril he does more thinking in
> one second than he would ordinarily do in a day. No man
> ever realized more fully than I did at that dreadful moment
> the truth of the adage: "Necessity is the mother of inven-
> tion."

Gordon includes two diagrams to help his reader understand "the unprecedented movement" he ordered his brigade to perform and sums up this episode in no uncertain terms.

> The situation was both unique and alarming. I know of no
> case like it in military history; nor has there come to my
> knowledge from military text-books or the accounts of the
> world's battles any precedent for the movement which
> extricated my command from its perilous environment and
> changed the threatened capture or annihilation of my
> troops into victory.

If Gordon had been a bully or had puffed himself up at the expense of other men, passages like this would be unbearable. But what's so disarming about his narrative is that it lavishes praise on everyone, friend and foe alike. A. P. Hill is "that brilliant soldier"; Clement A. Evans is "that intrepid leader"; Robert Johnson is "a brilliant young officer"; Generals Seymour and Shaler, captured during Gordon's May 6 flank attack, are "gallant Union leaders"; John W. Daniel, who wrote an account that largely contradicts Gordon's, is "brave and brilliant"; Grant is "so able a commander"; Longstreet's corps is "superb," as is the Texas brigade that ordered Lee to the rear in the Widow Tapp's field. No wonder Gordon became a successful politician. It's hard to grudge so generous a spirit its share of the accolades.

On the one hand, then, Gordon's memoir scores high marks as an individualized expression of personal memory. It makes good reading—better than most generals' memoirs, in fact—and it also scores high on the Stephen Crane test, since it brims with unembarrassed statements of how Gordon actually felt, statements such as "my brain was throbbing with the tremendous possibilities to which such a situation invited us." On the other hand, the author of *Reminiscences of the Civil War* isn't content simply to put his point of view on record and let it go at that. He also wants to serve history, to establish as a matter of fact who was responsible for delaying his flank attack on May 6 (the culprit, he says, was Early), and to align his memoir with the emerging official record. Gordon's case is particularly interesting because his narrative appeared after the government finished publishing the *Official Records* in 1901. In fact, Gordon quotes extensively from the *OR*, specifically from the reports of Federal officers, to demonstrate conclusively that, contrary to what Early claimed, Burnside's Ninth Corps was not placed on the Union right in support of Sedgwick's Sixth Corps and its exposed flank. Unfortunately for Gordon, although his appeal to the records confirms his observation that Burnside was nowhere near the Union right at the time Early claimed it was, historians have largely rejected the service he offers to perform for them. In the disagreement about what happened south of the Orange Turnpike on May 5, for example, Rhea follows Daniel rather than Gordon, and in assessing the contrary claims made by Early and Gordon about the significance of the May 6 flank attack, Steere likewise sides with Early against Gordon. With the historians' verdict in, Gordon's memoir goes back on the shelf, discredited as history and condemned to be ignored by those who judge Civil War memoirs by an ideal standard of objective omniscience.

As the case of Gordon's *Reminiscences* makes clear, the Civil War memoir has led a double life, trying to function as both a witness to subjective individual experience and a servant to objective historical narrative. For this reason, the memoir occupies a middle ground between the eyewitness letter or diary, on the one hand, and conventional historical narrative, on the other. This middle ground, for all its difficult tangles and uneven terrain, can nevertheless prove fertile for the reader willing to waive the requirement that a memoir always justify itself as official history. The memoirs of Longstreet, Grant, and Morris Schaff reveal other important features of this complicated genre.

The first edition of James Longstreet's *From Manassas to Appomattox: Memoirs of the Civil War in America* was published in Philadelphia in 1896 and the second in 1903, the same year that Gordon's memoir appeared and the year before Longstreet's death. Like Gordon, Longstreet refers to the war by its Northern name, his choice of epithets reflecting his reconciliation with the government of the United States after the war (for a time he served as Minister Resident to Turkey), a reconciliation for which many in the South never forgave him. Like Gordon, Longstreet refers explicitly to the *OR*, though still incomplete at the time of his first edition, noting in the preface that "the official War Records supply in a measure the place of lost papers." And like Gordon yet again, Longstreet produced a narrative that many historians view with misgivings. In *Lee's Lieutenants* (1942–46), for example, Freeman comments that the inaccuracies of Longstreet's account result in a book that is "even more unjust" to him than it is to any of the people he criticizes.

Despite the reservations of historians, however, *From Manassas to Appomattox* had a least one important sympathetic reader during the later twentieth century. In *Killer Angels,* Michael Shaara draws heavily on Longstreet's account of Gettysburg as he fashions the character of the Confederate First Corps commander into a military visionary who understands the emerging conditions of modern warfare and their implications, both strategic and tactical, much better than his superior, Robert E. Lee. As a result, millions of Americans who have either read *Killer Angels* or seen the film *Gettysburg* have been strongly influenced by Longstreet's memoir, whether they know it or not. In addition to the sections that Shaara uses, sometimes almost verbatim, Longstreet's account of Gettysburg contains many other memorable moments, such as the controversial characterization of Lee as "excited and off his balance" and laboring "under that oppression until enough blood was shed to appease him." But even this damning judgment sounds tame beside the thundering denouncement of Jubal Early, a verbal thrashing administered in the grand diction and implacable rhythms of Victorian English.

> There was a man on the left of the line who did not care to
> make the battle win. He knew where it was, had viewed it
> from its earliest formation, had orders for his part in it, but
> so withheld part of his command from it as to make co-

operative concert of action impracticable. He had a pruriency for the honors of the field of Mars, was eloquent,
before the fires of the bivouac and his chief, of the glory of
war's gory shield; but when its envied laurels were dipping
to the grasp, when the heavy field called for bloody work,
he found the placid horizon, far and away beyond the cavalry, more lovely and inviting. He wanted command of the
Second Corps, and, succeeding to it, held the honored
position until General Lee found, at last, that he must dismiss him from field service.

Whatever historians have decided or will decide about responsibility for the
failure of the Second Corps to take Culp's Hill on July 2, 1863, the rhetoric of
invective doesn't get much better than this, at least not in the stately idiom of
"pruriency for the honors of the field of Mars" and "the glory of war's gory
shield" that Longstreet wields throughout his memoir.

The elevation of Longstreet's language no doubt will alienate many contemporary readers, partly because it doesn't make for easy reading and partly
because it muffles the realities of lead or iron missiles traveling at high speeds
into human flesh. In his chapter on the Battle of the Wilderness, for example,
Longstreet mentions blood exactly twice, both times with reference to his own
wounding on May 6 along the Orange Plank Road. The second time he quotes
another officer's description of "the bloody foam" that he, Longstreet, blew
from his mouth. Here is the first.

The blow lifted me from the saddle, and my right arm
dropped to my side, but I settled back to my seat, and
started to ride on, when in a minute the flow of blood
admonished me that my work for the day was done.

Although one can admire the understatement here, the refusal to indulge some
readers' taste for the graphic details of violence, it is also possible to feel uncomfortable with a rhetorical chilliness that sometimes sounds like admirable coolness under fire but at others like monstrous cold-bloodedness.

Whatever one thinks of Longstreet's narrative coolness, his chapter on the
Battle of the Wilderness is weaker and less memorable than the chapters on
Gettysburg. Admittedly, Longstreet missed the fighting on May 5 altogether

and had to leave the battle before its conclusion on May 6. Still, he witnessed and must have felt much that he could have conveyed forcefully. Despite its shortcomings, however, the chapter does have its moments. One of these is the eulogy for Micah Jenkins, brigade commander in Charles W. Field's division of Longstreet's corps, who was mortally wounded by the same burst of friendly fire that hit Longstreet.

> He was one of the most estimable characters of the army.
> His taste and talent were for military service. He was intel-
> ligent, quick, untiring, attentive, zealous in discharge of
> duty, truly faithful to official obligations, abreast with the
> foremost in battle, and withal a humble, noble Christian. In
> a moment of highest earthly hope he was transported to
> serenest heavenly joy; to that life beyond that knows no
> bugle call, beat of drum, or clash of steel. May his beautiful
> spirit, through the mercy of God, rest in peace! Amen!

Sam Watkins punctuates his memoir with many such passages, and the com-bination of stock martial imagery with conventional expressions of Christian piety may not grip every reader forcefully. But in the context of Longstreet's coolness, exclamation marks stand out and signify an eruption of feeling that registers distinctly on the Stephen Crane test scale. Of the more than twenty-eight thousand casualties in the Wilderness, Jenkins is the only one Longstreet pauses over, reminding us that not even the coolest of commanders can remain impervious to his losses, in this case the loss of a fellow general officer and South Carolinian. The eulogy for Jenkins marks an inescapably personal moment and, as such, distinguishes Longstreet's memoir, at least here, from the emotionless records that Crane deplored.

Another feature that humanizes *From Manassas to Appomattox,* a feature that typifies many memoirs, especially those by generals, is one we could call the *What if?* moment. *What if* moments abound in both popular and profes-sional reflections on the Civil War, the most famous of them being, "What if Jackson hadn't been wounded at Chancellorsville?" Many people understand this particular *What if* to invite the response, "Then Jackson would have been on the left at Gettysburg, he would have taken Culp's Hill, Lee would have won the battle, and the South would have gained its independence." Since the bigger *What if*s tend to originate from the Southern point of view (What if the Confederates had chased the Federals back into Washington after First Manassas–Bull Run?), some people tend to forget that *What ifs* work both ways: What if McClellan hadn't been so timid during the Peninsula Campaign or Sharpsburg-Antietam? What if Joe Hooker hadn't lost his nerve and pulled back at Chancellorsville? What if John Reynolds hadn't been killed the first day of Gettysburg? What if James Wilson's Union cavalry division had watched the Orange Turnpike long enough to see Ewell's Second Corps arriving at Locust Grove on May 4, 1864, on its way to the Wilderness?

The fact that *What ifs* imply a simplemindedly naive view of cause and effect, a view that assumes one change among many causes will necessarily lead to specific predictable effects, doesn't really matter. What matters is that *What ifs* reflect the all-too-human desire to comprehend and control contingencies beyond comprehension and control. In Longstreet's case, the big *What if* of the Battle of the Wilderness involves the poor preparation of Hill's Third Corps on the Orange Plank Road during the night of May 5.

> Under that plan events support the claim that the Third
> Corps, intrenched in their advanced position, with fresh
> supplies and orders to hold their ground, could have
> received and held against Hancock's early battle until my
> command could have come in on his left rear and com-
> pleted our strongly organized battle by which we could
> have carried the Wilderness, even down and into the clas-
> sic Rapidan.

Could have . . . could have . . . could have. Although Longstreet doesn't spell it out, this conditional fantasy presumably continued: And the defeat of the Army of the Potomac in the Wilderness during the election year, when Lincoln had resorted to his last general, could have led to McClellan's presidential victory and independence for the South. At this moment Longstreet's memoir has departed from the path of objective historical narrative and become a wishful meditation on his own powerlessness to change the outcome of events; and no amount of stoic reconciliation can wholly efface his regret and remorse. Questionable history writing, perhaps, but a memorable moment full of the pathos that gives memoirs one of their defining qualities.

Longstreet's memoir is made up of more than elevated language, cool understatement, *What ifs,* and—as in the final pages of the chapter on the Wilderness—self-defense, in this case against the charge that he arrived on the Plank Road twenty-four hours late. One of the more attractive features of *From Manassas to Appomattox* is Longstreet's sympathetic portrait of Grant, who graduated a year behind him at West Point, served with him in the Fourth United States Infantry Regiment before the war with Mexico, and, in the Appomattox chapter of the memoir, "looked up, recognized me, rose, and with his old-time cheerful greeting gave me his hand, and after passing a few remarks offered a cigar, which was gratefully received." In the Wilderness chapter, Longstreet includes a short paragraph comparing Grant and Lee, a paragraph that concludes, "They were equally pugnacious and plucky,—Grant the more deliberate." Few students of the war could take issue with this characterization, but it is in the preceding sentence that Longstreet suddenly drops his reserve to offer a remarkable—some might say sentimental—description of the man so many in both the North and South vilified as a butcher.

. . . but the biggest part of him was his heart.

Although Longstreet doesn't quote from Grant's *Personal Memoirs,* which preceded both the publication of the *OR* and his own book, the simple, straightforward language of this statement reflects the writing of the man it describes. In many ways Grant's writing embodies the style that Whitman admires in the "Soldiers and Talks" paragraph of his *Memoranda,* "the superfluous flesh of talking" having long been worked off Grant not only by the rigors of war but also by the cancer in his soft palate, cancer that he was fighting during the writing of his memoirs. The clarity and concision of his style have received extensive praise, including the admiration of Gertrude Stein and Sherwood Anderson, whose modernism Grant, in some ways, influenced. To hear the difference between the old idiom and the new, one has only to compare the last sentences of the opening paragraphs of Longstreet's and Grant's chapters on the Wilderness. Both writers are setting the stage for the devastating campaign to come, but Longstreet does so in a lengthy sentence composed of several subordinate clauses connected by semicolons, the last of which runs, "that we should first show that the power of battle is in generalship more than in the number of soldiers, which, properly illustrated, would make the weaker numbers of the contention the stronger force." Grant puts matters more succinctly.

> The two armies had been confronting each other so long,
> without any decisive result, that they hardly knew which
> could whip.

But it is easy to overpraise Grant's style, especially for readers who have become so suspicious of rhetorical embellishment that they no longer hear the plain style as a style at all. At its best Grant's writing makes complicated events and movements easily accessible to the contemporary reader. At its worst it is, in the words of his own description of the country between the Rapidan and the James, "rather flat." In the Wilderness chapter, for example, we hear that "The country roads were narrow and poor," an unremarkable sentence repeated almost verbatim a few pages later: "The roads were narrow and bad." When such sentences alternate with longer ones, their brevity provides refreshing variation, but when they occur in unrelieved succession, they sound dull and somewhat undercooked.

For all their stylistic differences, Grant's account of the Wilderness has much in common with that of Longstreet, whom Grant describes, at the end of a chapter on Chattanooga, as "brave, honest, intelligent, a very capable soldier, subordinate to his superiors, just and kind to his subordinates, but jealous of his own rights, which he had the courage to maintain." Like his former comrade, Grant does little to make the individual sufferings of soldiers real for his reader—in his account the word "blood" doesn't appear at all—but, like Longstreet, he does permit himself to eulogize a single soldier, whose loss must stand in the reader's mind for all other losses. As in Longstreet's narrative, the eulogized soldier, Alexander Hays, is a brigade commander, one who served in Birney's division of Hancock's Second Corps.

> I had been at West Point with Hays for three years, and had
> served with him through the Mexican war, a portion of the
> time in the same regiment. He was a most gallant officer,
> ready to lead his command wherever ordered. With him it
> was "Come, boys," not "Go."

For all the terse precision and matter-of-fact sobriety that characterize this short paragraph, especially when we compare it with Longstreet's on Micah Jenkins, Grant cannot resist indulging elsewhere in his own version of *What if* any more successfully than his enemies, Gordon and Longstreet, each of whom believed that if his respective flank attack could have realized its full potential, he could have won the Battle of the Wilderness.

> I believed then, and see no reason to change that opinion
> now, that if the country had been such that Hancock and
> his command could have seen the confusion and panic in
> the lines of the enemy, it would have been taken advantage
> of so effectually that Lee would not have made another
> stand outside of his Richmond defences.

Like his Confederate counterparts, Grant believes that if things had been different, they would have been so different that the rest of the spring 1864 campaign would never have happened. Unlike them, however, he doesn't base his *What if* on criticism of an individual, as Gordon blamed Early and Longstreet blamed Hill (and by implication Lee, who presumably told Hill not to entrench because Longstreet would be up early enough to relieve him). Instead, Grant blames the Wilderness itself. In fact, Grant rarely blames anyone at all for anything, and not for lack of opportunities. He doesn't censure Wilson for failing to keep his cavalry across the Orange Turnpike or Burnside for being slow in moving toward the left or Gibbon for not supporting the rest of the Second Corps as quickly and strongly as he should have.

The choice, conscious or unconscious, to blame everything on the dense forest invites a closer look. On the one hand, it reflects extraordinary tolerance of other people's costly ineptitude, a tolerance that contrasts favorably with the nearly pathological blame-fixing of some other memoirists. On the other hand, shifting the blame to the nature of the ground, which, after all, also affected the Army of Northern Virginia adversely, neatly shields from censure all ineptitude, Grant's included. That terrible mistakes were made, some by the Union high command, some by subordinate officers, becomes apparent only in a muted acknowledgment that Grant connects with the wounding of Longstreet.

> Longstreet had to leave the field, not to resume his com-
> mand for many weeks. His loss was a severe one to Lee, and
> compensated in a great measure for the mishap, or misap-
> prehensions, which had fallen to our lot during the day.

For someone so highly praised as a straight talker, this is an oddly devious moment, for basically it claims that Longstreet's wounding leveled the playing field, which had tilted in favor of the Confederates not because the Union leadership on various levels made serious mistakes and miscalculations, but because "mishap, or misapprehensions"—the subtle and uncharacteristic wordplay sounds suspicious—fell to the Union "lot." It is as though the Army of the Potomac had been dealt a bad hand of cards or gotten a poor roll of the dice, and the implication is that Confederate bad luck simply offset Union bad luck, not Union blunders.

It is also revealing that the supposedly plainspoken Grant, who scores so well on Walt Whitman's test, doesn't score higher on Stephen Crane's. At one point he does admit, "I was anxious that the rebels should not take the initiative in the morning" of May 6; and yet, even though he also admits that "More desperate fighting has not been witnessed on this continent than that of the 5th and 6th of May," a judgment that the rest of the nineteenth and all of the twentieth centuries have done nothing to shake, Grant gives us no access to his interior world, a world that other witnesses represent as tumultuous. It is from James Wilson's *Life of John A. Rawlins* (1916), a narrative two steps removed from Grant himself, that we get the harrowing account of Grant breaking down in his tent on the night of May 6, and from Horace Porter's *Campaigning with Grant* (1897) the telling detail of Grant smoking twenty large, strong cigars during the same day. This last detail so impressed Gordon that he includes it in his *Reminiscences*.

> In after years, when it was my privilege to know General
> Grant well, he was still a great smoker; but if the nervous
> strain under which he labored is to be measured by the
> number of cigars consumed, it must have been greater on
> the 6th of May than at any period of his life, for he is said
> never to have equalled that record.

It's hard to argue with Gordon's interpretation, and yet where are the signs of "the nervous strain under which he labored" in Grant's *Personal Memoirs*? Depending on individual predispositions, readers can applaud or deplore or not care much about Grant's tight-lipped refusal to give us any indication of how he felt during what he himself later viewed as the most desperate fighting ever to take place on the North American continent, fighting for which in many ways he was both directly and indirectly responsible. Elsewhere in his book Grant does give us slight inklings of what was happening in the heart that Longstreet thought his biggest part. In the chapter on Cold Harbor, for example, he admits, "I have always regretted that the last assault at Cold Harbor was ever made," a confession somewhat diluted by his noncommittal use of the passive voice but still much more than Sherman ever said about the disastrous attack on the Dead Angle at Kennesaw Mountain. Then there is the great detail, perfectly delivered in a single sentence, about Grant's reaction upon reading the message in which Lee requests an interview to discuss the terms of surrender at Appomattox.

> When the officer reached me I was still suffering with the
> sick headache; but the instant I saw the contents of the
> note I was cured.

The scarcity of moments such as these, moments completely absent from the account of the Wilderness, makes me wonder how both Grant and his earliest readers understood the first word of his title. To my ear the word sounds as though it should have quotation marks around it, since Grant's memoirs aren't much more personal than those of Sherman, who avoids the word altogether. More than a hundred years after the publication of Grant's book, many Americans assume that "personal" must mean "intimate," but I for one am not questioning the absence of details about Grant's drinking or how much he missed his wife. I'm questioning the absence, or scarcity, of material that is private in the sense that it differs significantly from what is a matter of public record, material that could come only from the person writing the memoir. In other words, as writers and readers of Civil War memoirs understood them, should a typical example of the genre consist mostly of battle reports sewn together in a readable narrative, with some eulogies, *What ifs,* and self-defense thrown in for variety? If so, do Civil War memoirs still deserve the attention of a few general readers a hundred or so years after their publication, readers who could just as easily pick up a well-written history instead?

I still say yes, but with two qualifications. First, not all Civil War memoirs have an equal claim on precious time and eyesight, any more than all examples of any other genre do. In the Library of Congress subject headings, Civil War memoirs appear under "United States History Civil War 1861–1865 Personal Narratives," and when I last checked, I found 824 entries under that heading, a number that comes into perspective with the discovery that a search for personal narratives by Americans about World War II, the second most written-about war involving the United States, generated 429 entries. Anyone who sifted through the 824 entries would soon discover that "personal narrative" is a large, baggy category, one that also includes diaries, journals, biographies, and collections of letters, not to mention duplicates of works, some in multiple editions. But even with these items weeded out, there are still many, many memoirs to read, and most are only average because average is, by definition, what most things are. Confronted by this mass, general readers should treat themselves to the best examples of the genre, and here Grant's book serves well.

But my second qualification is that twenty-first-century general readers shouldn't choose a memoir that does only what a well-written version of the *OR* would do better. Instead, they should choose memoirs that do something different, that offer something missing from most memoirs written by people who think of themselves primarily as servants of accurate historical records. Sam Watkins's *"Co. Aytch"* is one good example. Watkins makes it clear at the beginning of his narrative, and frequently reminds his readers throughout it, that he writes "only from memory" and that if they want details that his memory can't deliver, they should see "the histories." Another good example is one that I came across reading histories of the Battle of the Wilderness, a memoir reduced in those histories to a few quotations that make it look unexceptional.

Morris Schaff's strangely rich memoir *The Battle of the Wilderness* contains much that contributes nothing to the historical record. As an ordnance officer, Schaff helped supply the Army of the Potomac before the Wilderness campaign and records that between April 4 and May 2, 1864, he ordered 2,325,000 rounds of musket and pistol cartridges for Meade's soldiers, or approximately three for every Confederate who served during the four years of war, if we accept E. B. Long's estimate of 750,000 for the number of Confederate soldiers. Historians who make use of Schaff rely on him primarily for his account of being assigned to lead the dilatory Burnside down the Parker's Store Road to the Chewning Farm on May 6 and for his description of meeting the Iron Brigade's Lysander Cutler in the woods and learning from him of Wadsworth's collapse along the Orange Plank Road, a collapse he subsequently reported to the high command at the Lacy House, only to find himself disbelieved. But using Schaff's memoir to supply only these meager details is, as Emerson would say, like using a volcano to cook eggs.

Like Watkins, Schaff makes it clear early on that he doesn't aim to serve the historical record.

> I am free to confess that the strategy, grand tactics, and mil-
> itary movements of the Civil War, stirring as they were, are
> not the features which engage my deepest interest, but
> rather the spirit which animated the armies of North and
> South. That, that is what I see.

With this disclaimer Schaff should attract many like-minded readers to his
memoir, but those who think they will find there a careful examination of the
psychological motivations of individual soldiers are in for a surprise. When
Schaff refers to "the spirit which animated the armies," he means something
large and even supernatural.

> Reader, if the Spirit of the Wilderness be unreal to you, not
> so is it to me. Bear in mind that the native realm of the
> spirit of man is nature's kingdom, that there he has made
> all of his discoveries, and yet what a vast region is unex-
> plored, that region along whose misty coast Imagination
> wings her way bringing one suggestion after another of
> miraculous transformations, each drawing new light and
> each proclaiming that nature's heart beats with our own.

If Emerson had brought his brand of transcendentalism to the Battle of the
Wilderness and survived to write about it, his account might have sounded
something like this. For Schaff, the natural world, in this case the dense Wilderness itself, reflects and symbolizes human spirit. Whereas for Grant the dense
forest amounts to a topographic impediment on which he can blame the
mishaps or misapprehensions that fell to the Union lot there, for Schaff it constitutes a sublimely terrifying realm that not only shapes local events but also
serves as the agent of national fate, which Schaff understands to be the destruction of slavery.

> And was there a Spirit of the Wilderness, that, as tears
> gathered in eyes of fathers and mothers over separation
> from children and home, recorded an oath to avenge the
> wrong? Else why did the Wilderness strike twice at the
> Confederacy in its moments of victory? Who knows!

As an interpretation of the fighting in the Wilderness that included, during Chancellorsville, the wounding of Jackson and a year later the wounding of Longstreet, this passage may strike the more historically inclined as little short of lunacy. The standard interpretation of the Wilderness terrain reads it as an ally of the smaller Army of Northern Virginia because it hobbled the gigantic and unwieldy Army of the Potomac. But in Schaff's spiritual world, the Wilderness transforms itself into an ally not only of the Federal forces but also of abolition itself.

In a weird and extraordinary passage, Schaff raises the ghost of Jackson and confronts him with both a personification of Slavery and the Spirit of the Wilderness. Placed at the close of Schaff's narrative of May 4, the first day of the campaign, the passage extends over several pages, but three short excerpts outline its contours.

I wonder, Reader, if the ghost of Stonewall did not really come back? You see, it was about the anniversary of the night on which he received his mortal wound, and the old armies that he knew so well were on the eve of meeting again. What should be more natural than that he should come to this side of the river, that river whose beckoning trees offered such sweet shade to the dying soldier? . . .

Abruptly, and with almost a gasp, he fastens his astonished gaze on a cowled figure that has emerged from the trees and is looking at him. Is it the Spirit of the Wilderness, whose relentless eyes met his as he fell, and does he read in their cold depths the doom awaiting Longstreet? . . .

Hark! he hears something. It draws nearer, and now we can distinguish footsteps; they sound as if they were dragging chains after them through the dead rustling leaves. Presently, off from the roadside where two oaks press back the tangle, admitting a bit of starlight, Stonewall sees a gaunt, hollow-breasted, wicked-eyed, sunken-cheeked being. Behold, she is addressing him! "Stonewall, I am Slavery and sorely wounded. Can you do nothing to stay

the Spirit of the Wilderness that, in striking at me, struck
you down?'"

This scene, in which military history meets *Macbeth,* may provoke nothing
but scorn in many readers, especially military historians. In the first chapter of
The Face of Battle (1976), for example, John Keegan asserts that, like a play, a
"battle must obey the dramatic unities of time, place, and action," but a few
pages later he also warns that "Imagination and sentiment, which quite properly delimit the dimensions of the novelist's realm, are a dangerous medium,
however, through which to approach the subject of battle." From Keegan's
point of view, the danger of approaching battle through sentiment and imagination, which Schaff explicitly invokes in a passage quoted earlier, is that they
can produce "some very nasty stuff indeed," stuff that indulges in the "pornography of violence."

Whatever else Schaff is—mystic, romantic, eccentric—he is no pornogra-
pher. If he views the Wilderness as a fateful region in which larger forces oper-
ate in ways we can neither completely understand nor completely explain, he is
hardly alone. In "The Bear" in *Go Down, Moses* (1942), Faulkner has his main
character, Ike McCaslin, list a series of events from the war in order to question
the proposition, advanced by another character, that God has turned his face
toward the South.

> '. . . and that same Longstreet shot out of saddle by his own
> men in the dark by mistake just as Jackson was. His face to
> us? His face to us?'

If using imagination to read the Wilderness as more than a topographic impediment makes questionable sense to the military historian, it nevertheless makes
good psychological, emotional, or spiritual sense, not only to many of the men
who fought there—the effects of religious revivals among soldiers of the Army
of Northern Virginia are well documented, and many soldiers of the Army of
the Potomac recorded their impressions of being haunted by the region—but
also possibly to many of the people who visit the area today.

> It is the holding of the secrets of butchering happenings
> like these, and its air of surprised and wild curiosity in
> whosoever penetrates the solitude and breaks its grim,

immeasurable silence, that gives the Wilderness, I think, its
deep and evoking interest.

This is Schaff again, now narrating battle in and around Saunders' Field on
May 5. I can't speak for every visitor to the Wilderness battlefield, and I certainly can't speak for military historians, but I find nothing to argue with in this
explanation of the "deep and evoking interest" of the woods between Route 20
and the Mill Branch. In fact, it's the best explanation, in any memoir I've read,
of the palpable uncanniness of the Wilderness. Of course, Schaff realizes, and
so do I, that some will object to this kind of talk.

"And is this history?" comes a peevish voice from the general level of those who are as yet only dimly conscious of
the essence and final embodiment of History. Yes, it is a little sheaf out of a field lying in one of its high and beautifully remote valleys.

No matter how many Civil War memoirs I read, and no matter how many other
people I get to read them, I don't think I'll ever feel that I'm in a position to
identify, let alone dismiss, all "those who are as yet only dimly conscious of the
essence and final embodiment of History," although I take pleasure in Schaff's
confident bravado. Still, I do feel quite strongly that Schaff's memoir, even at its
most extravagant, along with other memoirs that stray unconventionally from
generic norms, finally does teach me history, or at least a kind of history. If nothing else, it teaches me a little more about the history of how people looked back
on May 1864, and for whatever reasons, I need to know that, too.

ELEVEN

Histories

E VEN THOUGH MOST Civil War memoirs appeared before most Civil
War histories, the emergence of the former contributing significantly to
the production of the latter, it's a good bet that general readers who
want to learn more about the war will reverse this chronology, reading histories
first and then, if they choose to dig deeper, picking up the memoirs that fill out
the footnotes of those histories. Having passed the Wilderness sign, for example, someone who wanted an overview of the battle there would be more likely
to visit the public library and start with Bruce Catton's text in *The American
Heritage Picture History of the Civil War* or the third volume of Shelby Foote's
The Civil War: A Narrative or James McPherson's *Battle Cry of Freedom* than
with the memoirs of Gordon or Longstreet or Grant or Schaff. In some ways,
of course, this choice makes perfect sense, since most of us depend on histories to introduce us to the people who wrote memoirs and to the memoirs they
wrote.

But in other ways this choice is odd and ironic, since it distorts history by
putting first what came second. By using a book from the last forty years of the
twentieth century as a lens through which to view, and perhaps as a standard
against which to judge, books from the last forty years of the nineteenth or the
first thirty of the twentieth, we risk losing sight of the place of Civil War histories in the spectrum of written representations of, say, the Battle of the Wilderness, a spectrum that includes all the documents from Katherine Couse's letter
on. If we lose sight of the place of Civil War histories in this spectrum, we risk
repeating the error of the young David Copperfield, who, in answer to a question from the transcendently naive Mr. Dick, "'I suppose history never lies does

it?'" answers decisively, "'Oh dear, no, sir!'" Since Civil War histories usually don't lie in the same way that histories officially sanctioned by totalitarian regimes often do, we may need to remind ourselves that the writing of history, like all writing, is a creative and to some degree subjective exercise rather than merely an objective recording of facts. The writing of history as much as of fiction works according to principles and conventions (though different ones) that create a world within which a reader moves.

In the case of Civil War history, appreciating these creative principles and conventions involves special complexity because the keen appetite of general readers in the United States for that history directly opposes the prevailing academic scorn for it in many college and university history departments. This scorn, based first on the simplistic distinction between social and military history and second on the reductive assumption that military history is written exclusively by and for people with militaristic and reactionary tendencies, presents yet another irony, since, at least in the western tradition, all history begins with military history. Without Herodotus on the Persian Wars or Thucydides on the Peloponnesian War or Xenophon in his *Anabasis* we wouldn't have history, at least in the forms in which we know it, and those forms reflect principles and conventions that ultimately trace their origins to these Greek writers of military history.

Chief among these principles and conventions is the organization of history into prose narrative, as opposed to, say, lyric poetry or musical theater. We so take for granted that writing history involves storytelling in prose that it's hard for us to imagine it taking any other form. In the case of Civil War history, general readers bear out this taking-for-granted by responding most positively to books that offer them a "narrative synthesis" of events. This phrase is James McPherson's and comes from the chapter "What's the Matter with History?" in his collection of essays, *Drawn with the Sword* (1996). In that chapter McPherson examines the success of his own *Battle Cry of Freedom,* published eight years earlier, which by 1996 had sold six hundred thousand copies. To put this figure in perspective, we need to understand that it amounts to approximately twenty-two or twenty-three people out of every ten thousand in the United States. Still, as book sales go, the figure is undeniably impressive. McPherson bases his judgment about the importance of narrative synthesis on some five hundred letters he received about his book. He quotes one of these fan letters with becoming modesty but without any hint of being troubled by its implications: "Your book read like a novel."

Although Herodotus fathered western history, it would be quite a stretch to say that he fathered the western novel, and yet it makes sense that twenty-five centuries later a Civil War historian could be proud of the compliment that his historical narrative was as readable, as enjoyable, as a book of fiction. Even so, McPherson's fan letter raises some significant questions, first among them, should the prose narratives of history aspire to the condition of prose fiction? If the answer is yes, as McPherson's testimony suggests it is, then David Copperfield's error deserves a closer look, since it implies more than the failure to recognize the fairly obvious fact that histories create a world within which a reader moves. It also implies the failure to recognize, and to appraise, the affinity between historical writing and creative writing. History cannot consciously lie and be good history, but apparently it can consciously fictionalize, in the sense of adopting the narrative strategies of fiction, and still be good history. In fact, not only can it, but, at least in the case of Civil War history, many people seem to think it should.

Wanting history to offer a narrative synthesis and wanting it to read like a novel may not be incompatible desires, but they aren't necessarily the same thing. Narrative synthesis has to do with putting together, with assembling separate elements into a coherent whole, whereas getting a piece of writing to read like a novel has to do with propelling a reader through that whole. Synthesis implies not getting lost in close analysis, not missing the whole for the parts, whereas novels have to do with designing words and stories into compelling shapes and structures. No attentive reader of Charles Dickens or Henry James or James Joyce or William Faulkner or Virginia Woolf could long defend the claim that novels avoid close analysis, and no regular reader of weekly news magazines, which specialize in synthesis, could mistake those magazines for novels. When he claims that general readers want narrative synthesis, McPherson cannot mean that they want narratives that avoid the analysis of particulars, for, as Aristotle argues in the ninth section of the *Poetics,* it is the business of history to express the particular, not the universal, which Aristotle associates with poetry and some of us might associate with novels.

How does a particular history balance analysis with synthesis or particularity with generalization, and by what features of language and storytelling does it propel a reader through that balance? People who want to read about the Civil War have two basic options available to them: wide-angle histories and close-up histories. Wide-angle histories attempt to narrate the entire war or a significant portion of the war, sometimes in one volume, sometimes in several.

People interested in the Battle of the Wilderness, for example, can find anywhere from a few pages to a chapter or two on that battle in a wide-angle history. Along with the *American Heritage Picture History,* the final volume of
Foote's trilogy, and McPherson's book, the third volume of Douglas Southall
Freeman's *R. E. Lee* (1935), Winston Churchill's *The American Civil War*
(1958), Catton's *Grant Takes Command* (1969), and the fourth volume of Allan
Nevins's *The War for the Union* (1971) provide twentieth-century examples of
narratives that include the Battle of the Wilderness in wide-angle surveys,
expanding a category that emerged soon after the war with William Swinton's
Campaigns of the Army of the Potomac (1866).

Close-up histories, by contrast, set out to narrate a single moment in the
war. In the case of the Battle of the Wilderness, examples include Edward
Steere's *The Wilderness Campaign: The Meeting of Grant and Lee* (1960),
Robert Garth Scott's *Into the Wilderness with the Army of the Potomac* (revised
in 1992), Gordon Rhea's *The Battle of the Wilderness, May 5–6, 1864* (1994),
and John Michael Priest's *Nowhere to Run: The Wilderness, May 4th and 5th,
1864* (1995). As the dates of these studies suggest, the close-up approach,
though not without earlier precedents, has become more popular recently,
prompting McPherson to lament in "What's the Matter with History?" that
more and more is being written about less and less. While this response is predictable coming from someone committed to a certain brand of narrative synthesis, one that tries to squeeze the entire war between two covers, to dismiss
close-up histories as being about less and less makes as much sense as criticiz-
ing a good map of Virginia because it won't help with a trip through the Rock-
ies. A close-up history can include abundant narrative synthesis, and it can read
like a good novel, as Stephen Sears's treatments of Sharpsburg-Antietam and
Chancellorsville make admirably clear. If the business of history is particulars,
then the close-up approach simply provides greater particularity within a limited area. Turning McPherson's formulation around, it would make just as
much sense to complain that wide-angle surveys deliver less and less about
more and more.

As with any sorting into categories, the boundaries between the wide-angle
and the close-up aren't rigid. For the person who wants to read about the
Wilderness, Clifford Dowdey's *Lee's Last Campaign* (1960) and Noah Andre
Trudeau's *Bloody Roads South* (1989) are books that deliver more pages and
greater particularity than most of the wide-angles but fewer pages and less particularity than the close-ups. In general, however, a useful rule of thumb for

distinguishing between wide-angles and close-ups is the Regiment Test: A book that describes a Civil War battle without frequently identifying particular regiments by number is a wide-angle book. In his nine-hundred-page synthesis *Battle Cry of Freedom,* for example, McPherson mentions particular regiments rarely and usually only in the most famous cases, such as the Fifty-fourth Massachusetts or the Twentieth Maine or First Minnesota at Gettysburg. The person driving north on Route 20 who wants to know what regiments filled Saunders' Field needs another book. Likewise, Freeman, Catton, and Nevins make few or no references to particular regiments, although Catton's account of the Wilderness does mention the Fifth Maine, but only in the singular context of a sergeant who shoots a wounded comrade, stranded between the opposing lines, to keep him from being burned to death. Even Foote, whose narrative reflects a novelist's eye for the defining detail, tells his version of the Wilderness without identifying regiments, although he does mention an Alabama battalion that helped stop Wadsworth near the Plank Road.

Although the Regiment Test provides one way to measure different degrees of particularity, and so to distinguish between wide-angles and close-ups, it doesn't reveal significant differences in the methods of historical storytelling. For both wide-angles and close-ups the ingredients are basically the same: plot summary, analysis, anecdotes, memorable lines, and battle pieces. Different histories mix these ingredients in different ratios according to different recipes, and the success of the mixture depends on the skill of the storyteller. But whatever the variations, Civil War histories have resolved the art of Herodotus into these components, and it is by means of these components that they represent to the rest of us the violence we may have trouble imagining.

In the *Poetics,* Aristotle claims that history relates what has happened. Unfortunately, "what has happened" isn't as simple as this simple statement makes it sound, since what happens to a general can differ greatly from what happens to a private, and what happens to our enemies, in their own eyes, often bears little resemblance to what happens to them in ours. Nevertheless, we can use Aristotle's description to think of plot summary as the simplest continuous recitation of something that happened, the kind of recitation that a child gives when asked to describe a movie: This happened, then this happened, then this happened. If we think of historical narrative as a solution, then plot summary is the solvent and the other components are the solutes. Obviously, no Civil War history could consist only of plot summary, both because it would be impossible to summarize everything that happened to everybody and because, even if it were possible, the monotony of a flat narrative unrelieved by selection and omission would be unbearable. But if we start by looking at Swinton's early *Campaigns of the Army of the Potomac,* we can use it to isolate and appraise some of the features that characterize later narratives.

Although Swinton's narrative recipe lacks generous helpings of the ingredients that might make it read like a novel, it does have at least one distinguishing quality. Because it appeared so soon after the war, its "sources of information are entirely manuscript," as Swinton explains in the preface. Consequently, the narrative includes none of the moments derived from books published later, moments that have become staples, if not clichés, in subsequent histories and have helped to make the return to manuscript sources a professional requirement for Civil War historians. For example, the section on the Wilderness doesn't include the obligatory staging of "Lee to the rear" or Griffin storming into Union headquarters and mouthing off at Meade or Grant snapping that he's tired of hearing people worry about what Lee is going to do.

Instead, *Campaigns of the Army of the Potomac* delivers the kind of straightforward journalistic account one might expect from a man who reported the war for the *New York Times.* In Swinton's case, the what-has-happened of history limits itself to what has happened to the generals of the Army of the Potomac, and he tells his story without much dramatization or rhetorical embellishment.

> Against this naked flank the Confederates made a vigorous
> attack upon Ayres' brigade of Regulars, and this giving way,
> Bartlett's brigade also was beaten back. Two guns that had
> been advanced on the turnpike to take advantage of the first
> success, their horses being killed, were left between the
> lines, and fell into the hands of the enemy.

Swinton bases these two sentences, which describe action in Saunders' Field during the afternoon of May 5, on Bartlett's notes and Meade's report respectively, and the bare-bones storytelling typifies his general-centered, or what John Keegan calls "strategocentric," plot summary.

But it would be a mistake to characterize Swinton's narrative as wholly lacking in personality. In anticipation of Crane's impatience with the dullness of Civil War records, the Wilderness chapter serves up this sentence to represent the feelings of Northern soldiers upon crossing the Rapidan.

The barrier that had so long divided the opposing armies
was passed, and with the mingled emotions which grand
and novel enterprises stir in men's breasts, the troops
looked out, hopefully, yet conscious that a terrible struggle
was before them, into a region yet untrodden by the hostile
armies, but soon to become historic by a fierce grapple of
armed hosts and bloody battles in many tangled woods.

Although it's not clear what Swinton means by "a region yet untrodden," since
Hancock's Second Corps camped on the old Chancellorsville battlefield before
moving down the Brock Road, and since, for example, Warren led the Fifth
Corps into the Wilderness over much of the same ground he had covered with
the Second Corps during the Mine Run campaign five months before, the sentence gives some sense of how this early Civil War historian mixes other ingredients into his narrative, as when he describes the action of May 5 as "not so
much a battle as the fierce grapple of two mighty wrestlers suddenly meeting,"
a description that combines a figurative image with a modest attempt at analysis. Not so happily, it also shows that the ready-made tag "fierce grapple" comes
a little too easily to Swinton's mind.

Despite other moments that break up simple plot summary—moments
such as a paragraph on what military art has to say about the defense of rivers
or the description of the Wilderness as "a region of gloom and the shadow of
death" or the statement, "There is something horrible, yet fascinating, in the
mystery shrouding this strangest of battles ever fought"—Swinton's narrative
synthesis shows us Civil War military history at an early stage of its development. At this early stage, many conventions and motifs that become familiar in
later narratives, for better and for worse, have yet to appear.

To Swinton's credit, however, his wide-angle survey of events in the eastern theater distributes its attention proportionately, with the three days at Gettysburg getting more space than the two in the Wilderness, and the two in the
Wilderness getting more than the one at Sharpsburg-Antietam or Fredericksburg. By contrast, some of the other wide-angle histories achieve narrative synthesis by pinching certain parts of the war and stretching out others. This
pinching is especially noticeable in treatments of the Wilderness. McPherson,
for example, gives the two-day battle all of two pages, whereas he devotes five
to First Manassas–Bull Run. But in paying the Wilderness little attention,
McPherson and other wide-angle histories are not alone. In Whitman's *Memo-*

randa, for example, which narrates the Battle of Chancellorsville for nearly four pages, the Wilderness appears only once, referred to as "the bloody promenade of the Wilderness" in a list of other battles under the heading, "The Million Dead, too, summ'd up—The Unknown."

Without selection and omission, without pushing some moments into the foreground and others into the background, no historical narrative of the Civil War would achieve narrative synthesis or read like a novel. One of the first distinctions any narrator must master is the one between narrative time and time narrated, a distinction that children absorb from hearing fairy tales make the predictable shift from general background to a particular instance, from "Once upon a time there lived a queen who was X" to "One day she did Y." In the case of Swinton's *Campaigns of the Army of the Potomac,* the ratio between narrative time and time narrated is simple and direct: the longer a battle takes, the more space it gets. In the case of McPherson's *Battle Cry of Freedom,* the ratio has changed and become more complicated.

The point here is not to praise or damn McPherson or Whitman or Ken Burns, whose eleven-hour documentary spends about eight minutes on the Wilderness, but to recognize what it is about narrative synthesis and what it is about the Battle of the Wilderness that don't suit each other. For one thing, many wide-angle narratives zip through the Wilderness for the same reason that so much rode on the campaign that began there. By the time we as readers get to the Wilderness in a wide-angle narrative, we're in the same position as many people were in 1864. We've had enough killing, enough news of killing, and we're just about numb. Someone who was war-weary in 1864 couldn't do anything about it, but someone writing a narrative that includes 1864 can avoid wearying readers by speeding up narrative time. For another thing, the Wilderness wasn't decisive. No one won or lost, no one retreated back across a river, and so the Wilderness offers the storyteller no opportunity to tell a larger story in microcosm. As Aristotle tells us in his discussion of plot, a whole is something with a beginning, a middle, and an end, but these are precisely the features that the Battle of the Wilderness makes so hard to identify, unlike Gettysburg, which offers a storyteller the dramatic unity of its neat three-day structure. As others have argued, in some ways the Battle of the Wilderness wasn't a battle at all but rather the opening of a nearly continuous forty-day battle. With full awareness of its biblical resonance, Foote gives the title "The Forty Days" to the chapter that includes his account of May 5–6, 1864.

Too much of the killing we've already seen. Too little of the decisiveness and closure that many associate with good stories. No wonder the Wilderness fares so badly in some narratives, and yet what makes the battle bad for wide-angle storytelling is also part of what makes it, in Swinton's words, horrible yet fascinating, "the strangest of battles ever fought." For the reader of Civil War histories, then, the Battle of the Wilderness represents a telling paradox: its minor position in a wide-angle narrative that aims at readable synthesis reflects and confirms its unique significance.

How then does the wide-angle historian narrate what resists narrative synthesis? One hundred twenty-two years after Swinton, McPherson has a repertoire of stock lines and anecdotes to represent the strangest of battles, and he makes efficient use of them, having set the scene with condensed plot summary.

> But the southerners knew the terrain and the Yankees' preponderance of troops produced only immobility in these dense, smoke-filled woods where soldiers could rarely see the enemy, units blundered the wrong way in the direction-less jungle, friendly troops fired on each other by mistake, gaps in the opposing line went unexploited because unseen, while muzzle flashes and exploding shells set the underbrush on fire to threaten wounded men with a fiery death.

Having synthesized the events of two days into this single, well-crafted sentence, which culminates in the sensational if not necessarily original flourish, "fiery death," McPherson moves from plot summary in his first paragraph to anecdote in his second, telling yet again the story of the Texas brigade shouting, "Go back, General Lee." Next comes a paragraph on the Confederate use of the unfinished railroad cut, the subsequent flank attack on Hancock, and Longstreet's wounding. Finally, a fourth paragraph shifts from the Plank Road to Gordon's flank attack on the Union right and closes the account with the memorable lines from Grant, quoted from Horace Porter's *Campaigning with Grant* (1897), about Lee turning a double somersault and landing on the Union rear, lines that end, "Go back to your command, and try to think what we are going to do ourselves, instead of what Lee is going to do."

If the Army of the Potomac could have moved through the Wilderness at the same brisk pace McPherson does, there would have been no battle there, and the brisk pacing of *Battle Cry of Freedom* has much to do, no doubt, with the enjoyment of the person who wrote that the book reads like a novel. Nevertheless, the wide-angle account that reads most like a novel is not McPherson's but Foote's. To say so is not simply to redirect fan mail from the former to the latter, but to acknowledge that Foote himself has done his best to dissolve the distinction between history and novel. Having read and admired his novel *Shiloh* (1952), especially the technique of narrating from multiple points of view, which Foote passed on to Michael Shaara for use in *Killer Angels,* I turned to Foote's account of Shiloh in the first volume of *The Civil War* (1958) and discovered that the novel and the history have several phrases, sentences, and entire passages in common. Often the difference between a passage in the novel and one in the history consists of nothing but a change in pronouns, with a first-person speaker in *Shiloh* making way for a third-person narrator in *The Civil War.*

This convergence of history and fiction will make some people uncomfortable, and a few will dismiss Foote's trilogy as a popularization that has no place in the ranks of serious professional histories. But they need to think again, at least about what it is they're dismissing. If people want to quarrel with Foote over matters of interpretation—for example, does he accept without question Gordon's account of events in the Wilderness?—they're free to do so, as they would be with any other historian. But if they dismiss him because they get nervous when a novelist goes to work on history, they may have lapsed into David Copperfield's error. The ingredients of Foote's narrative are the same as those of Freeman, Catton, Nevins, McPherson, and other close-up historians. Foote simply mixes those ingredients in a more skillful and memorable way.

Two features of Foote's narrative synthesis stand out right away. The first is the quality of the language, which uses several techniques to avoid the flatness of cliché, among them the hyphenated coinages that startle with their freshness. In the account of the Wilderness, for example, we find soldiers "anticipating a quick pink-yellow stab of flame and a humming, bone-thwacking bullet from every shadow up ahead." Likewise, Foote gives us "narrow, jungle-flanked, moonless roads," "bullet-shattered legs," "a Wilderness-hampered halt," "jungle-foundered soldiers," "brush-choked interval," "bullet-flailed brush," and "morale-shattering repulse." Then there are all the phrases that take the form "the X of Y," many of them metaphors Foote reserves for representing the Wilderness itself: "the blind tangle of the Wilderness," "this green maze of vines and briers and stunted oaks and pines," "the green toils of the Wilderness," "the briery hug of the jungle," and "that leafy sea of green."

These examples of Foote's linguistic self-consciousness may inspire nothing but distrust in those who feel that history, especially the history of men killing each other by the thousands, has no business fiddling with aesthetic distractions as the Wilderness burns, and it may not help to remind them that no writer, whether of history or novels, writes without linguistic self-consciousness. But even these skeptics cannot object to a second characteristic feature of Foote's narrative, since it delivers more of the particularity that Aristotle claims it's the job of historians to deliver. Like other wide-angle histories, Foote's narrative tends toward generals and strategocentricity, but unlike many of the other wide-angles, Foote humanizes his generals and other high-ranking officers in a simple yet ingenious way: Each time he introduces a new one, he gives his age. Consequently, the Wilderness isn't just a matter of Wadsworth and Griffin and Hancock and Poague and Smith and Sorrel and Jenkins and Johnston, all names that for many readers may feel like little more than empty ciphers; it's an encounter with Wadsworth at fifty-six, Griffin at thirty-eight, Hancock at forty, Poague at twenty-eight, Smith at forty-four, Sorrel at twenty-six, Jenkins at twenty-eight, and Johnston at twenty-seven. Age is obviously important to Foote—in the last paragraph on the last page of the trilogy he tells us that he was "two years younger than Grant at Belmont" when he began the project and "four months older than Lincoln at his assassination" when he finished it—and he makes it important to us as well, since he shows that, along with all the other swirling contingencies that affect the combat and killing, we need to remember the contingencies implied by particular men fighting at particular moments in their own lives.

For all the features that make Foote's narrative read like a novel—and there are others, such as the chummy references to Longstreet and Hill as Old Peter and Little Powell—its synthesis of images and moments depends heavily on older books, as Foote freely admits in his bibliographical note. Some of these images and moments are familiar ones, like the skeletons exposed on the Chancellorsville battlefield or Griffin complaining to Meade as Grant overhears or "Lee to the rear" or Kershaw shouting "Friends!" to the Virginia soldiers who shot Longstreet and Jenkins or Grant breaking down in his tent. But for all their familiarity, Foote also manages to present many of these images and moments in fresh ways. For example, in the account of Griffin complaining to Meade about the lack of support for his division in Saunders' Field on May 5, for which Foote, like everyone else, relies on George R. Agassiz's selection of Theodore Lyman's letters, *Meade's Headquarters, 1863–1865* (1922), Foote adds the sentence, "The air was full of God-damns," a product of his own imagination rather than Lyman's account. Similarly, in managing the account of Grant sobbing in his tent, an account based on James Wilson's memory of what John Rawlins told him, Foote's dramatically short sentence, "He broke," recalls the power of "Jesus wept" in the gospel of John.

Along with familiar images and moments recast in his own way, Foote's narrative recipe calls for liberal quantities of memorable lines, all of which appear in other narratives. He quotes an unnamed veteran who calls the Wilderness "A battle of invisibles with invisibles" and another who refers to it as "simply bushwhacking on a grand scale," the first of which appears in Catton's *Grant Takes Command* and both of which reappear in Gordon Rhea's close-up history. We find, in a passage carved directly out of Gordon's memoir, Ewell calling out "'General Gordon! . . . the day depends on you!'" and Gordon responding, "'These men will save it, sir.'" There's also the one-liner Hancock delivered to Longstreet after the war, "You rolled me up like a wet blanket," and, just as in McPherson's narrative, a full quotation of Grant on the subject of Lee turning a double somersault, a quotation that Foote relished enough to repeat again on camera with Ken Burns fifteen years later, adding at the end, "Grant's wonderful."

One ingredient that Foote's account of the Wilderness goes light on is analysis or commentary. This is not to say that no ideas inform his trilogy. The largest idea, that a narrative of the war needs to represent more of the war outside of Virginia, emerges in Foote's balancing of the eastern and western theaters. But he doesn't give us anything like Swinton's paragraph on the military art of defending rivers or the harsh judgment that Churchill delivers on "Grant's tactics of unflinching butchery" during the spring of 1864: "More is expected of the high command than determination in thrusting men to their doom." In itself, there is nothing about wide-angle narration that necessarily prevents a narrator from analyzing a particular moment closely, especially in a footnote. In *Grant Takes Command,* for example, Catton devotes a lengthy note to raising doubts about Wilson's account of Grant's breakdown on the night of May 6. A particular narrator may interrupt the momentum of storytelling to include analysis and commentary in the writing of history just as in the writing of fiction, and the proportion of analysis to storytelling helps to identify and define a particular narrator.

But the simple limitations of space mean that a wide-angle narrative synthesis of the entire war, especially if the narrator wants to tell a briskly paced story, cannot skimp on plot summary, anecdotes, and memorable lines in order to analyze as generously as some readers might like. For more analysis, readers need to turn to the close-up histories, which can afford to interrupt plot summary with larger amounts of other ingredients. Here an excellent example is Charles Royster's chapter "The Death of Stonewall" in *The Destructive War* (1991), a chapter that opens with some of the most memorable lines of the war, Jackson's last words about passing over the river and resting in the shade of the trees. From this opening, Royster then builds a chapter that alternates paragraphs summarizing the plot of Jackson's wounding and death with paragraphs devoted to analysis of these moments, their implications, and various representations of them. Pushing the ratio of plot summary to analysis close to fifty-fifty, Royster's experiment is a daring one. The chapter doesn't provide the uninterrupted storytelling of a good page-turner, yet it is powerful enough to challenge the view that narrative synthesis must always aspire to read like a popular novel.

Analysis isn't the only ingredient that close-up histories can deliver more of than their wide-angle counterparts. They can also devote more space to what Keegan calls "the battle piece," the extended description of actual combat in which a storyteller suspends the larger narrative of a battle or war in order to dilate a particular moment in the fighting. In Swinton's *Campaigns of the Army of the Potomac,* the two sentences narrating the fighting in Saunders' Field on May 5, the first of which begins, "Against this naked flank," provide a small example from a wide-angle survey. But now let's compare descriptions of that same moment from two of the close-up histories. Here is Edward Steere's version in *The Wilderness Campaign:*

> One of the fiercest hand-to-hand grapples of the Wilderness battle flared around the battery position. A number of stout-hearted Zouaves paused in flight to lend a hand. Bayonets crossed over dead horses. Artillery sabers clashed on rifle barrels. Some went home in deadly stabs; others slashed into red gaping wounds. The roaring detonation of revolvers, hoarse imprecations, and sharp outcries of agonized pain all mingled in a frightful uproar. "It was claw for claw and the Devil for us all," wrote a Confederate participant. Gunners and Zouaves were overborne by the weight and fury of Confederate steel. Lieutenant Shelton fell with

a wound and was taken prisoner. Severely wounded, Captain Winslow surrendered the guns.

And here is Gordon Rhea's paragraph about the same moment in *The Battle of the Wilderness:*

> A whirlwind of hand-to-hand combat swirled around the Federal guns that were still blazing away from the middle of Saunders' Field. Steuart's 1st and 3rd North Carolina regiments pitched in with clubbed muskets and bayonets. "'Twas claw for claw, and the devil for us all," one of the Southern combatants remembered. Abandoned by Ayres's infantry, the stubborn gunners managed to get off a few final shots, fighting alone until they were overrun by graycoats. Jamming two pistols in Shelton's face, an officer from the 6th Alabama demanded that the lieutenant surrender. As he was being led away, Shelton saw an Alabama regiment in "butternut suits and slouch hats, shooting straggling and wounded Zouaves." Only after nearly all the artillery horses were killed and the officers wounded did the cannon fall into rebel hands. "The guns were fought to the last," the 5th Corps artillery chief Wainwright noted in his report, "and lost as honorably as guns could be lost."

No one could argue that these two paragraphs deliver more particularity than Swinton's two sentences, and certainly more than do Freeman, Catton, Nevins, Foote, and McPherson, who don't mention the contested guns at all. Such particularity follows predictably from two accounts that pass the Regiment Test, with both Steere and Rhea focusing on regiments (the Zouaves belonged to the 146th New York) and officers below the rank of general. But although these two battle pieces differ from wide-angle histories in the degree of their specificity, do their close-up narratives differ in kind from other versions of narrative synthesis?

In looking closely at these two passages, we notice right away some obvious similarities and some obvious differences. Similarities include the characterization of this particular moment as one of "hand-to-hand" fighting, a characterization that immediately suggests a special degree of ferocious intensity; the reference to bayonets, which accounted for a very small percentage of wounds in the Civil War; and the use of the same memorable line from a Confederate soldier, a line that both writers take from Walter Clark's edition of *Histories of the Several Regiments and Battalions from North Carolina in the Great War 1861–1865* (1901). Among the differences, we find more quotations representing more points of view in Rhea, along with more references to particular regiments. But we also find in Rhea no indication that Shelton was wounded—in fact, the image of the Alabama officer jamming two pistols in his face suggests that Shelton is still active enough to require the aggressive application of force against him—and no mention of the badly wounded Captain Winslow, who doesn't appear anywhere in Rhea's book.

If we look more closely, however, differences and similarities become complicated. In his account Steere attempts to describe the actual physical effects of fighting, as that fighting occurred, on the bodies of the men involved, whereas Rhea's only references to wounding and killing appear late in the paragraph and describe not the hand-to-hand fighting itself but the aftermath, such as the shooting of "straggling and wounded Zouaves." But Steere's description of the fighting also employs a point of view that detaches weapons and wounds from the soldiers using and suffering them. Bayonets cross and sabers clash, and both inflict "deadly stabs" and "red gaping wounds," but they do so in a way that leaves not only specific people out of the picture but in fact any people at all. Between the reference to the Zouaves in the second sentence and the attribution of the memorable line to a "Confederate participant," actual men vanish altogether from Steere's battle piece, which represents them and what they undergo in Saunders' Field by substituting parts for wholes.

In addition, although both Steere and Rhea quote the same line about claws and the Devil, they do so for different purposes. For Steere the line sums up the violence he has been narrating. With its reduction of men to claws, it also helps to erase those men, or at least their humanness, from the account. But Rhea relies on the quotation to substitute for description of the hand-to-hand combat that supposedly characterizes this episode. The North Carolina soldiers pitch in, the quotation comes and goes, and by the time it has passed, so has the hand-to-hand fighting.

Both passages also show a tendency to use well-worn words, phrases, and metaphors to heighten the drama of the narrative. Having lumped all the Zouaves under the cheerful heading "stout-hearted," Steere opts for the Swintonian word "grapples," which with its reminder of grappling hooks has a certain appropriateness for hand-to-hand fighting, but suddenly he has the grapple giving off heat and light as it flares. Rhea chooses the meteorological image of a whirlwind for combat and, predictably enough, has that whirlwind swirl around the two canons. Not surprisingly, the use of conventional words and epithets leads both authors onto shaky literary ground. Steere describes the overpowering "weight and fury of Confederate steel," by which he presumably means the swords and bayonets used in hand-to-hand fighting. But his swashbuckling substitution of "steel" for the men who wield the weapons also risks unintended irony, since in the industrially challenged South genuine Confederate steel would have been a rare item indeed. Rhea, for his part, adopts the heavily used epithet "graycoats," also a favorite of Freeman's, for soldiers dressed in the motley clothing worn by the Army of Northern Virginia, then subverts his own image of unlikely uniformity two sentences later by quoting Shelton's observation of Alabama soldiers dressed in butternut suits.

This kind of close reading may appear hypercritical or ungenerous, but it isn't meant to be. Both of these books are excellent close-up histories; Steere's was deservedly reprinted more than thirty years after its original publication and Rhea's won a prestigious award. Anyone who wants to learn about the Battle of the Wilderness will benefit greatly from reading them, and we can only hope that other battles will find such competent, thorough narrators, if they haven't already done so. But taking a close-up look at the writing of close-up histories may prevent us from slipping into David Copperfield's error and forgetting that historians, no matter how careful their research into published and unpublished sources, are writers drawing on the writings of other writers, and that when they write, their art is primarily a literary art. In our unguarded moments, we may believe that they offer us narrative synthesis of what has happened, but in fact they offer us narrative synthesis of earlier writing about what has happened.

Although close-up histories may differ from wide-angles in the degree of particularity they offer, they don't differ significantly from them in the kinds of assumptions they make about storytelling. Neither Steere nor Rhea, for example, explicitly announces that he wants to write a narrative that reads like a novel, but both reveal the operations of literary sensibility in their undertakings. Rhea's readers discover his self-consciousness as a storyteller in the final sentence of his introduction to *The Battle of the Wilderness:* "The tale is one of the most thrilling in American military history." With its connotation of pleasant diversion, even entertainment, the word "tale" alerts us to one aspect of the attitude that shapes the subsequent narrative. Meanwhile, the adjective "thrilling" is an odd choice for the Battle of the Wilderness, since so much of what happened on May 5 and 6 had to do with the slow, frustrating work of trying to get thousands of men organized in dense woods. True, the near capture of Lee, Hill, and Stuart in the Widow Tapp's field, or Lee attempting to lead the Texans against Hancock, can get the adrenalin pumping, but the confusion, chaos, and error of the battle, not to mention the grinding attrition of Grant's larger strategy, are not likely to strike many readers as very thrilling. Rhea's sentence tells us more about the way he wants to present his material than about the inherent quality of the material itself.

As for Steere, the passage from *The Wilderness Campaign* quoted above appears in a section headed "Tragedy and Comedy in Sanders' Field" (Steere calls the field by this name throughout), and at the close of the same chapter he quotes Shakespeare's Henry the Fifth at Harfleur ("Once more unto the breach"), commenting that the "drama of Harfleur and Agincourt was not to be reinacted in the Wilderness." His taste for theatricality now established, Steere closes the chapter with his own version of Griffin's protest to Meade and Grant's subsequent recommendation that Meade arrest Griffin, the same incident that prompted Foote to invent "The air was full of God-damns." To Lyman's original version of the incident, Steere adds the description of Meade "seeking as it were to placate an angry child" in his attempt to mollify Grant, who, in this version, "lit a fresh cigar and lapsed into meditation." In a note Steere adds, "The author admits a slight embellishment of Lyman's account."

Slight embellishment? How slight does embellishment have to be before it becomes lying, or if not lying, then pure fiction? Steere is a very careful, scrupulous historian, as his note admitting embellishment confirms; many historians who embellish wouldn't bother to call attention to a practice that many readers take for granted. In fact, one of the most attractive features of his narrative is Steere's insistence on acknowledging what we still don't know, and probably won't ever know, about what happened in the Wilderness. He concludes the account of Griffin, Meade, and Grant, for example, with the sentence, "The manner of General Griffin's exit is not recorded." Unlike Rhea, Steere doesn't aim to fashion the Battle of the Wilderness into a thrilling tale. Instead, he allows the gaps in our knowledge to stand both for the limitations imposed on certainty by the Wilderness itself and for the limitations of any effort to narrate the past to the present.

What is the point of adding slight embellishments or writing histories that read like novels? For that matter, why write histories at all? This second question has too many answers: because the historian was present at the events narrated and feels both qualified and obliged to narrate them; because the historian, though not present at them, feels strongly that the events narrated must not be forgotten; because the historian wants to promote a certain version of events; because the historian takes pleasure in writing history; because the historian must write history to meet someone else's demands for productivity. As for the first question, in the case of the Civil War at least, Foote himself may answer it best when he describes his purpose as "re-creating the war and making it live in the world around us."

But the next question is, do the embellishments and heightenings and shadings and manipulations that Civil War historians have always practiced necessarily help to re-create the war and make it live in the world around us? Much of the time the answer has to be yes. A well-written, briskly paced narrative that reads like a novel or thrilling tale will stimulate the imaginations of most readers better than a collection of dull, dusty records will. But for some readers, and I include myself in this group, the embellishments and heightenings and shadings and manipulations also call attention to the fact that a narrative is always only a screen of language woven from earlier language, and that screen can cut us off and distance us from the particularity of what has happened. When I drive by the Wilderness sign, all the histories I've read help me envision some of what happened, or what may have happened, fifty-one miles up Route 20. But they also make me wonder if I've been had by the historian's art, if my habits of reading have only led me further and further into a world of plot summaries, anecdotes, memorable lines, and battle pieces in which it's all done with mirrors, one piece of writing reflecting another.

Nagged by these doubts, I find myself wanting a different kind of language, not one without conventions of its own, since such a language would be impossible, but one unfamiliar enough to me to push me through the alienating screen of novel-like narrative synthesis. In a small historical society on an island off the coast of Maine, I found an example of what I was looking for.

G. S. W. of right shoulder. Ball struck at outer third of clavicle, carrying away 1 ½ in. of clavicle, and a portion of spine of scapula, and all underlying tissues, scar tender, adherent, dragging, covered with scaly eruption, 4 in. long, 3 in.

wide. Voluntary motion in shoulder totally lost, elbow
pronation and supination normal, flexion and extension
limited ⅞, fore arm carried at right angle to upper arm,
wrist motion limited ¼, thumb motion in thumb and fingers normal, can pick up a knife or fork with hand but can
not use it. There is total disability of shoulder arm and
hand.

Surgeon's Certificate. Pension Claim Number 59,863. Address of Board: Rock-
land, Maine. Date of Exam: July 1, 1903. Name of Claimant: Asa O. Candage.

Asa Candage fought in the Wilderness with the Seventh Maine, Third
Brigade, Second Division, Sixth Corps of the Army of the Potomac. According
to notes left by his daughter Florence, he received the wound described above
on May 6, having already been shot in the foot that morning. Florence claims
that the Seventh Maine fought all day long through swamps, the men around
Candage falling by the dozen, until finally he and a Penobscot Indian were left
alone in a bad spot. When Candage called for reinforcements, a bullet struck
the Indian in the arm. Candage then saw a sharpshooter in a tree, drawing a
bead on him, but before he could act, a bullet struck him in the shoulder. He
lay in the woods north of Saunders' Field and Route 20 for three days before
help came.

I don't know if Florence is slightly embellishing what happened. I don't
know if Candage slightly embellished what happened when he told her about
it. Even to repeat this much of Florence's version of her father's story is to begin
to construct a battle piece, to shape it into readable form, and I don't want to
do that. But whatever happened to Candage on the Union right in the Wilderness on May 6, 1864, it produced the G. S. W., or Gun Shot Wound, described
in the Surgeon's Certificate. Nine hundred pages of such language would be
tough going for me, but this one paragraph, which lacks any of the emotion
Crane wanted, any of the pornographic sensationalizing Keegan dislikes, any of
the techniques that make a narrative synthesis read like a novel, suddenly
pushed me through phrases like "withering fire" or "decimated in seconds" to
something on the other side. I've never seen a document like this quoted in any
history of the Wilderness I've read. Multiply it by fifteen or twenty or twenty-
five thousand. Make the war live in the world around us.

TWELVE

Fictions

THERE'S A FAMOUS moment in *The Red Badge of Courage* that has always puzzled me. It appears near the end of the seventh chapter, after Henry Fleming has run from the fighting, overheard his division commander celebrating the subsequent success of his regiment, and wandered off into the woods feeling sorry for himself. Walking through the deep thickets of the Wilderness somewhere between what is now Route 3 and the Rapidan or Rappahannock, Henry reaches "a place where the high, arching boughs made a chapel," a place of "religious half light" that promises some kind of epiphany or revelation.

> Near the threshold he stopped, horror-stricken at the sight of a thing.
> He was being looked at by a dead man who was seated with his back against a columnlike tree. The corpse was dressed in a uniform that once had been blue, but was now faded to a melancholy shade of green. The eyes, staring at the youth, had changed to the dull hue to be seen on the side of a dead fish. The mouth was open. Its red had changed to an appalling yellow. Over the gray skin of the face ran little ants. One was trundling some sort of a bundle along the upper lip.

People who write about *Red Badge* professionally have had plenty to say about this moment, reading it according to various interpretations of the novel, and though everyone agrees that the image of the corpse is gruesome and hideous, no one seems bothered by the timing of Crane's introduction of a decomposing Union soldier.

I'm bothered. If Crane's novel takes the Battle of Chancellorsville for its setting—and since the publication of Harold R. Hungerford's 1963 essay "'That Was at Chancellorsville': The Factual Framework of *The Red Badge of Courage*," no one has argued publicly that it doesn't—then something's wrong. The last time I read the novel I had the pleasure of talking about it with several doctors, and I asked them how long they thought the Union soldier had been dead, assuming the usual conditions of early May in central Virginia. One man, to whose expertise on the subject the others deferred, said he thought about two or three days, and no one else disagreed with this estimate. Certainly, none of the people who have written about the novel seems to doubt that the body has been decomposing for some time. One eminent Crane scholar refers to it explicitly as a "rotted corpse."

But this is only the second day of Chancellorsville, and the first one of fighting for Henry's regiment, the movements of which correspond to those of several units in the Second Corps. Even if we assume that the dead Union soldier belonged to a unit engaged in brief skirmishing east of Chancellorsville the day before, he can't have been dead much more than twenty-four hours. And what about his uniform "that once had been blue, but was now faded to a melancholy shade of green"? We can't know for sure who the soldier was, but if he was a veteran whose uniform had faded during previous service, what was he doing alone in the woods west of the site of skirmishing on the first day of battle? If he'd been killed on the spot where Henry finds him, how likely is it that he'd be the only casualty there? If he'd been wounded in the fighting east of Chancellorsville, why wouldn't his veteran instincts have led him to the hospital tents for medical attention? Or if he was a new, untried recruit like Henry, a wounded man who had also fled the fighting and hidden himself in the woods, his relatively new uniform couldn't have faded from blue to melancholy green in a single day, or even in two or three days. Curious to see how Hollywood visualized this puzzling scene, I watched John Huston's 1951 black-and-white version, which stars Audie Murphy, the most decorated GI of World War II, as Henry Fleming, only to discover that Huston omitted the encounter altogether.

What kind of nitpicking is this? After all, *The Red Badge of Courage* is fiction, isn't it? Don't we expect a novelist to invent? Should we make a case of every questionable detail in Crane's novel, such as the preposterously high number of Henry's regiment, the 304th New York, or should we relax and take the novel on its own terms? When Aristotle distinguishes between history and poetry, he distinguishes between what has happened and what may happen. In the case of the Battle of Chancellorsville, it certainly may have happened that a single Union soldier wearing a uniform already faded to green somehow got himself killed somewhere in the Wilderness two or three days before Henry Fleming discovers him. Perhaps he served as a scout. Perhaps he was a deserter with a bad sense of direction.

Certainly these are plausible explanations, and perhaps they explain why no one else seems troubled by the scene. But in the case of Civil War fiction my question is, how does the fictional representation of what may have happened, with all its accuracies or inaccuracies, enlarge or diminish our sense of what actually happened? Let's take another case, also one that may puzzle only me. In *Killer Angels* Michael Shaara has Lee, at the close of the second day of Gettysburg, thinking thoughts that will lead him to formulate the plan for Pickett's Charge the next afternoon.

> He saw that in his mind's eye: his boys backing off, pulling
> out, looking up in wonder and rage at the Yankee troops
> still in possession of the high ground. If we fall back, we
> will have fought here for two days and we will leave know-
> ing that we did not drive them off, and if it was no defeat,
> surely it was no victory. And we have never yet left the
> enemy in command of the field.

Wrong. And not just a little wrong, either. After the standoff at Sharpsburg-Antietam, not quite nine months before the time of this meditation, the Army of Northern Virginia retreated back across the Potomac and in fact did leave the enemy in command of the field, enabling Alexander Gardner's team to take the photographs that shook the North in October 1862 and Lincoln to issue the Emancipation Proclamation.

When I asked a reenactor about this moment, the same man who worked on the film *Gettysburg* and told me about the spontaneous cheering of Martin Sheen as Lee, he dismissed it quickly and simply as Shaara's mistake. But I'm not so sure. I have no particular reason to think Michael Shaara infallible, but that's an awfully big mistake for anyone with even moderate knowledge of the eastern theater to make, let alone someone who did as much research as Shaara obviously did.

In this case, the novelist's version of what may have happened has everything to do with how he wants us to imagine what actually happened. Of course Lee remembered Sharpsburg-Antietam. Shaara shows him explicitly recalling it twice, once when he worries that "Rhodes might be attacking half the Union army" and thinks to himself "Another Sharpsburg," once when he consults with Longstreet over a map, saying, "I am suspicious of written orders since that affair at Sharpsburg," an allusion to the famous loss of Special Order 191 and its passing into McClellan's hands. But it may have happened that at a crucial moment late at night Lee's great pride in his army, a pride attested to elsewhere by Shaara's Lewis Armistead ("'But the Old Man is just plain, well, too *proud*'"), momentarily affects his recollection of the past. In turn, by focusing on the grave consequences of too much pride, Shaara sets up his reading of Lee's error as hubris and the Battle of Gettysburg as Aristotelian tragedy, a reading made explicit in Chamberlain's thoughts at the end.

> Professors' minds. But he thought of Aristotle: pity and terror. So this is tragedy. Yes.

As Charles Royster has argued in *The Destructive War,* many people have a particular investment in calling the Civil War, or any part of it, a tragedy, since they feel that doing so allows them to view the war as an anomaly rather than as the result of something intrinsic to the nature of their nation. In the context of the early 1970s, when *Killer Angels* appeared, Shaara also may have had in mind yet another instance of the tragic consequences of pride, as Lee's declaration that "we have never yet left the enemy in command of the field" would have resonated with what many people were thinking about the war in Vietnam.

Although not everyone likes it, Shaara's version of what may have happened doesn't violate anyone's version of what actually happened, since in this scene he operates in the realm of the private thoughts of a man who never made those thoughts a matter of official record. When it comes to matters of official record, *Killer Angels* scores high marks among several professional historians. James McPherson teaches the book to his Princeton undergraduates, for example, and the bibliographic essay at the end of *The Third Day at Gettysburg and Beyond,* edited by Gary Gallagher and published in 1994, includes Shaara's novel among the historical books and essays cited, describing it as "among the most popular books ever written on the battle," one that "explores the roles of R. E. Lee, James Longstreet, and Lewis Armistead on July 3 in fascinating and sometimes controversial portraits." Stephen Crane, born more than eight years after Chancellorsville, was gratified by reviews that praised *The Red Badge of Courage* as a work that only a veteran of the war could have produced. Were Shaara still alive, he would probably find the approbation of Civil War historians similarly gratifying.

The enthusiastic piece of fan mail quoted by McPherson in "What's the Matter with History?" implies that good historical narrative should read like a novel, but is the converse also true? Should Civil War fiction try to pass as historical narrative, or at least aim for inclusion in history course syllabi and scholarly bibliographies?

Authors of fictional works on the Civil War have addressed this question in various ways. In his own note "To the Reader," for example, Michael Shaara claims that he has "not consciously changed any fact" and "not knowingly violated the action," although he admits that he has modernized the language of his characters and closes with the crucial statement, "The interpretation of character is my own." Similarly, at the end of *Jacob's Ladder* (1998), Donald McCaig admits forthrightly that he is "no historian" but adds that he has "tried to stick tight to the facts." In the note to the reader that opens *The History of Rome Hanks* (1944), Joseph Stanley Pennell anticipates questions about historical accuracy when he assures readers that "All anachronisms are conscious, as the narrative is filtered through the memories and desires of several narrators who may be either ignorant or untruthful—or both." In his "Author's Note" at the beginning of *Oldest Living Confederate Widow Tells All* (1989), Allan Gurganus complicates the matter still further by including "A word to the reader about historical accuracy," which describes former slaves' testimony that they had seen Lincoln in the South during the war. Gurganus then comments, "Such visitations remain, for me, truer than fact," and he closes with the richly suggestive statement, "History is my starting point."

Not all Civil War novels include such notes. Many let their attitudes toward history and historical accuracy surface in their acknowledgment of the books consulted. Thomas Keneally's *Confederates* (1979), which lists several titles and concludes with the wonderful benediction, "May all these authors, the living and the dead, flourish in reputation," and Charles Frazier's best-selling *Cold Mountain* (1997), which ends with Frazier's brief apology for taking liberties with the life of his main character, fall into this category, as does Shelby Foote's *Shiloh*. But many others say nothing, leaving their attitudes toward history unexamined and unexplained. This may be the largest category of all, and it includes both older and more recent works, among them Crane's *Red Badge of Courage,* Ellen Glasgow's *The Battle-Ground* (1902), Mary Johnston's *The Long Roll* (1911) and *Cease Firing* (1912), Evelyn Scott's *The Wave* (1929), Margaret Mitchell's *Gone with the Wind* (1936), William Faulkner's *The Unvanquished* (1938), Mary Lee Settle's *Know Nothing* (1960), Robert Penn Warren's *Wilderness* (1961), and Thomas Dyja's *Play for a Kingdom* (1997).

Whatever its stated or unstated attitude toward historical accuracy, a piece of fiction reveals much about its intentions and aspirations in the way it approaches the Civil War. Does it place the war in the foreground or the background? If in the foreground, what part or parts of the war does it focus on? Battles and military campaigns? If so, from the perspective of generals or privates? If not, then on civilian life? Politics? If in the background, how far back and for what purpose? Does it approach the war directly by looking straight at it? If so, from an omniscient point of view or from multiple limited points of view? To what extent does it present the war using the same ingredients as do histories that rely on plot summary, anecdotes, memorable lines, and battle pieces? If it approaches the war indirectly, as Whitman always said he preferred, how does it convert the seemingly peripheral or marginal—what Sam Watkins calls a side show of the big show—into something significant and representative? These are some of the questions that keep cropping up as I read fictional treatments of the Battle of the Wilderness.

Contemporary with *The Red Badge of Courage* is Harold Frederic's longish short story "A Day in the Wilderness," written in 1893 and subsequently published in *The Deserter and Other Stories: A Book of Two Wars* (1898). For those who insist on historical accuracy, Frederic's story presents some obstacles. In the third section of the story, we learn that all of the main characters belong to the First Division of the Union Fifth Corps, but earlier Frederic tells us that a brigade of this division, commanded by the fictional General Boyce, forms the rearguard of the "great army" and has only just arrived on the second day of the battle. In fact, the First Division of the Fifth Corps opened the battle the day before in Saunders' Field. Also, it is crucial to the plot that one of Boyce's regiments comes from Ohio, and the Fifth Corps included no regiments from that state. Finally, Frederic shows a poor sense of the topography of the Wilderness, since the action involves a "murderous ravine" so precipitous that the steepness makes the fourteen-year-old drummer boy, Lafe Hornbeck, dizzy as he looks down on it from above.

> The other side of the gulf spread out before him could not
> be seen for the smoke—but the tops of tall pines growing
> on its bottom were far below him.

Although the Wilderness has plenty of troublesome gullies and ravines, this particular plunging chasm sounds altogether unlikely, as if one of the gorges of upstate New York had suddenly strayed south.

But even if Frederic reveals a rather casual attitude toward historical accuracy, he clearly appreciates the reputation of the Wilderness.

> In this gloomy and sinister wilderness men did not know
> where they were, nor whom they were fighting. Whole
> commands were lost in the impenetrable woods. Mounted
> orderlies could not get about through the underbrush, and
> orders sent out were never delivered.

Like Crane, Frederic had a version of history available to him in *Battles and Leaders of the Civil War* (1884–1888), the fourth and final volume of which includes contributions on the Wilderness by Grant, E. M. Law, Alexander Webb, and Charles Venable. But with all the other battles also represented in this collection, why would Frederic choose the Wilderness for the only piece of fiction he focused entirely on soldiers in the field, especially since he obviously had no special commitment to getting the specific facts of the battle right?

The answer may have something to do with his description of the gloomy and sinister wilderness as a place where "men did not know where they were, nor whom they were fighting." Frederic's story, in which Lafe Hornbeck discovers that the "young, fair-faced officer" from Ohio is actually his uncle Lyman whom he saves from the burning woods, treats the Civil War as the setting for the same mixture of uncanny coincidence, recognition, and discovery that characterizes the surprise endings of many stories in Ambrose Bierce's *Tales of Soldiers and Civilians,* published two years before Frederic wrote his story. If Frederic's story is an imitation of Bierce, it's a weak one at best, but it does suggest that for Frederic, as for Bierce, representing the massive complex-

ity of the war comes down to dramatizing the accidental discovery of connections between and among individuals. On a literal level, accounts of such discoveries are plentiful in Civil War records, and so Frederic may be fictionaliz-
ing the kind of incident that frequently occurred. But on a figurative level, he
may also be representing the war as an intricate network of connections, despite
its appearance as total confusion and chaos. Perhaps such a representation is
accurate; perhaps it is nothing more than Frederic's wishful attempt to manage
confusion and chaos. Either way, the Wilderness provides him with an extreme
version of the confusion and chaos he needs to make tracing a single thread of
connection all the more remarkable.

Published almost twenty years after Frederic wrote "A Day in the Wilderness,"
Mary Johnston's *Cease Firing* also confronts sticklers for historical accuracy
with some challenges. In a chapter called "The Wilderness," Johnston, grand-
daughter of Joseph Johnston's cousin, shifts the scene from Georgia, where
Désirée Gaillard reads a newspaper account of the battle to Edward Cary and a
railroad carful of Confederate wounded, to Virginia, where the sun is setting on
May 4, 1864. Like Frederic, Johnston wastes no time in presenting her version
of the terrain, but whereas Frederic's version is "gloomy and sinister," Johnston's description luxuriates in romantic intensification of exotic richness.

> Night fell. Far and wide rolled the Wilderness. An odour
> rose from the dwarf pine and oak and sweet gum and
> cedar, from the earth and its carpet of the leaves of old
> years, from the dogwood, the pink azalea, and the purple
> judas-tree, from rotting logs and orange and red fungi, from
> small marshy bottoms where the frogs were croaking, from
> the dry, out-worn "poison fields," from dust and from
> mould,—a subtle odour, new as to-day, old as sandalwood
> cut in the East ten thousand years ago. Far and wide
> stretched the Wilderness.

Despite the syntactic savoring of the same flora that Frederic makes repellent,
describing it as "foul underfoot with swamp or thicket," Johnston gets some
basic features of the landscape and the battle badly wrong. Even if one could
overlook the blunder of "Ewell and A. P. Hill moved westward, deeper into the
Wilderness"—Johnston has the Army of Northern Virginia coming from the

direction of Fredericksburg, as it did in May 1863 but not a year later, when it moved east into the Wilderness from Orange—her lengthy evocation of what she calls "eve-of-battle mood" in the Confederate camp includes the conversation of men looking at "the pale light along the northern horizon."

> "It's like the lights of a distant city over there."
> "A hundred and forty thousand men make a city. . . . Not so distant either."

If Crane had written *The Red Badge of Courage* from a Confederate point of view, this image of enemy campfires would have suited a description of looking across the Rappahannock towards Falmouth during the winter of 1863, but the most significant aspect of May 4, 1864, is that Ewell's Second Corps and Warren's Fifth Corps camped only a few miles from each other without Grant or Meade having the least idea of their proximity. If, as Johnston imagines the scene, "The grey soldiers, too, had their camp-fires" and the "light of these flared, to the eyes of the blue, on the southern horizon," Grant and Meade would have known what they were facing, and the Battle of the Wilderness could not have unfolded as it did.

When the battle does unfold in *Cease Firing,* it follows the familiar recipe of many historical narratives. Having opened with Ewell's memorable lines ("just the orders I like—to go right down the Plank Road [actually, the turnpike] and strike the enemy wherever I find him"), quoted by both Johnston and Gordon Rhea from Robert Stiles's *Four Years under Marse Robert* (1903), Johnston then gives a one-page plot summary of the fighting in order to hasten to May 6 and a page devoted to the anecdote of "Lee to the rear." Then comes the wounding of Longstreet, followed by an extensive quotation from Stiles, which also appears in Rhea's narrative, a quotation describing Longstreet in the ambulance. As the chapter closes, Johnston turns to the feature of the battle so basic to both verbal and visual representations of the action on May 5 and 6.

> Night was not so black in all parts of the Wilderness. In
> parts it was fearfully red. The Wilderness was afire.

Unlike Frederic, who focuses on a few characters not involved in combat, Johnston works to put actual fighting in the foreground of her novel, temporarily suspending the stories of her characters to deliver a strategocentric narrative that reads like many wide-angle historical syntheses. Although that narrative lacks an instance of the battle pieces that characterize close-up histories, it reflects Johnston's ambitious attempt to give her story an epic scope that anticipates Margaret Mitchell's *Gone with the Wind.* Few readers will find *Cease Firing* a rival to Mitchell's novel, but Johnston's evocation of the Wilderness includes at least one poetic touch that Morris Schaff, whose memoir appeared two years earlier, would have admired.

> The Wilderness lay awake. She communed with her own
> heart. But the men whom she harboured slept.

Seventeen years after *Cease Firing* appeared in 1912, another Southerner, Evelyn Scott, published *The Wave* to high praise from many, some of whom ranked it alongside works by Faulkner, Hemingway, and Thomas Wolfe that appeared the same year, and most of whom agreed that it set a new standard for the writing of Civil War fiction. Although the latter claim feels reasonable, I have trouble endorsing the former.

> First the houses stalked by in lines, one after another,
> wedges with brilliantly orificed fronts.

Orificed? This sentence describes the view out the window of the train that Grant is riding east in March 1864, and the impressionist technique of transferring the movement of the train to the houses it passes is one Crane might well have admired. But "orificed"? Scott's prose strains self-consciously toward novelty, and that self-consciousness can make the reading tough going, as in the case of the nervous twitch that signals a movement into Grant's mind with single quotation marks.

> What he insisted to himself constantly was that nobody
> could 'shake' him. A certain blandness recent in the atti-
> tude of his associates he distrusted heartily. Still—it was a
> fine thing, the way officers and men alike had 'stood up' for
> him. He could not tolerate 'sentimental talk.' The results of
> the war would be 'good' for everybody. The country, and
> particularly the 'hidebound South,' needed a 'shaking up.'

When Shaara takes invention into Lee's mind, he enlarges my sense of what actually happened by persuasively imagining a version of what may have happened, but when Scott takes invention into Grant's mind, too many reminders of her authorial supervision interfere with my suspension of disbelief.

Still, *The Wave* does represent a development in fictional representation of the war as a whole and of the Wilderness in particular. Having acknowledged in her "Foreword" that "In the insertion in this text of the characters of mythical military leaders side by side with those who existed in fact, and in other deliberate inaccuracies of time and place, this book takes a number of liberties with 'history,'" Scott introduces her novel with a long epigraph from Philip Lake's *Physical Geography* (first edition 1915). In this epigraph, Lake distinguishes between the action of a cork bobbing in the ocean and the action of waves traveling over its surface. In constructing her book, Scott presents characters who bob like corks as the wave of war sweeps by. But unlike Mary Johnston or Harold Frederic or Stephen Crane, Scott doesn't follow the same characters all the way through her six-hundred-page novel, which has no plot aside from the chronology of the war itself. Instead, characters come and go as the wave moves under, over, and around them, propelled by larger forces and motions.

In theory, it's a good idea, as literary modernism meets the Civil War and refrains from imposing a single point of view or a single coherent narrative on events that resist both. Instead of using the war as a backdrop for a conventional plot, such as a love story, or narrating battle according to the conventional recipe of wide-angle histories, Scott momentarily isolates particles in the tidal wave of war. In the case of the Wilderness, for example, she represents the battle with a sequence of four short episodes. In the first, she focuses on Earl Marbray, a Southerner from near Orange, Virginia, but a soldier "in one of Burnside's corps" (Burnside had only one corps). As he approaches his home and crosses the Rapidan, Earl thinks about his killing of another man before the war "in a fit of craven anger" and has the premonition *"I'm gonta die today."* In the second episode, Scott stages a somewhat comic scene, as Grant and Meade stumble through the thick woods discussing strategy and revealing themselves as caricatures. The third focuses on Beverly, a Confederate soldier in Ewell's corps, whose horse has joined a wild stampede in the middle of which Beverly falls and gets trampled, his brain "pulped to quietness." Finally, the fourth turns to the story of Bob, a Confederate flag-bearer caught in the fires of the Wilderness. Intent on saving the flag, or at least on being seen as trying to save it, Bob climbs a tall pine, attempts to attract the attention of "'Uncle Robert's' men" somewhere in the distance, and, as the episode closes, slips toward the smoke below.

No plot summary of battle, no memorable lines, no "Lee to the rear" or wounding of Longstreet or Griffin protesting to Grant or Grant snapping that he's tired of hearing his subordinates worry about what Lee is going to do next. Mixing generals with enlisted men and historical figures with fictional characters, Scott evokes the Battle of the Wilderness by flashing discrete moments at her readers. Since three of the moments involve characters in extreme physical or psychological crisis, Scott's sketch of the Battle of the Wilderness leaves us with the impression of frenzied intensity, an impression that will have the most power over readers who don't find the episodes overwritten. But even readers who find the linguistic barrage of Scott's style a little overwhelming will have to credit her with making them more sensitive to the name of the battle.

'Wilderness.' Sounds jes' like somethin in the Bible.

And that word—*wilderness*—always seemed to him to
mean something. . . . *Wilderness*. Words. All different. All
seeming to be 'concerned' with something or other. And no
'sense' to anything. This tortured him, voluptuously—*wil-
der-ness*.

These sentences appear in Earl Marbray's section, but they also connect with the Grant-Meade episode, since Meade says the word "Wilderness" to himself, and Grant, as Scott portrays him "in his hardy unimaginativeness," rejects the deeper undertones of *wil-der-ness*. Scott's achievement here is to bring those undertones and their figurative possibilities into the foreground. She isn't the first to hear the biblical resonance of the name "Wilderness." In *Campaigning with Grant* (1897), for example, Horace Porter recalls a drum corps striking up the camp-meeting air *"Ain't I glad to get out ob de wilderness!,"* and the unsigned poem "Battle of the Wilderness" in *Harper's Weekly* for May 28, 1864, takes as its epigraph the line "The wilderness shall bloom," a line the poet attributes to the Bible, apparently a condensed paraphrase of Isaiah 35:1. And who knows how many sermons preached from pulpits North and South on May 15, 22, and 29, 1864, made use of scriptural references to wilderness in order to read the trial of battle in a larger context?

By the time we get to Robert Penn Warren's *The Wilderness,* published in 1961, the same year that his book *The Legacy of the Civil War: Meditations on the Centennial* appeared, allegorical, or at least figurative, meanings of the Wilderness dominate. The story of Adam Rosenweig, "the crippled Jew from Bavaria," Warren's three-hundred-page novel follows its main character through his departure for North America to fight for freedom, the discovery of his disability—despite the wearing of a special corrective shoe—which disqualifies him for service, his firsthand experience of the New York draft riots, his encounter with a wealthy New York financier, his subsequent employment by a sutler headed for Virginia, his visit to Gettysburg a few months after the battle there, his sojourn with the Army of the Potomac during the winter of 1863–64, and his decision not to leave when Grant orders the sutlers back toward Washington but to cross the Rapidan and join the fighting. Since the novel doesn't reach the Battle of the Wilderness until its last twenty-five pages and represents it only as distant sound when it does, Warren's title points beyond the immediate context of the spring 1864 campaign toward another kind of wilderness, a vast, trackless state of existential bewilderment.

> "The Wilderness?" Adam asked. "What they call the Wilderness?"
> "Yeah," the man said. "And they don't call hit that fer nuthen. It is that-a-way. It is shore-God a place a man can wander and not know."

For Adam Rosenweig, wandering through this interior wilderness involves the collision of his youthful idealism with the brute facts of the war in North America. "They wouldn't let me fight," he explains to an unnamed woman whose husband will guide him across the Rapidan. When she asks him, "Fight fer what?" he answers, "Freedom."

> "Freedom," she repeated at last, trying the word on her tongue, musing on it.
> Suddenly, she rose.
> "Killen," she said bitterly, "that's what they is fighten

fer. They all done got the habit. They is killen fer killen. Anything else they done long forgot."

In *The Legacy of the Civil War,* Warren gives convenient labels to the psychological bequests left to the South and North, calling them the Great Alibi and the Treasury of Virtue respectively. Throughout *The Wilderness,* as in this passage in particular, Adam Rosenweig speaks on behalf of the Treasury of Virtue, which Warren admits may not be as "comic or vicious" as the Great Alibi but calls it "equally unlovely." The unloveliness of Rosenweig's position extends to the surge of manly pride he feels when he finally kills a man, a beardless Confederate "scarecrow," on the outskirts of the Battle of the Wilderness. By the time he resolves on the last page "to walk out of the Wilderness," Warren's narrator is spinning the same kind of ambiguity around his young killer that Crane's narrator spins around Henry Fleming when he leaves the Wilderness. Rosenweig's realization that "He knew, however, that he would have to try to know what a man must know to be a man" is no more conclusive and no less flecked with irony than Henry Fleming's feeling "a quiet manhood, nonassertive but of sturdy and strong blood" on the last page of *Red Badge of Courage.*

For all of Warren's lack of figurative subtlety in his choice of setting or in his crippling of his main character, another version of the archetypal Wandering Jew, and for all of his inclination towards heavily introspective indirect discourse that yields large pronouncements such as "History needed forgiveness," the novel does contain memorable images of battle. Having heard the eruption of fighting in Saunders' Field on May 5 as "a dry, nagging crackle, like green briar burning" and awakened at dawn on May 6 to find the air "trembling and clotted," Rosenweig's imagination compresses into a few lines the same fires that Evelyn Scott ignites around her Confederate flag-bearer for several fraught pages.

the heave of far flame on a darkening sky above thickets
where, miles away, the steam of sap in vernal wood would
be exploding festively like firecrackers, and wounded men,
those who were able, would drag, pull, claw, hunch, hump,
roll themselves, inch by inch, over the ground in a lethargic
parody of flight until the moment of surrender when the

summarizing scream of protest would be uttered, but heard
by no ear.

But compression isn't everything. In his 1988 novel *Traveller,* Richard
Adams also packs his description of the burning Wilderness into a few lines,
closing that description with the not very compelling sentence, "I guess a lot of
our wounded must 'a died in them woods—yeah, burned in the fires." No matter how strong one's preference for the understatement of Hemingway or the
lean, sinewy narratives that Whitman admired, such a sentence in such a context flattens itself beyond understatement into a casual offhandedness that feels
wholly ineffective and out of place. As throughout the novel, the first-person
speaker of the sentence is Lee's most famous horse, Traveller, and one might be
tempted to attribute any descriptive flatness to the necessary limitations of
Traveller's imagined point of view and sensibility. Even with this excuse, however, Evelyn Scott's longer version does more to keep a reader focused on the
awful details of death by fire.

In some ways, Adams's experiment in point of view looks ingenious, and it
does produce original moments. Yes, *Traveller* does give us yet one more version of "Lee to the rear" in the Widow Tapp's field, but not one of the myriad
other versions considers what it could have felt like to be the horse that Lee
tried to urge into Hancock's Second Corps.

> "Forward, men!" he shouts. "I'll lead you myself!"
> Snakes alive! Like thunder you will! I thought. Marse
> Robert personally leading a charge agin the Blue men? I'd
> never figured on this. 'Course, I'm an awful coward, Tom,
> you know. Gunfire I'd more less got used to—'much as I
> ever did—but leading a charge? I wonder who offers the
> biggest mark, I thought. The General's horse, I guess. Well,
> here we go!

Traveller contains other interesting touches as well, such as the horse's epithets
for various Confederate generals. Longstreet, Hill, and Ewell become Old Pete,
Red Shirt, and the Bald General respectively, all these nicknames familiar or
predictable, but the designations of Stuart and Jackson as Jine-the-Cavalry and
Cap-in-the-Eyes reveal an extra dash of ironic cleverness. Still, Adams's exper-

iment makes me uncomfortable. Although he opens each chapter with historical plot summary, which sets the scene and grounds his equine ventriloquism
in something like reality, too often the monologues delivered by Traveller to
Tom Nipper, the cat who frequents his stall in Lexington, Virginia, after the
war, remind me of conversations between Wilbur the pig and Charlotte the spi-
der in E. B. White's *Charlotte's Web*—a great book to be sure but not one
through which to try to imagine the American Civil War. In *Patriotic Gore*
(1962), Edmund Wilson observes of Thomas Nelson Page's children's story
Two Little Confederates (1888) that it "was hard to make the Civil War seem
cosy, but Thomas Nelson Page did his best." Richard Adams's version of the
Wilderness does its best to make the battle, if not quite cosy, a little too funny
and easy.

By the time we get to a talking horse, the relation between Civil War fiction and
historical accuracy has entered a new dimension, and the liberties that Richard
Adams takes with what may have happened far exceed those exercised by his
predecessors. In the case of *Traveller* those liberties don't enlarge my sense of
what actually happened, but not because I object in principle to the taking of
great liberties. Harry Turtledove's triumphant blending of science fiction with
so-called alternate history in *The Guns of the South* (1992) makes *Traveller* look
like a model of historical accuracy and restraint, and yet Turtledove's extravagant invention of what never could have happened helps me understand the
nature and significance of what did happen.

A professional historian who has published both history and speculative
fiction, Turtledove takes on the greatest *What If* of all, at least for a student of
the Civil War: What if the South had won? To bring about a Confederate victory, he doesn't settle for any strategy as tame as letting Jackson survive Chancellorsville or causing Lee to decide against launching Pickett's Charge.
Instead, he transports several white supremacists from late-twentieth-century
South Africa to Orange, Virginia, during the winter months of 1864. With them
the South Africans bring a new weapon, the AK-47, which they give the Army
of Northern Virginia before the Wilderness campaign.

The Guns of the South could have imagined Confederates armed with auto-
matic weapons at any moment during the war. Since the novel envisions the
capture of Washington, it makes sense that those weapons need to appear in the
eastern theater, but their effect at Sharpsburg-Antietam or Gettysburg would
have been no less devastating. In choosing the Battle of the Wilderness for the

beginning of his alternate history, however, Turtledove sharpens our understanding of how crucial and pivotal the battle was, despite—or perhaps because
of—its inconclusiveness. As for his reimagination of the actual fighting, which
focuses on the Brock Road–Plank Road intersection, sticklers for historical
accuracy don't have to wink at the kinds of gaffes made by Frederic or Johnston
or Scott. In fact, they may find themselves on the defensive, as Turtledove
includes at least two moments that test the knowledge and historical sophisti-
cation of his readers. In the first, he takes Hancock's memorable line "We are
driving them beautifully," spoken to Theodore Lyman around 5:30 on the
morning of May 6, and slips it quietly into the mouth of Confederate Major
General Henry Heth, who exclaims it to Lee on May 5. In the second, the members of the Forty-seventh North Carolina, whose names Turtledove has taken
from official records, greet the approaching men of the Third Arkansas, the
only non-Texas regiment belonging to Gregg's Brigade of Field's Division of
Longstreet's Corps. This greeting subtly alludes to the "Lee to the rear"
episode, of which Turtledove's alternate history has no need, since it reminds
us that in shouting another memorable line, "Texans always move them!," as he
supposedly did when Gregg's Brigade appeared, Lee allowed his enthusiasm to
erase from popular memory the presence of the Third Arkansas.

If *The Guns of the South* were a different kind of book, moments like these
might come off as little more than in-jokes for historians. But in following events
from Lee's countermove north across the Rapidan to the capture of Washington to the armistice to the election of Horatio Seymour over Lincoln in November 1864 (for which Turtledove provides detailed returns in an appendix) to
Lee's victory over Nathan Bedford Forrest in the Confederate election of 1867
to the violent confrontation with the men from South Africa, Turtledove is not
simply spinning out a well-researched fantasy. He is also meditating on the
nature of history and historical narrative itself. No sooner has Lee been elected
president of the Confederacy than a veteran of the Forty-seventh North Carolina shows him a copy of *The American Heritage Picture History of the Civil
War* taken from the South Africans.

> This Bruce Catton's style was less Latinate, less ornate,
> more down-to-earth than Lee would have expected from a
> serious work of history. He soon ceased to notice; he was
> after information, and the smooth, flowing text and aston-
> ishing pictures made it easy to acquire. He had to remind

himself that Catton was writing long after the war ended
and that, to the historian, it had not gone as he himself
remembered.

Floated free from its immediate context, this last sentence threatens the neat
distinction between what may have happened and what actually happened, a
distinction without which, in turn, the boundary between history and fiction
cannot long remain clear. In context, Catton's version of the war differs from
Lee's because the time-traveling South Africans tampered with events. But even
if they hadn't tampered, how would Lee read Bruce Catton? If a nineteenth-
century participant could read a twentieth-century history, how much of it
would feel like fiction to him? For that matter, if he could read twentieth-century fiction, how much of it would feel like what he remembered? In Turtledove's masterful representation of Lee's historical uncertainty, we see the reflection of a North Carolina soldier's thoughts on May 5, 1864: "In the Wilderness,
certainty meant little."

According to Albert J. Menendez's *Civil War Novels: An Annotated Bibliography* (1986), the war has generated over a thousand novels, and yet I often hear
someone say that we have yet to see the great Civil War novel, adding something
like, "Where is the *War and Peace* of the American Civil War?" This question
makes as much sense to me as asking, Where is the *Moby-Dick* of the Russian
whaling industry? But even if I could take the question seriously, I wonder how
many people who ask it have come from recent readings of *War and Peace,*
which contains long philosophical stretches that make the cetology chapters of
Moby-Dick look like light reading. Besides, who knows how many good Russian novels about the Napoleonic wars never got written because other novelists
felt intimidated by *War and Peace*? If the price of an American counterpart to
Tolstoy's tome were the loss of most of the books we now have, would we be
willing to pay it? To be sure, there are many hundreds of mediocre American
Civil War novels, but there are also several excellent ones, and the new novels
coming out are getting steadily better. The most recent treatment of the Wilderness appears in Jeff Shaara's *The Last Full Measure* (1998), which devotes
about ninety pages to the battle and repeats many of the familiar features and
motifs of strategocentric, wide-angle historical narratives: "Lee to the rear,"
Longstreet's flank attack, the wounding of Longstreet, Gordon's flank attack,
and Grant's anger at his officers' preoccupation with worry about Lee's next

move. But two earlier novels, both from 1997, give us fine examples of the steady improvement in Civil War fiction.

The first and better known is Charles Frazier's *Cold Mountain*. Like *Guns of the South*, *Cold Mountain* tells a good story at the same time that it also does something more, reflecting on its own attempt to represent what necessarily exceeds any one representation.

> When Inman reached the war years, though, he accounted
> for them in only the weak detail of a newspaper account—
> the names of the generals who had commanded him, the
> large movements of troops, the failure and success of vari-
> ous strategies, the frequent force of blind luck in determin-
> ing which side prevailed. What he wanted Ada to know
> was that you could tell such things on and on and yet no
> more get to the full truth of the war than you could get to
> the full truth of an old sow bear's life by following her sign
> through the woods. . . . No one could know the entirety
> any more than we can know the life of any animal, for they
> each inhabit a world that is their own and not ours.

In following out the spirit of its own wisdom, *Cold Mountain* does many things well. Leaving aside "the weak detail of a newspaper account," the kind of weak detail that too often characterizes the narration of battles or campaigns in other novels, Frazier manages to make his characters "each inhabit a world that is their own." In some ways, his narrative strategy corresponds to that of Evelyn Scott. By telling the stories, and stories within stories, of Ruby, Veasey and Laura Foster, Blount, Odell and Lucinda, the captive, Monroe and Claire Dechutes, Junior and Lila, the goatwoman, Stobrod and the burned girl, Sara, and the sow bear, Frazier creates his own version of many corks bobbing in and around and over a single gigantic wave. The difference is that Frazier subordi-nates these narrative particles to the continuous stories of Inman and Ada, whose points of view alternate chapters, as well as to the inevitable—and by the middle of the novel, predictable—convergence of Inman's desertion from a Confederate hospital with the patrollings of the villainous Teague and his henchmen in the Home Guard.

But as Inman knows, no one can know the entirety, and readers of *Cold Mountain* won't come away from it knowing much more about the face of battle than they did before they read it. Set in 1864 in North Carolina, the novel includes references to Fort Sumter, Williamsburg, Malvern Hill, Sharpsburg, Fredericksburg, Gettysburg, Cold Harbor, and Petersburg, where Inman receives the wound that has him in the hospital when the novel opens. Of these battles, Inman thinks most often about Sharpsburg, Fredericksburg, and Petersburg, but the only one that Frazier gives us in the form of the conventional battle piece is Fredericksburg, leaving us to gather from Inman's occasional thoughts of and oblique references to the other battles their devastating effects on him. Speaking for myself, I wish that he had adopted this strategy with Fredericksburg as well, since his gift for originality—so evident in the linguistic texture of a late-twentieth-century novel that manages to include muntins, tarboosh, tompion, snath, froe, harquebus, skeps, travois, flews, stook, yaupon, sisal, puncheon, and sputcheon among its nouns—doesn't extend to descriptions of battle. Having lapsed almost immediately into "withering fire," one of the top five clichés in Civil War battle writing, Frazier then sets a collision course for the memorable line that Ken Burns helped make famous to forty million people, the line that Jeff Shaara uses to close his Fredericksburg chapter in *Gods and Generals* (1996), the only wartime line of Lee's to appear in *Bartlett's Familiar Quotations:* "It is well that war is so terrible, or we should get too fond of it." True, Frazier shows Inman taking irreverent exception to Lee's line, but convention has already dulled the edge of novelty, and by the time the aurora borealis appears and a band strikes up "Lorena," the script has become too familiar.

Missing from Inman's thoughts and references are any about or to the Wilderness, where Inman's unidentified North Carolina regiment could have fought with either Ewell's or Hill's Corps. Frazier's omission of the Wilderness may not have the same kind of ominous significance as the blank in Timothy O'Sullivan's photographic record, but given Inman's strong reactions to the fighting of 1862, I can't help wondering about his responses to the fighting of May 1864. By a strange coincidence, Thomas Dyja's *Play For a Kingdom* focuses on nothing but the fighting of May 1864. In its relatively young shelf life, this novel hasn't yet attracted the same attention as *Cold Mountain,* perhaps because it had the bad luck to appear in the same year as the best-seller, perhaps because it lacks the central love story of the best-seller, perhaps because too many people think that *Killer Angels* left no room for subsequent fictionalizations of a small group of men engaged in a particular battle. Whatever the reason, Dyja's novel stares unblinkingly at the face of battle, and the results are both original and powerful.

This last statement doesn't mean that *Play for a Kingdom* has no familiar or conventional elements. In focusing on a small unit of twenty men, the survivors of Company L (a neat touch, since regiments with ten companies get only as far as "K," as "J" was never used), Fourteenth Brooklyn, during the final days of their three-year enlistment, Dyja constructs a miniature world that recalls many global microcosms in fiction and film from Melville's *Pequod* to the Fifty-fourth Massachusetts in *Glory*. This particular microcosm includes a Portuguese Catholic, a Jew from Hungary, two Irishmen, and two Germans, as well as a Whitmanian sample of occupations: butcher, druggist, housepainter, grocer, undertaker, pickpocket, prizefighter, horse trainer, accountant, cook, actor, janitor, baker. In addition, during scenes at a Union hospital after the fighting at the Bloody Angle of Spotsylvania, May 12, 1864, Dyja gives us the rising pile of amputated limbs that has become the mark of authenticity for representations of the Civil War in fiction and film, especially recently, although it shows up as early as Whitman's *Memoranda during the War*. There's also a passage about a war between black and red ants, which any reader of Thoreau's *Walden* will recognize. Finally, in the sections devoted to the five baseball matches between the Fourteenth Brooklyn and the Twelfth Alabama, matches played surreptitiously during picket duty, one can even catch an occasional whiff of Ernest Lawrence Thayer's "Casey at the Bat" (1888).

Fiction would be impossible without convention, however, and Dyja's novel also gives us much that's either startlingly new—as in the case of a Confederate spy passing information to the second lieutenant of the Fourteenth Brooklyn in spoken Latin—or an unusually good version of an already established convention. Take, for example, the battle pieces in *Play for a Kingdom*. The novel includes three major representations of combat, one in Saunders' Field during the afternoon of May 5, one at Laurel Hill the evening and night of May 8, and one at the Bloody Angle. The fighting in the Wilderness, which Dyja calls "an army of pine" and "a desert of trees," takes him over the same ground that Edward Steere and Gordon Rhea try to cover in their paragraphs about the hand-to-hand fighting around the two Union guns north of the Orange Turnpike, and *Play for a Kingdom* reconstructs the scene more memorably than either of the histories. But Dyja's most horrifying version of hand-to-hand combat comes with the fighting at Laurel Hill, which Katherine Couse could hear all too well from her house.

Butts of muskets swung like clubs and shattered skulls,
spraying brains and teeth. Men bit and clawed, they pulled
at eyes, ripped into flesh, tore beards off, and all the while
they screamed. They screamed in fear; they screamed in
horror at what they saw and what they did and what they
had become. . . .

A Reb had both hands around Lyman's throat, close
enough for Lyman to smell the fetid breath and years of
sweat. Choking, Lyman leaned forward and bit a chunk out
of the Reb's face, then spit it back at him, screaming his
name as though introducing himself to the man who'd just
tried to kill him.

Would John Keegan call this an example of the pornography of violence?
Perhaps, but what Keegan criticizes in the typical battle piece—disjunctive
movement, uniformity of behavior, simplified characterization, and simplified
motivation—Dyja has avoided by focusing exclusively on a small group, as one
man falls unconscious, another collapses from fatigue, two crawl away weeping
with shame, and several punch and stab and club in various states of frenzy and
madness. Shattering the opaque screen of memorable lines such as "'Twas claw
for claw, and the devil for us all," Dyja's picture destroys the simple and uniform with a continuous sequence of individual moments of clawing, moments
that are brutally graphic but not, in my judgment, pornographic. Did the hand-
to-hand fighting at Laurel Hill or Saunders' Field actually include such
moments? I don't know, but Dyja's images help me imagine something much
closer to what must have happened than the passages in Steere or Rhea do.
With the face of battle thrust so close, it's hard to believe that a man crazed with
adrenalin could keep from baring his teeth and sinking them into it.

More than once *Play for a Kingdom* shifts its gaze from the face of battle to
take a wider look at the war and its causes, although it always does so through
the eyes of a particular character at a particular moment. In one scene, for example, the racist Irish housepainter finds himself attached to a burial party of black
soldiers whose conversation causes him to rethink his relation to both racism
and the Fourteenth Brooklyn. In another, one of the members of the Twelfth
Alabama scores several good hits in a final conversation with one of the Brooklyn men.

"If'n you been telling the coloreds that y'all come down
here to save 'em, and then you don't wanna have nothing to
do with 'em, you're as bad as some damn slave owner."

But whatever Dyja does, whether up close or from a distance, historical accuracy and fictional invention cooperate to make what actually happened and what could have happened hard to separate.

As for Henry Fleming and the decomposing Union soldier, it's hard for me to believe that Fleming could have stumbled so unexpectedly on the corpse without some warning from his nose, a sensory organ that Dyja's more persuasive version of realism addresses continually. And I don't really think that Crane had in mind a veteran whose uniform had turned green before the action of Chancellorsville. Throughout *The Red Badge of Courage,* Crane insists so often on the anonymous uniformity of the "vast blue demonstration" of the Army of the Potomac that he clearly associates "the melancholy shade of green" with weathering since the soldier's death. But again the sequence is all wrong, since by the time the blue uniform had absorbed enough sun and rain to turn it green, the decomposing body would look more like a fleshless skeleton than the figure Henry confronts.

In other words, no matter how much I admire *The Red Badge of Courage,* no matter how much it has helped me imagine the fear of battle (a Vietnam combat veteran once told me that he felt Crane had gotten the fear exactly right), I have to conclude that the famous scene with the decomposing soldier is a mistake, one that violates historical accuracy, breaks the contract of fictional realism, and exposes the limits of Crane's attempt to transfer what he felt as a football player to the context of the American Civil War. He may have felt fear every bit as overwhelming as what some men experience in combat, but in itself that fear couldn't have taught him about the realities of physiological decomposition in the Wilderness. And yet, I wouldn't change a single detail in the scene or wish for a moment that Crane had omitted it, not because I need it to symbolize "the great death," as Henry thinks of it on the last page, or to typify the antiromantic tendencies of Crane's realism or naturalism. I need the passage, with its clumsy handling of time and detail, because its flaws confess something in the Wilderness no story can master.

THIRTEEN

Poems

PEOPLE WHO COMPLAIN that we have yet to produce a *War and Peace* of the Civil War will have an even easier time putting down Civil War poetry. Despite Whitman's claim in *Memoranda during the War* that the war furnished material "far more grand, in my opinion, to the hands capable of it, than Homer's siege of Troy, or the French wars to Shakspere," Civil War poetry has nothing to rival the *Iliad* or *Henry the Fifth*. In *Patriotic Gore*, Edmund Wilson puts the matter bluntly, dismissing thousands of lines of wartime verse as "barren reading" and claiming that the "period of the Civil War was not at all a favorable one for poetry." I happen to think this judgment spectacularly wrong, since the period of the Civil War gave us the greatest poems of Emily Dickinson and they are more than enough to redeem any period. But Wilson doesn't share my opinion of Dickinson, whom he thinks "a little overrated." Fair enough, but respect for his opinion would come more easily, at least to me, if Wilson didn't then confess the unreliability of his reading with the statement that Dickinson "never, so far as I know, refers to the war in her poetry."

> When I was small, a Woman died—
> Today—her Only Boy
> Went up from the Potomac—
> His face all Victory

Numbered 596 by editor Thomas H. Johnson in *The Poems of Emily Dickinson* (1955) and dated by him to around 1862, this poem refers to the death of

Francis H. Dickinson of Amherst, Massachusetts, who was killed at Ball's Bluff, Virginia, on October 21, 1861. To appreciate the achievement of Dickinson's small elegy, we have only to compare it with a contemporary piece by Caroline Augusta Ball, whose elegy "The Jacket of Grey" gave its title to a volume published in 1866.

> Fold it up carefully, lay it aside;
> Tenderly touch it, look on it with pride;
> For dear must it be to our hearts evermore,
> The jacket of grey our loved soldier boy wore.

To the ears of the 1860s, Ball's end-stopped rhyming couplets, which waltz along in the same one-two-three meter as "The Star-Spangled Banner," would have sounded much more like what poetry should be than Dickinson's imperfectly rhymed version of ballad or hymn meter. And to the sensibilities of most poetry readers in the 1860s, Ball's archaic diction, which, for example, refers to combat as "the fray" (conveniently rhyming with "grey"), would have sounded appropriately elevated rather than hackneyed and stale. But beyond historical differences in taste between then and now lie more important differences that involve the representation of death in combat and the presence or absence of partisanship.

In Ball's vision, combat is a matter of unsheathed swords and lighted brands but no actual image of killing with lead or iron projectiles. Instead, she gives us a theatrical tableau of the aftermath of battle: "But our treasured one on the red battle field lay, / While the life-blood oozed out on the jacket of grey." By contrast, Dickinson's vision is unsentimental and matter-of-fact in its compressed blending of geometry with the modern technology of bullets.

> How slowly
> The Seasons must have turned
> Till Bullets clipt an Angle
> And He passed quickly round—

Ball elegizes with effusive lamentation ("Ah! vain, all, all vain were our prayers and our tears"), Dickinson with terse understatement that reflects the increasingly impersonal and mechanical nature of combat. Not all readers will necessarily prefer Dickinson's method to Ball's, but they should agree that whereas

Ball's elegy is limited by partisanship ("Can we ever forget when he joined the brave band, / Who rose in defence of our dear Southern land"), Dickinson's moves beyond the death of one man from a small town in a small battle toward a generalized contemplation of perpetual death everywhere.

> I'm confident that Bravoes—
> Perpetual break, abroad
> For Braveries, remote as this
> In Scarlet Maryland—

Those who believe with Wilson that Dickinson is overrated might also find her geography a little fuzzy in the final line, since Ball's Bluff lies on the Virginia side of the Potomac, but my guess is that she wrote this poem about a year after Francis Dickinson's death, when the fighting at Sharpsburg-Antietam had turned Maryland "scarlet" (a definite improvement over "Yonder Maryland" in another version of the poem), and no Northerner who read the newspapers as avidly as Dickinson could have missed the exhibit of Alexander Gardner's photographs from the battlefield there. If I'm right, Dickinson uses the death of someone known to her to approach the vast enormity of so many thousands unknown to her.

With the exception of Dickinson, however, I have to agree with Wilson that the period of the Civil War was not a golden age for American poetry. Whitman published *Drum-Taps* in 1865 and Melville followed with *Battle-Pieces* in 1866, but for all their memorable moments neither of these books is an unqualified success. Aside from the work of these poets, the only two war poems from the 1860s, other than the lyrics of the minstrel song "Dixie," that general readers in the United States might still be able to recognize today are Julia Ward Howe's "The Battle Hymn of the Republic," composed, according to a plaque on the building, on November 21, 1861, at Willard's Hotel in Washington, and John Greenleaf Whittier's "Barbara Frietchie," originally collected in the volume *In War Time* (1864). Excepting these popular favorites, what there is plenty of is bad poetry.

In the case of the Wilderness, for example, a modern reader familiar with "The Battle Hymn of the Republic" has to struggle hard to read, or hear, James D. Gay's "The Battle of the Wilderness," which I happened across one day in the University of Virginia Special Collections (the poem is dated between 1864 and 1869). Gay, who resided at 300 North 20th Street, above Vine Street,

Philadelphia, advertised himself as "the celebrated Army song publisher and dealer," who sold his songs "beautifully illustrated with Battle scenes" in "large or small quantities" at his residence. The words for "The Battle of the Wilderness," unaccompanied by any music, appear on a single sheet that measures just under 5½ by 9½ inches. At the top of the page appears one of Gay's battle scenes, which shows Federal soldiers, led by a sword-wielding officer on horseback, advancing in perfect order across an open space toward a distant line of Confederates, identified by the Stars and Bars rather than the more familiar battle flag. Between the opposing lines lie two apparently dead bodies and one wounded man. Behind the Confederates stands a single row of leafless trees through which one can see a range of high hills or low mountains resembling nothing visible from anywhere in the actual Wilderness. At the bottom of the page one sees that "J. D. Gay also publishes the different Army Hospitals Views which are beautifully colored" and which "will be sent by Mail." The song itself consists of ten four-line stanzas, not necessarily the worst of which is the sixth.

> They met them in the Wilderness, just at the break of day sirs,
> And fought them on the right and left, till Lee he ran away sirs,
> And left some thousands on the field, he could not get away sirs;
> But our Union boys they dressed their wounds, their dead they put
> away sirs.
> CHORUS—And that's just so—Ri, fal, de ral de laddy and that's just so.

But perhaps it's not fair to pick on song lyrics unaccompanied by music, especially the song lyrics of someone self-employed and self-promoting. Perhaps we should look instead to a poem in the "journal of civilization," *Harper's Weekly*. In the issue of May 28, 1864, appears the unsigned poem "The Battle of the Wilderness," which opens with the biblical epigraph mentioned in the last chapter. Unfortunately, however, the shift from unaccompanied song to self-contained poem doesn't significantly improve the quality. "The Battle of the Wilderness," which celebrates with no doubts or second thoughts a Union victory on May 5 and 6, begins and ends with the same stanza.

> Victory! shout for victory
>   On the battle-field again;
> For the bloom of the Wilderness
>   Glory to God! Amen!

Between the initial and final appearances of this stanza fall five others, each of which begins with the same line that opens the poem. Of the remaining fifteen lines, none manages to get beyond either convention or a partisanship that spills over into overt propaganda. The second stanza offers to those who mourn one of Grant's 17,666 casualties the consolation that "Only by Death's dark roses / The lilies of peace shall grow"; the third urges, "Let a nation's heart rejoice"; the fourth finally descends from abstraction to mention the actual men who bade victory grow "From the bloom of the Wilderness / To the fruitage of the Po"; the fifth identifies Freedom as what can blossom from the bloody "flowers / That have so purpled the Wilderness"; and the sixth caps the celebration with an unequivocating image of the victory "That flashes a morning light / From the bloom of Wilderness / Far into the years of right."

But again perhaps it's not fair to pick on an unsigned poem that appeared in a journal catering to a general readership. What about a poem from a real poet? Born in Richmond in 1823, John Reuben Thompson purchased the *Southern Literary Messenger* and became its editor in 1847. Before the launching of both *Harper's Magazine* and the *Atlantic Monthly,* the *Southern Literary Messenger,* which Edgar Allan Poe edited from December 1835 until January 1837, emerged as a leading literary journal. In addition to editing the *Messenger* longer than anyone else (1847–1860), Thompson also flourished as a poet, and his poems were collected, edited, and published by John S. Patton in 1920. Published in the New Orleans journal the *Crescent Monthly* in May 1865, when Thompson was living in London and editing the Confederate newspaper the *Index,* one of his poems focuses on the most famous moment, at least from a Confederate perspective, in the Battle of the Wilderness.

> Dawn of a pleasant morning in May
> Broke through the wilderness cool and grey,
> While, perched in the tallest tree-tops, the birds
> Were carolling Mendelssohn's "Songs Without Words."

Although some might wince at the unlikely closing line of this opening stanza, Thompson's eighty-line poem "Lee to the Rear" still had admirers in the early twentieth century. According to Allan Nevins's *The Evening Post* (1922), almost seventy years after its publication nearly every Southern schoolboy still knew the poem.

Thompson's grasp of actual conditions in the Wilderness is pretty weak. He locates the famous incident "Down on the left of the rebel lines" when in fact Lee was on the right at the Widow Tapp's farm, and his quaint evocation of "the tide of battle" rolling "Over the Wilderness, wood and wold" obscures the reality that there was precious little wold, or unforested land, on the battlefield, especially along the Orange Plank Road near the Brock Road. Thompson also erases Longstreet from his representation altogether, so that his version of the incident has none of the actual drama of Lee learning the identity of the Texas brigade and realizing that the anxiously awaited First Corps had finally arrived just in time to prevent the total collapse of the Confederate right. Finally, Thompson's image of "Calm and resolute Robert Lee" bears no resemblance to the man whom many later described as having temporarily lost his sense of balance and perspective.

Despite these historical quibbles, however, and despite too many lines that recall Caroline Augusta Ball, both in their conventional language and their metrical predictability, "Lee to the Rear" marks an advance over the achievement of John Gay or the anonymous poet in *Harper's Weekly*. Although he stages the incident from a Confederate perspective, at least Thompson discards the egregious partisanship of Ball's "dear Southern land," and he avoids altogether the distasteful self-righteousness of the *Harper's Weekly* poet, a remarkable feat of restraint for someone also editing a newspaper devoted to Confederate propaganda. Furthermore, at least twice in his twenty stanzas Thompson manages to break through the crust of clichés like "banners rent," "columns riven," and "foemen slain." The couplet describing the roar of Federal artillery ("For still with their loud, deep, bull-dog bay, / The Yankee batteries blazed away") freshly transforms the mechanical into the animal, anticipating Crane's extensive use of the same technique in *Red Badge of Courage*—never mind that Federal artillery saw limited action in the Wilderness—and the quatrain in which Lee's soldiers tell him to go to the rear attempts a tonal pungency that Patton makes even more noticeable with genteel censorship in the 1920 *Poems*.

"We'll go forward, but you must go back"—
And they moved not an inch in the perilous track:
"Go to the rear, and we'll send them to h---!"
And the sound of the battle was lost in their yell.

Whatever its other failings, Thompson's "Lee to the Rear" helps fulfill the prophecy of its own final stanza, "But the fame of the Wilderness fight abides," in part by mythologizing history but also in part by focusing on a specific moment and personalizing it in a way that differs completely from the faceless anonymity of Gay's song or the *Harper's Weekly* poem. Some might argue that to value a nineteenth-century poem for the kind of personalized specificity and focus that characterizes so much twentieth-century poetry is to judge that poem by historically inappropriate standards. But the twentieth century is not unique in valuing personalized specificity and focus. With the development and spread of photography during the war, poets who wanted to write about the fighting found themselves confronted by two different modes of representation, one involving the familiar rhetorical formulas of conventional battle poetry, the other involving the minimal framing and description of arresting visual images.

That the photographic mode of representation held powerful attractions for at least one poet confronting the war is clear from the achievement of Whitman's shorter poems in *Drum-Taps*. Such superbly realized pieces as "Cavalry Crossing a Ford," "Bivouac on a Mountain Side," "An Army Corps on the March," and "By the Bivouac's Fitful Flame" compensate for many of the poems, especially early in the volume, that succumb to the rhetorical excesses of Harper's-Weeklyism. (Significantly, the awful poem "Beat! Beat! Drums!" first appeared in *Harper's Weekly*.) As the ordering of poems in *Drum-Taps* makes clear, Whitman himself perceived all too clearly the discrepancy between his loud belligerence and his quieter watching. In the often anthologized poem "The Wound-Dresser," he admits parenthetically that "Arous'd and angry, I'd thought to beat the alarum, and urge relentless war, / But soon my fingers fail'd me, my face droop'd and I resign'd myself, / To sit by the wounded and soothe them, or silently watch the dead." But even in "The Wound-Dresser," despite this apparent insight into his own motives and transformation, Whitman awkwardly pairs conventional battle rhetoric ("Soldier alert I arrive after a long march cover'd with sweat and dust, / In the nick of time I come, plunge in the fight, loudly shout in the rush of successful charge") with some of the greatest and most terrible lines to come out of the war.

From the stump of the arm, the amputated hand,
I undo the clotted lint, remove the slough, wash off the matter and
    blood,
Back on his pillow the soldier bends with curv'd neck and side-falling

> head,
> His eyes are closed, his face is pale, he dares not look on the bloody
>   stump,
> And has not yet look'd on it.
> . . . .
> I dress the perforated shoulder, the foot with the bullet-wound,
> Cleanse the one with a gnawing and putrid gangrene, so sickening, so
>   offensive,
> While the attendant stands behind aside me holding the tray and the
>   pail.

It's hard to believe that only a slight shift in the stressing of "amputated," placing emphasis on the second syllable rather than on the first and third, would render the first line a metrical match for any in "The Jacket of Grey," and Whitman's artistry shows in many other touches as well, such as in the auditory fusion of prominent sounds from "perforated" and "wound" into "putrid." But the proof of these lines lies in their power to stun with a visual clarity wholly distinct from familiar rhetorical conventions about life-blood oozing, a clarity that momentarily blinds us to their artistry.

Although flawed, *Drum-Taps* differs vastly from the poetry of Caroline Augusta Ball, as does Melville's *Battle-Pieces,* published a year later. When it comes to managing the competing tendencies toward, on the one hand, familiar rhetorical formulas and, on the other, specifically focused clarity, Melville had many of the same problems as Whitman. But because Melville was not as good a poet as Whitman, his successes are fewer and more qualified. "The Portent," which closes with the image of John Brown as "The meteor of the war," and "Shiloh" are both short enough to avoid major catastrophes and to justify their inclusion in anthologies. But unlike Whitman, Melville constructed his book by writing poems to follow the chronology of the war. As a result, many of his poems, especially the longer ones, feel as though they were written merely in obedience to that chronology rather than in obedience to deep observation and feeling. A good example of Melville at both his best and worst is the two-part poem, "The Armies of the Wilderness."

> Like snows the camps on Southern hills
>   Lay all the winter long,
> Our levies there in patience stood—

They stood in patience strong.
On fronting slopes gleamed other camps
    Where faith as firmly clung:
Ah, froward kin! so brave amiss—
    The zealots of the Wrong.

As Dickinson makes abundantly clear to any skeptic, American poetry in any century can put the common meter of hymnody to good use, but although one can sing these opening lines to the tune of "O God, Our Help in Ages Past," Melville stumbles badly in this first stanza. If the only problem were his ignorance of the terrain and troop dispositions on both sides of the Rapidan (Lee's tent stood on the southern slope of Jerdone Mountain, north of the Plank Road and just west of where the Orange County Airport lies today, but the Union army wintered on relatively flat ground), the lapse wouldn't exceed any of those in Thompson's "Lee to the Rear." But the much bigger problem that haunts not only "The Armies of the Wilderness" but all of *Battle-Pieces* is the bad fit between Melville's Union partisanship and his antiwar sentiments. The former gives us numerous clanky occurrences of the capitalized abstractions Right and Wrong, while the latter generates some of the more convincing lines in the volume, such as "All wars are boyish, and are fought by boys" ("The March into Virginia") and "What like a bullet can undeceive!" ("Shiloh").

The first part of "Armies of the Wilderness" has little to recommend it, other than an image of Federal soldiers, through "the pointed glass," watching Confederates play baseball ("They could have joined them in their sport / But for the vale's deep rent") and one of the few images in Civil War poetry of the massive deforestation caused by encamped armies: "And stumps of forests for dreary leagues / Like a massacre show." But in the second part, when May arrives and Melville introduces Grant, the poem moves toward some of the best lines in *Battle-Pieces,* lines that Ken Burns admired enough to have George Plimpton read them during Burns's eight-minute recounting of the battle in his documentary.

In glades they meet skull after skull
    Where pine-cones lay—the rusted gun,
Green shoes full of bones, the mouldering coat
    And cuddled-up skeleton;
And scores of such. Some start as in dreams,

And comrades lost bemoan:
By the edge of those wilds Stonewall had charged—
But the Year and the Man were gone.

Sung to the tune of "O God, Our Help," only two of these lines, the first and the sixth, would fit the pattern, and with the welcome shift into metrical variation, Melville momentarily discards his Unionist boosterism, although unfortunately it returns soon after Longstreet arrives on the scene ("But Heaven lent strength, the Right strove well, / And emerged from the Wilderness"). As in the case of the excerpt from Whitman's "Wound-Dresser," what makes these lines so great, especially the first four, is the photographic focus on specific visual details that the men of Hancock's Second Corps would have seen during their passage through the Chancellorsville battlefield toward the Brock Road. Furthermore, like Whitman, Melville delivers their visual force in conjunction with dense auditory patterning, as, for example, he binds the first four lines together by redistributing the prominent sounds of "skull" among the words "cuddled-up skeleton."

Two memorable passages from Whitman and Melville may not be sufficient to dissuade anyone from accepting Wilson's judgment that the Civil War was a bad time for poetry. But anyone who does accept that judgment needs to understand that American poets during and after the war didn't just fail to produce memorable war poetry. Most of them failed to produce memorable poetry, period. I understand that some will want to make a case for Stephen Crane or Edward Arlington Robinson or Trumbull Stickney or Adelaide Crapsey, but the fact is that between the time Whitman and Dickinson reach the heights of their powers and the time Robert Frost, Wallace Stevens, William Carlos Williams, Ezra Pound, T. S. Eliot, and Marianne Moore reach the heights of theirs, it's pretty slim pickings. In frankly acknowledging this lapse in American poetry, however, we need to guard against easy conclusions about either cause and effect in literary history or cause and effect in the relation of war to poetry. It gets us nowhere to say that the Civil War produced realism and that realism, particularly the realism of war, simply doesn't foster lyric poetry.

Despite the boundary-drawing in most recent anthologies of American literature, and despite the narratives endorsed by many teachers and scholars, the Civil War did not produce realism. I acknowledge that losing 2 percent of the population to disease and combat, as urban industrialism ground up rural agrarianism, led many among the maimed, the bereaved, and the dispossessed to discard certain kinds of romantic tendencies in favor of certain kinds of realistic ones. But it's too easy and too naive to conclude that because the war was ugly and brutal, writers and readers suddenly awoke from the dreams of romance into the harsher light of realism. For one thing, all wars are ugly and brutal, but not all wars have been followed by greater realism in literature. If they had been, then we would expect to see realism flourishing after the Revolution, the War of 1812, and the Mexican War. In the twentieth century, we associate World War I with the birth of modernism and Vietnam with the dislocations of postmodernism, neither of which is quite the same thing as realism.

And what about the influences on literary realism that have nothing to do with the Civil War? What about the invention of photography in 1837 and the development of the wet-plate negative in 1845? In numerous discussions of the new technology, we read that, unlike painting, photography captures reality itself. What about the discovery of gold in California in 1848, the massive westward migrations, and the development of a new kind of realistic observation in frontier literature? What about the influence of the French novelists—Balzac, who died the year of the Compromise of 1850; Flaubert, whose *Madame Bovary* appeared the year before the Dred Scott decision; and Zola, whose experiments in naturalism reflect nineteenth-century developments in science? Rather than claim that the Civil War engendered literary realism, it makes much more sense to say that some of the conditions that combined to produce war in North America during the nineteenth century also combined to produce realism there.

As for the claim that something inherent in lyric poetry makes it incompatible with realism and, specifically, with the representation of war, I can't agree. If anything, a genre that intensifies brief bits of individual experience stands an excellent chance of producing memorable representations of events that far exceed the power of any one observer to comprehend the whole. Of course, the sweep of long novels and histories and memoirs can accomplish many things that a few lines of verse cannot. But as the undiminished power of Civil War photographs shows us, small, specific glimpses can also speak volumes. So then why aren't there more great Civil War poems?

One reason is that the first generation of major modern American poets didn't focus on the Civil War, perhaps because the two world wars eclipsed it in their awareness, perhaps because they were busy looking abroad much of the time. Also, among Frost, Stevens, Williams, Pound, Moore, and Eliot, there isn't a single Southerner, and although one doesn't have to be a Southerner to write about the war, I wonder what Williams's insistence on discovering the universal in the local might have meant if he had come from Virginia rather than New Jersey, or how our sense of Civil War poetry might differ if Faulkner's muse had caused him to keep developing his verse rather than devoting his energies to prose. Frost touched on the war in "The Black Cottage," a dramatic monologue included in *North of Boston* (1914), and in his polemical statements Pound often pointed to the Civil War as the beginning of American economic corruption and decadence. But otherwise the poets who now dominate anthologies of modern poetry mostly ignored the war.

This blank doesn't mean, however, that no poets born late in the nineteenth century ever turned their attention to the war. In Richard Marius's edition of *The Columbia Book of Civil War Poetry* (1994), William Vaughn Moody, Edgar Lee Masters, Edward Arlington Robinson, Paul Laurence Dunbar, Carl Sandburg, Vachel Lindsay, John Gould Fletcher, Donald Davidson—Marius twice lists Davidson as having been born in 1922, but he was actually born in 1893—and Stephen Vincent Benét all have poems, and poems not wholly without merit. The title poem of Davidson's volume *Lee in the Mountains* (1938), for example, shows Lee thinking to himself, "I heard the tangled / Cry of the Wilderness wounded, bloody with doom," more compelling lines than anything in Gay, Thompson, or *Harper's Weekly*. But few of these poems have managed to establish themselves in general anthologies.

Of these particular poets, the one who deserves a closer look here is Stephen Vincent Benét, whose epic poem *John Brown's Body* (1928) won the Pulitzer Prize in 1929. In his anthology, Marius represents the poem with two excerpts, "The Congressmen Came Out to See Bull Run" and "John Brown's Prayer," neither of which is especially likely to entice a contemporary reader into plowing through the entire poem. In his headnote to "The Congressmen Came Out to See Bull Run," Marius comments that Benét's "reputation has not endured." Twenty years before Marius's postmortem, Daniel Aaron described the poem in *The Unwritten War* (1973) as "still widely (and I think mistakenly) regarded as the great Civil War epic." The juxtaposition of these comments is a little confusing, since their chronology suggests that Benét's star, still shining brightly as late as Richard Nixon's presidency, suddenly fell during the subsequent twenty years. In fact, however, Aaron's statement, which appears in a footnote, remains ambiguous. It doesn't say that *John Brown's Body* was still widely read in 1973—it wasn't—and it doesn't say whether Aaron thinks that someone else's mistake lies in thinking Benét's epic great or in thinking it the best of all the other Civil War epics that come to his mind. If he means the latter, it's hard to see why, since in 1973 it would have been difficult to name another serious contender.

Whatever others think of Benét's reputation, the United States Postal Service thought enough of him to honor the centennial of his birth with a 1998 commemorative stamp. It's not clear that anyone in the Postal Service actually read the poem, since the background for Benét's young, bespectacled face is a few of the black soldiers from Saint-Gaudens's monument to Robert Gould Shaw and the Fifty-fourth Massachusetts. It's true that the cast of characters in *John Brown's Body* includes the unfortunately named Spade, a slave who runs away and ends up fighting at the Battle of the Crater in Petersburg. It's also true that despite the attention he pays to Southerners in his narrative, the title of Benét's poem, along with a prelude called "The Slaver," makes it clear where his sympathies lie. But the message that the designers of the commemorative stamp seem to want to send has more to do with an idealized image of John Brown's legacy than with the poem that Benét actually wrote.

The poem Benét actually wrote contains much of value. Especially when one considers that it appeared not long after the first flush of modernist free verse, the broad spectrum of traditional poetic forms employed by Benét is impressive, from the opening sonnets of the "Invocation" to the common meter of "John Brown's Prayer" to the blank verse used throughout the poem. Inevitably, the technique of varying verse forms causes the epic to fragment into smaller poems, some of which do little more than advance the narrative, some of which dilate a particular moment, as in the case of the short lyric that accompanies Jack Ellyat's return to consciousness after he has been taken prisoner by the Confederates at Shiloh, escaped, and been given food and shelter by Melora Vilas.

> Cold comes back and pain comes back
> And the lizard, too,
> And the burden in the sack
> May be meant for you.
> Do not play the risen dunce
> With unrisen men.
> Lazarus was risen once
> But earth gaped again.

Lyrics like the one from which this excerpt comes make a strong bid for memorability, and other remarkable moments and touches abound in *John Brown's Body*. In a prose section of Book Two, for instance, Benét introduces Whitman in a passage based on a section from the notes to *Memoranda during the War,* later incorporated into *Specimen Days* (1882), about the return to Washington of exhausted Federal troops after the defeat at First Manassas–Bull Run; in Book Three, as Jack Ellyat thinks about escaping from the column of Federal prisoners, he confronts the ironic discrepancy between the reality of his situation and visual representations of the war in *Harper's Weekly:* "You had to escape like a drawing in *Harper's Weekly* / With stiff little men on horses like sickle-pears / Firing round frozen cream-puffs into your back"; and in Book Six Benét offers, in the midst of images of people for whom the war is not a daily reality, a wonderful portrait of Dickinson.

> A moth of a woman,
> Shut in a garden, lives on scraps of Eternity
> With a dog, a procession of sunsets and certain poems
> She scribbles on bits of paper. Such poems may be
> Ice-crystals, rubies cracked with refracted light,
> Or all vast death like a wide field in ten short lines.
> She writes to the tough, swart-minded Higginson
> Minding his negro troops in a lost bayou,
> "War feels to me like an oblique place."

As for the Battle of the Wilderness in *John Brown's Body*, Benét's narrative pinches it in much the same way that Ken Burns's documentary film does. Book Eight contains an abridged version of "Lee to the rear," but otherwise, in a poem that gives so many pages to First Manassas–Bull Run, the Wilderness is only a name in a list of names.

> Follow the agony if you must and can
> By the brushwood names, by the bloody prints in the woods,
> Cold Harbor and Spottsylvania [*sic*] and Yellow Tavern
> And all the lost court-houses and country stores
> In the Wilderness, where the bitter fighting passed,
> (No fighting bitterer)—

The criticism that Benét's ambitious poem is better in some places than in others should hardly disqualify it from the generous consideration of readers who have learned to live with the drastic ups and downs of Pound's *Cantos* (first collected, including Canto 120, in 1972), Hart Crane's *The Bridge* (1930), or Williams's *Paterson* (first collected in 1963). But even if the modernist competitors of *John Brown's Body* have crowded it out of most anthologies, one can see in those anthologies that with the next generation of American poets an important shift takes place in Civil War poetry. Instead of the major poets ignoring the war while only the minor ones write about it, the major poets begin to pay more attention. Beginning with Allen Tate, born the year after Benét was, many important American poets wrote poems about the war, including (in order of birth) Langston Hughes, Robert Penn Warren (whose 1953 volume *Brother to Dragons* includes five powerful lines on the fires he also describes in *Wilderness*), Charles Olson, Elizabeth Bishop, Randall Jarrell, John Berryman, and Robert Lowell. Of their poems, the two most familiar to anthology readers are Tate's dense, symbol-heavy "Ode to the Confederate Dead" (1928), and Lowell's sparer, more accessible response, "For the Union Dead" (1959), which meditates on Saint-Gaudens's monument to Colonel Shaw and the Massachusetts Fifty-fourth against the immediate backdrop of construction on Boston Common, as well as against the larger backdrop of desegregation.

> Their monument sticks like a fishbone
> in the city's throat.
> Its Colonel is as lean
> as a compass-needle.

The second generation of modern poets found in the war many opportunities for good poetry, and subsequent generations have followed with notable poems of their own, so that we now have numerous poetic representations of the war that successfully avoid sentimentality or partisanship or cliché. In the midst of this promising plenitude, the most important development in recent Civil War poetry, and the one that would be my nomination over *John Brown's Body* for the best Civil War epic, assuming that a book-length narrative sequence of shorter poems qualifies as an epic, is Andrew Hudgins's *After the Lost War* (1988).

As Hudgins explains in a preface and headnote, this volume consists of a sequence of forty-four poems "based on the life of the Georgia-born poet and musician Sidney Lanier," who joined the Macon Volunteers, was sent to Virginia, fought in the Battle of Chancellorsville and various smaller engagements, was transferred to the Signals Corps and then, in 1864, to the blockade-runner *Lucy,* was captured and sent to Fort Lookout, Maryland, where he spent three months, and returned to Macon in broken health after the war. As Hudgins freely acknowledges, many of the biographical details in the sequence derive from two biographies he found especially useful, Edwin Mims's *Sidney Lanier* (1905) and Aubrey Harrison Starke's *Sidney Lanier* (1933). Although he protects himself in the preface with the disclaimer that "the voice of these poems will be unfamiliar to anyone who knows the writings of this historical figure," in fact Hudgins's version of Lanier deserves credit for often preserving many of the original tones. In his chapter "A Confederate Soldier," for example, Mims quotes from a letter of June 11, 1866, Lanier's fond recollection of life at Fort Boykin on Burwell's Bay with his brother Clifford: "Cliff and I never cease to talk of the beautiful women, the serenades, the moonlight dashes on the beach of fair Burwell's Bay, and the spirited brushes of our little force with the enemy." Hudgins's version of this letter, which opens the sixth section of "Serenades in Virginia: Summer 1863," sharpens the language into regular iambic meter while it still traces the contours of Lanier's voice.

> When Cliff and I discuss the war,
> we talk of lovely women, serenades,
> the moonlit dashes on the beach,
> the brushes of our force with theirs,
> with whom we clashed with more élan
> and consequence.

Of the many fine poems in *After the Lost War,* several stand out for their ability to push a contemporary reader beyond naive idealization of the war toward keener awareness of the physical and psychological conditions behind the combat in Virginia, particularly "At Chancellorsville: The Battle of the Wilderness," "After the Wilderness: May 3, 1863," "Burial Detail," and "Reflections on Cold Harbor." Although the title of the first poem is puzzling—apparently Hudgins has confused the battles of 1863 and 1864—the poem itself transforms an instance of battlefield scavenging, as recounted by George Herbert Clarke in *Some Reminiscences and Early Letters of Sidney Lanier* (1907) and quoted in Starke's biography, into a scene of initiation for the young soldier. His uniform "shabby with / continuous wear, worn down to threads," Lanier comes upon a dead Indiana corporal, shot in the thigh, whose shirt consists of "good / stout wool, unmarked by blood." His brother Cliff advises him to take the shirt, but Lanier cannot bring himself to do so.

> Imagining
> the slack flesh shifting underneath
> my hands, the other-person stink
> of that man's shirt, so newly his,
> I cursed Clifford from his eyeballs to
> his feet. I'd never talked that way before
> and didn't know I could.

Just as it initiates him into angry swearing, Chancellorsville initiates Lanier into something larger that cannot afford the luxury of squeamishness. Although another Confederate has taken the dead man's shirt when the brothers return to the corpse, the poem snaps closed with two cool lines that serve as shorthand notation for the profound changes that war effects in a man's sensibility.

> By autumn, we wore so much blue
> we could have passed for New York infantry.

Hudgins excels at this kind of closure in which all the superfluous flesh of talking—all the embarrassing flourishes of Caroline Augusta Ball or John D. Gay or the *Harper's Weekly* poet or even Melville and Whitman at their respective worst—has long been worked off, leaving ample room for what Wallace Stevens, in a prose statement on the poetry of war published in *The Palm at the End of the Mind* (1971), calls "a consciousness of fact" to do its imaginative work. Writing in 1942 in the shadow of the Second World War, Stevens realized that "consciousness of an immense war is a consciousness of fact" and that in "the presence of the violent reality of war, consciousness takes the place of imagination." Stevens himself felt threatened by the encroachment of consciousness upon imagination and continually exhorted poets to resist the overwhelming reality of facts. And certainly when the brutal weight of brutal facts threatens to deaden the imagination altogether, such resistance is a matter of survival. But in *After the Lost War*, Hudgins shows us again and again that in the context of an immense war, the simple consciousness of simple fact can also startle the imagination into places it could never reach on its own.

The close of "After the Wilderness" furnishes my last example. After Chancellorsville, Lanier looks frantically for his brother Clifford "among the fields of dead / before we lost him to a common grave." When he finally finds him, Clifford is bent above a dying squirrel ("A battlefield is full of trash like that— / dead birds and squirrels, bits of uniform"), and in his obsessive attention to burying all the dead squirrels he finds in "a dozen, tiny, separate graves," he shows all too clearly that his collision with immense war has momentarily burned his mind. When the two young men finish the last of the tiny graves, Clifford breaks, as Grant supposedly did after the Wilderness, and "sobbed as though they'd been his unborn sons." And then Hudgins, in iambic pentameter lines that refuse to flinch under the nearly unbearable weight of what they lead us to imagine, gives mere fact the last and overwhelming word.

I wiped his tears and stroked his matted hair,
and as I hugged him to my chest I saw
he'd wet his pants. We called it Yankee tea.

As the large achievement of *After the Lost War* shows, American poets may yet fulfill the spirit, if not quite the letter, of Whitman's hyperbolic prophecy, finding in the Civil War "indeed the Verteber of Poetry and Art, (of personal character too,) for all future America." As the twenty-first century opens, they may discover, or rediscover, what Whitman called "the inexhaustible mine" of "native passion, first-class pictures, tempests of life and death." And if they do, and if they can make room in themselves for a consciousness of the facts of an immense war, the Wilderness may bloom and keep blooming.

Skirmish at Rio Hill

How lovely Custer must have looked
that extra day in February
cantering into Albemarle County
the third uncivil winter. Leap year
and in all of Virginia the only bright spot
brighter than blond curls against blue wool
must have been the first crocus
spiking yellow out of the rusty mud.
Not much happened. The pretty general
burned a few bridges, plundered the cabins
of hibernating Horse Artillery
for harnesses, axle-grease, skillets,
and got himself commended by Meade,
neglecting to mention in official reports
the exploding caisson that scared him off.
The shaken ladies of Charlottesville
bought a silk flag and bestowed it
on their defenders, but on the hill
not a single place came out of that day
with capital letters. Charlottesville has no
Wheatfield, Cornfield, Peach Orchard,
no Bloody Lane or Bloody Pond or Bloody Angle.
But Charlottesville has the Rio Hills
Shopping Center. Peace is hell
on those who never get it, so why make
matters worse by pacing the asphalt
and howling to cars apportioned by acre
You cannot serve both memory and Mammon?
Forget the lament and settle for reading
historical markers, I warn myself,
but by the time I finish this one
my two bored sons are slugging it out
on the shabby back seat, each snarling
He started it and both so crazed

I'll never determine the causes
they can't remember or know for sure
why I hated this place until I saw
a bloody nose in my rearview mirror
and turned to minister amidst the booming.

"War, Effect of a Shell on a Confederate Soldier"

Bodies make good business, Gardner knew
after his Antietam show took the North
and sealed the break with Brady.
But the long hiatus of losses that followed
meant those with the cameras and chemicals
couldn't get at the damn battlefields.
He sat in the capital and stewed into summer
till Pennsylvania started brewing and a chance
to scoop his old boss, that bastard,
sent him moving the wagons through Maryland
so fast he bumped into Stuart at Emmitsburg.
Detained, questioned, released, he slogged
the last muddy miles, lucky to reach
Rose's farm before the burial detail.

Thirty-four Georgians from Semmes's brigade
laid out by their buddies for burial
but abandoned. After three days
of decomposing Gardner, Gibson, O'Sullivan
found them fattened by gasses but otherwise
neatly arranged in rows around the field
on their backs, their features intact
except for those odd O's the mouths shape
when jaws go slack and lips stretched tight
by bloating cheeks make faces of men
who've stuffed themselves at a picnic
and before nodding off for naps in the sun
amuse themselves with minstrel routines.
At least they have each other, all together

except for one who would have spoiled the fun,
his belly blown away, the camera angle
asking us into his thorax. O'Sullivan shot
the eight-by-ten, Gardner the stereo

the War Photograph and Exhibition Company
of Hartford, Connecticut, would market
to collectors with a blurb beginning
"This poor fellow" and closing with
"A Word as to Prices." But first they placed
a shell on the ground above the right knee
and laid a rifle across both legs, the same gun
they propped by the Devil's Den Sharpshooter,
those bastards. In the right foreground
a severed left hand gropes toward the trigger.

Whenever I Smoke a Cigar

Whenever I smoke a cigar I think
of Grant in the Wilderness writing
orders out in fatless prose without revision,
then chewing on a burn-out stub and weeping
as numbers flooded in and names piled up
on lists the Northern papers printed
along with the outcry *Butcher, Butcher,*
but by the time he hooded himself
in a shawl on the porch to finish a book
that provided the wife he couldn't stand
to part from with nearly half a million,
before the sore throat he'd nursed for four months,
the thirty pounds gone, and the vomited blood
finished him, everybody up there loved Grant,
and yet whenever I smoke a cigar I wonder
what it takes to be happy in marriage
and march through the woods making widows.

Except I Shall See

Black-maned, black-tailed, a gray horse stands
tied to a locust tree outside St. Thomas.
Inside, in the usual pew, his white-haired master
bows his head as the organ plays Brahms,
"My Heart Abounds with Joy," but hard as he prays
he cannot dodge the image of a farmboy,
shot in the cheek or the groin,
laid in that pew after Cedar Mountain
or Chancellorsville, the house of the Lord
become the house of chloroform and amputation.

Winter sky the color of the horse
with small feet, delicate ears, quick eye
curls over the brick church as the man prays
that his mind might quiet, might free itself
from the hobble of loss, from remorse
that he ordered Pickett on, might somehow escape
the distraction of the farmboy or the sense
that all around him the mahogany pews
with cushioned kneeling-bars, racks
of red hymnals, black Books of Common Prayer
begin to hum with the passion of the wounded
rising out of the groan-logged wood

as I pray now that the plaque on his pew
across the aisle, or the one by the locust tree
where the gray horse waited, not just lift
my heart to history, and strand it there,
abandoned to annals, but reveal to me in worldliness
the world without end, for if I cannot come to Thee
through thoughts of another man on his knees,
I doubt that I can come at all.

FOURTEEN

The Ground

M AY 5. The anniversary. Ever since I began looking closely at the pictures—O'Sullivan's photographs of the Rapidan crossing, Homer's *Skirmish in the Wilderness,* the drawings by Forbes and Waud—I've been waiting for May 5, the day I could travel up Route 20 and see for myself how far the trees had leafed out. Then I could decide once and for all who got the Wilderness right. I've worked hard to keep this day free and have no other obligations.

It's not Ascension Day, though, as it was for the people of 1864. For May 5 to be Ascension Day, Easter has to fall on March 27, and it's done so only three times since men began killing each other around one o'clock in Saunders' Field: in 1910, the year Morris Schaff published his memoir; in 1921, the first year of Warren Harding's administration; and in 1932, which like 1864 was a leap year. The next time will come in 2005. After that, I've probably got only one more shot at observing the alignment of the Gregorian calendar with the 1864 liturgical calendar. 2016. If all goes well.

This isn't my first visit to the Wilderness. I've gone up several times in the last few months, hoping to match the place I'd read so much about with the actual ground. On my first visit, last November, I drove up Clark's Mountain Road, just outside of Orange, to the mountaintop orchard. Local lore has it that on a very clear day, with powerful binoculars, you can see the Washington Monument from Clark's Mountain, seventy-five or eighty miles away, especially if the sun hits the white obelisk just right. The day I went wasn't that clear, but it didn't matter much, since I drove up to get a sense of what Lee wanted to show Longstreet, Ewell, Hill, and his eight division leaders on May 2, 1864, and the Washington Monument wouldn't have figured in his aerial view.

Clark's Mountain marks the northeastern end of the Southwestern Mountains, a low range east of the Blue Ridge and the last significant elevation between central Virginia and Chesapeake Bay. There may be a few better views in the world, but none can teach as much about the Wilderness campaign as this one. Shelby Foote calls the view a living map, and so it must have been to men fighting before airplanes, helicopters, and satellite reconnaissance. But maps have names and labels on them, and the terrain below Clark's Mountain has none. With binoculars and compass, I did my best to pick out Culpeper, Stevensburg, Brandy Station, where the Army of the Potomac spent the winter. The carpet of fall foliage still hid the Rapidan. To the east and a little north, where that foliage showed the fewest gaps and clearings, spread the Wilderness. A van of early apple pickers bounced past. Clark's Mountain has no historical markers, interpretive maps, or telescopes that take a quarter.

When I reached the Wilderness on that November day, I passed a Park Service sign marking where Longstreet was shot and just beyond it an impressive monument to Union Brigadier General Wadsworth, mortally wounded near the spot. I then took a left onto Longstreet Drive. The problem is that Longstreet Drive runs through a gated opening in a large brick wall into Fawn Lake, a "club community" that offers, according to its brochure, families of all ages a lifestyle overflowing with recreational activities, especially golf on an eighteen-hole course designed by Arnold Palmer. Promotional material available at the welcome center informs the prospective buyer that Fawn Lake sits on the site of a Civil War battlefield, the peacefulness of which is mirrored by the peacefulness of the community. The promotional material also celebrates the working relationship that the community enjoys with the National Park Service and asserts the commitment of Fawn Lake to historic preservation. It's true that the developer preserved the Confederate trench line south of the Plank Road by incorporating it into the grassy median of Longstreet Drive. But when I stopped at the gated entry, manned twenty-four hours a day, to ask permission to walk the unfinished railroad cut that Longstreet's aide, Moxley Sorrel, used on May 6 to help roll Hancock up like a wet blanket, the guard looked as though I'd told him I wanted to hunt for leprechauns. He directed me to the welcome center, where a smiling young lady asked questions about the battle and granted permission.

I'd imagined the railroad cut as a deep trench or ravine that would hide four brigades from observation, but it isn't. I'd forgotten that the woods will do all the screening, if one can only find a way through them. The cut doesn't cut into the ground; it cuts into the trees, a compressed roadbed, barely visible now, that tunnels through them. Several yards into the woods someone had dumped large chunks of concrete. Nearby someone was building a huge house. I hope the people who inhabit it, sleeping soundly when they can, watching their diets, thinking over their drives and putts, either know nothing about the Battle of the Wilderness or have better nerves than I do. For their sake.

My second visit to the battlefield came in January, when I went back with my friend Frank to hunt for traces of the Parker's Store Road, at the time of the battle a narrow dirt track that zigzagged through the woods to connect the Orange Turnpike and the Orange Plank Road. On some maps it looks like a lightning bolt slashing across the battlefield from just west of the Lacy House in the north to just east of the site of Parker's Store in the south. On May 5, 1864, Warren's Fifth Corps, headed by Samuel Crawford's Third Division, was threading its way south along Parker's Store Road, as Hancock's Second Corps moved south along the Brock Road not far to the east. If Warren's corps, followed by Sedgwick's, could have gotten through the Wilderness to Parker's's Store, as Hancock's corps swung west from Todd's Tavern to Shady Grove Church on the Catharpin Road, the Army of the Potomac would have united in the open country below the Wilderness and turned west to face the Army of Northern Virginia encamped around Orange. But it couldn't.

The tactical significance of Parker's Store Road wasn't its only attraction, however, at least not for us. Because of the way the National Park Service has developed the Wilderness battlefield, and because of the way residential development has devoured and continues to devour much of the area—Spotsylvania is one of the fastest growing counties in Virginia—most people who visit the Wilderness can't help but see it as a sketchy collection of roadside markers and exhibits. The interpretive shelter along Route 20 in Saunders' Field gets the most use, and some of those who stop to read the signs there may also take the hour-long walk through the woods north of Saunders' Field to get some sense of General John B. Gordon's May 6 flank attack on the unprotected Union right. A few may find their way down Hill-Ewell drive for a walk around the field at the Widow Tapp's farm. Still fewer may walk up the farm lane to the ruins of the Higgerson House. But for the most part visitors stick to the edges of the Wilderness, and the Parker's Store Road runs through the interior.

Not every day lends itself to exploration of the interior. We held out for just the right conditions and got them on January 5: a weekday after the leaves had fallen and recent snow had packed them down so that depressions in the earth, such as those revealing a road trace, would be visible. We didn't require a sunny, seventy-degree day during January thaw in Virginia, but we took it anyway. No one around. The twelfth day of Christmas. Vacations over. Children back in school. The day before Epiphany. In his prayer book for January 5, 1864, Lee would have read Psalms Twenty-four through Twenty-nine. Psalm Twenty-four, which begins, *Domini est terra,* or "The earth is the Lord's," also appears among the readings for Ascension Day, May 5, 1864, the first day of fighting in the Wilderness.

Who is the King of glory? It is the Lord strong and mighty,
even the Lord mighty in battle.

Having left the car at a roadside picnic area, we headed east from Higgerson's farm into the woods, at first following the blue blazes of a walking trail, but when they started to lead us north toward Route 20, we abandoned the trail, turned southeast by the compass, and struck the Mill Branch of Wilderness Run, which runs east into Wilderness Run proper, which in turn flows north between the Lacy House and Wilderness Tavern into the Rapidan. Since the Parker's Store Road crossed the Mill Branch not far south of the Orange Turnpike, if we stuck to the bank of the branch, we'd have to step on the Parker's Store Road sooner or later.

The woods have opened since the war, and the forest floor is largely clear, especially in January, so moving along the branch through the trees doesn't present the same problems it gave James Wadsworth's division the morning of May 5. Passing in the opposite direction over the same ground, Lysander Cutler's First, or Iron, Brigade had to hack through a thick tangle of dwarf pine, thornbush, and briars before Gordon's counterattack broke it and sent it scrambling backwards for the first time in its history. But for us the route consisted of well-spaced oak, poplar, ironwood, shortleaf pine. Beech trees still held their parchment leaves, and hollies with red berries provided some green. Twice, in the distance, knots of deer unraveled suddenly. In the early morning the woods steamed off the overnight chill through spokes of sunlight. At one point I saw a large tree illuminated just like the central one in Winslow Homer's *Skirmish in the Wilderness. Domini est terra.* On such a morning in such a place it's hard to believe otherwise.

But if this part of the Wilderness Run valley doesn't give much of a sense of wartime flora, it still has plenty to teach about topography. Anyone who walks around the Widow Tapp's farm or wanders through the woods north of Saunders' Field, the ground where David Huffman of the Thirty-third Virginia and Asa Candage of the Seventh Maine came closest to one another, could be excused for thinking that despite the impenetrable growth and forest fires, at least the Battle of the Wilderness took place on level ground. Not so. The north bank of Mill Branch climbs ridges and tumbles into gullies again and again. At one point the bank looks down from a height too high to fall from, as the branch cuts through a deep ravine or gorge below. A map in Gordon Rhea's book shows the Twenty-fourth Michigan working its way west with its left on Mill Branch. In the two-dimensional world of a map the formation of regiments, each represented as a solid black rectangle, looks so clean, simple, and geometrically satisfying, but in three dimensions the uneven, undulating ground must have disfigured that neat Michigan rectangle as though it had been punched in from below.

But what of the Parker's Store Road? At least three times we found sunken road traces, the indented wheel ruts unmistakable, once for a short stretch on the north bank of the Mill Branch and twice after we slid down the bank, splashed across both the bridgeless branch and Wilderness Run, and climbed up into a land of houses and barking dogs. But there aren't any signs or markers. A mile or so to the north the visitor interested in Gordon's flank attack meets a sign identifying the trace of the Culpeper Mine Road, but for some reason the Park Service has left this part of the Wilderness unmarked and uninterpreted. Does anybody know for sure where a road that carried thousands of men and horses, many of them toward death or wounding, used to run? Nobody at the Chancellorsville Visitors Center did. Does it matter? After all, what's the loss of an obscure dirt road compared to all the other losses? Not much probably, but it still bothers me. Does it count if we see something but don't know that we see it? All the books, all the historians, all the enthusiasts— and still, deep in the interior, no identification or interpretation.

After returning to the car, we drove to the Chancellorsville Visitors Center to pay the new entrance fee now charged by Fredericksburg and Spotsylvania National Military Park. The Park Service estimates that the fees will generate at least $150,000 annually to help carry out such projects as rehabilitating the trail that Stonewall Jackson followed during his Chancellorsville flank march. Rehabilitating Parker's Store Road doesn't appear on the list of projects. Actually, I'd settle for some of the fee money going toward the production of a good map of

the Wilderness: large, clear, topographic, in color, with detailed troop dispositions superimposed on wartime features and an overlay that shows contemporary ones. The man behind the counter showed me new computer-generated
maps of Fredericksburg, which look good, and said that they were working on
a set for Chancellorsville. Maps for the Wilderness, he admitted, are still a few
years off.

As we paid the fee, we told him that we hadn't seen any signs to tell visitors
who didn't know about it that they had to come to Chancellorsville to pay. He
grimaced and said, "The Wilderness is hard to police." On my way out I
bought a copy of the April 1995 issue of *Blue and Gray,* a magazine "for those
who still hear the guns." This particular issue describes a tour of the first day of
the Wilderness. Flipping to a map labeled "Orange Turnpike / May 5, 1864, 3
p.m. to Dark," I found a sketch of the area Frank and I had covered. On the
north bank of the Mill Branch, where it intersects the Fifth Corps earthworks,
sit the small words, "Trail beyond this point not recommended."

After the January visit, I went back twice more. Once I returned with Frank, this
time to walk as much of the Culpeper Mine Road trace as we could. The
Culpeper Mine, or Spotswood, Road ran southwest-northeast north of the
Orange Turnpike and linked the Rapidan to the turnpike. It's the narrow dirt
track that Sedgwick's Sixth Corps traveled through the thick growth towards
Saunders' Field on May 5, and so Asa O. Candage, from Sedgwick, Maine,
must have received his gunshot wound in the shoulder somewhere in its vicinity. Unlike the Parker's Store Road, the trace of the Culpeper Mine Road is
marked in one spot by a sign. Swinging northeast from the sign, Frank and I
walked what we took to be the right track through the woods to the park
boundary, where the Culpeper Mine Road suddenly ends in a development
and someone's garage.

The other time I came back to the Wilderness, I came with my older son.
He's in fifth grade, and in fifth grade Virginia public school students have to
take several days' worth of tests based on the so-called Standards of Learning,
or SOLs, developed by the board of education. According to the book put out
by the board, fifth graders have to know certain things about United States history to 1877, including "causes, key events, and effects of the Civil War and
Reconstruction." The guidelines specify an emphasis on "economic and philosophical differences between the North and South"; "events leading to secession and war"; "leaders on both sides of the war" (Lincoln, Grant, Davis, Lee,

Frederick Douglass, and William Lloyd Garrison are singled out); "critical developments in the war, including major battles, the Emancipation Proclamation, and Lee's surrender at Appomattox"; and "life on the battlefield and on the homefront."

Faced with such a tall order, my son thought it might be helpful to visit a battlefield or two, so I offered to drive him up to the Wilderness. I had resolved in advance to do my best to keep my mouth shut and let him lead. For one thing, I didn't want to come on too strong and make him wish he'd never shown any interest at all. I know plenty of people whose parents dragged them mercilessly from battlefield to battlefield when they were young, and now they can't stand the thought of ever visiting a national military park again. But I also thought it best to keep quiet and speak only when spoken to because when I talk about the war, even in the most general and superficial way, I find I can't always count on controlling my voice. So I hid behind sunglasses and tried not to think about what fathers thought in 1864, especially fathers born in Connecticut and raising sons in Virginia.

At the Brock Road intersection, he noticed the big bronze compass that shows both Richmond and Washington fifty-eight miles from the spot, and in the Widow Tapp's field we saw a young couple with a baby lounging near a cannon. The man was flying a kite. But it was in Saunders' Field, after he finished reading the casualty figures on the monument to the 140th New York, that he gave me the sign I was half hoping for and half fearing. "Let's go, Dad. I've got those shivers again." As it turned out, the SOLs included only one question on the war: What was the real name of the Confederate general nicknamed "Stonewall" after the battle of First Manassas?

Who got it right? When battle erupted in Saunders' Field on May 5, 1864, did it do so against a bleak background of leafless trees and vines and bushes, as O'Sullivan's photographs of Germanna Ford imply, or against a luxuriant setting of blooming dogwoods and redbuds, as Mary Johnston suggests in *Cease Firing*? An image that got it badly wrong was one I discovered in the Louisiana Historical Association's Confederate Museum in New Orleans. The museum is housed in Memorial Hall, where Jefferson Davis's body lay in state in May 1893 and where in one glass case sits the crown of thorns woven by Pope Pius IX for Davis. Predictably enough, the museum devotes itself primarily to the war in the west and to artifacts that reflect the role of Louisiana. But even amidst relics such as John Bell Hood's spur, P. G. T. Beauregard's uniform and smoking cap, Braxton Bragg's bone toothpick and Bible, and a tree trunk from

Chickamauga embedded with balls, the Wilderness makes itself felt. There are the flags of the Tenth and Fifteenth Louisiana regiments, for example, both of which belonged to Leroy Stafford's brigade of Ewell's Corps and found themselves fighting near the Culpeper Mine Road. Eerily, however, the Wilderness is missing from the list of battle names sewn onto either flag.

Then there's the picture I found in the museum bookstore. Accompanied by the caption "Desperate Fight on the Orange C. H. Plank Road, Near Todd's Tavern, May 6th 1864," this color print, copyrighted by Kurz and Allison Art Publishers of Chicago in 1887, muddles everything. As if the mistaken caption (desperate fighting on May 6 took place near the Brock Road intersection—four miles north of Todd's Tavern), the impeccably uniformed Confederates in the foreground, the charging cavalry impossibly intermingled with infantry, and the misrepresented wounding of a general I take to be Longstreet in the lower left (three stars on his saddle blanket) weren't all bad enough, there are the trees. Fully leafed, well-spaced, and with no branches lower than ten feet, these deciduous giants, towering over an unobstructed forest floor, make it look as though the Battle of the Wilderness violated an Edenic bower of California redwoods.

But even though I know Kurz and Allison's image must be wrong, it turns out that I've waited for May 5 in vain. We've had a disorientingly mild winter this year, one with none of the harshness of 1863–64. The dogwoods and redbuds are long gone, and even the tardy oaks have fully greened. I've heard some people say that we're weeks ahead of normal, but how many? Sometime during this last month, on some ordinary, unremarkable day, I must have passed, without knowing it, the moment when the trees had leafed out exactly as far as the trees of May 5, 1864, had. Maybe I was doing my taxes or washing the dishes or arguing with someone about picking up his room. The *Farmer's Almanac* tells me how to correct for sunrise and sunset at different latitudes, and I know how to figure out what time it is on the other side of the world, but nothing in the Wilderness shows me how to convert the leaves of the present into the leaves of the past. Nothing. I was watching so closely and still missed them.

FIFTEEN

Sesquicentennial

ONDITIONS IN the Wilderness prevented Timothy O'Sullivan from making any photographs there during May 1864, and yet we have photographs from the Wilderness nevertheless. The harshest one I've seen appears in Roy Meredith's *Mr. Lincoln's Camera Man: Mathew Brady* (1946) above the caption, "REMAINS OF THE DEAD OF CHANCELLORSVILLE," and the note, "Photographed by Brady during Grant's Wilderness campaign." The photograph shows half a dozen skulls scattered like white helmets across the forest floor. They rest at different angles, so that the one at the far left, for example, faces toward the camera in three-quarters profile while the next one to the right rests on what would have been a left ear and stares toward the first. In the background stand the dark lower trunks of several larger trees, and in the foreground saplings and suckers are leafless. Among the skulls lie bones and other pieces of nondescript debris, including what looks like a shell casing to the right of center. Whether or not the photographer arranged the remains to heighten their effect, as Alexander Gardner's team did at Gettysburg, I can't say, but either way his picture has passed beyond the uncanny familiarity of Gardner's dead, who still look like people someone might have recognized, to the bleak desolation of anonymous human ruin.

The caption tells us that this picture shows what the soldiers of Hancock's Second Corps would have seen, having marched south from Ely's Ford on May 4, 1864, swung east at the remains of the Chancellorsville Tavern, where a recently installed traffic light now regulates this famous nineteenth-century intersection, and camped for the night somewhere near where Henry Fleming

"Remains of the Dead at Chancellorsville." Reprinted from Roy Meredith, *Mr. Lincoln's Camera Man: Mathew Brady* (1946) with permission of Russell and Volkening, Inc.

fled and where Sidney Lanier searched for his brother Clifford. It is also, however, a picture of how the present always takes place on other people's graves. "Everything is founded on the death of men," wrote Oliver Wendell Holmes, Jr., a sentence that Donald McCaig uses as the epigraph for his novel *Jacob's Ladder,* and the men of Hancock's Second Corps would have experienced the truth of Holmes's statement all too literally, as they founded their camp on a graveyard. But even the most casual of tourist visits to Washington, DC, can hardly escape the figurative truth of Holmes's statement. Washington Monument, Jefferson Memorial, Lincoln Memorial, Vietnam War Memorial, Korean War Memorial, Roosevelt Memorial, the little *tholos* commemorating the men of the city who died in World War I—the United States has founded itself and sustained itself on the deaths of millions, if we count not only the casualties suffered but also those inflicted.

The last time I visited Washington, I went to see the two most recent additions to its public monuments, the Korean War Memorial, with the poncho-clad platoon of eighteen soldiers advancing through the rain, and the Roosevelt Memorial, with its representation of ruins on which the words "I Hate War" have been carved repeatedly. But I also saw some things I hadn't anticipated. In the Lincoln Memorial I noticed for the first time that Lincoln has his left hand closed into a fist. On the Red Cross building at 17th and D, I saw the inscription, "In Memory of the Heroic Women of the Civil War." And passing the east end of the Mall I stumbled upon—how could I have missed it so many times before?—the Grant Memorial, in the center of which, between the great cavalry and artillery groups, towers Henry Merwin Shrady's equestrian statue, erected in 1920.

Charlottesville, Virginia, has two excellent equestrian statues of its own, one of an Apollonian Lee who rides Traveller with slow, stately dignity, his hat held in one hand, the other of Jackson, also hatless, galloping Little Sorrel furiously toward battle, his face full of passionate intensity. By contrast, Shrady's impassive Grant sits with slouched shoulders on his horse, who unlike Lee's and Jackson's horses, stands still, head up, ears forward, as though smelling and hearing distant battle. Grant wears not only a battered hat but also winter clothing and looks as he does in representations of him at Fort Donelson (February 1862). If we throw in Saint-Gaudens's statue of Sherman near the Plaza Hotel in New York, the uniqueness of Shrady's Grant becomes even more apparent. Unlike the dashingly caped Sherman, also hatless, he is not processing in triumph behind the figure of Victory. Unlike Lee, he is not moving with sublimely composed stage presence through great drama, as through the ranks of his hushed soldiers after the surrender in the McLean House at Appomattox. Unlike Jackson, he is not a participant caught up in the transfiguring adrenalin of battle. Instead, with neither pomp nor romance, Grant is going about the practical business of supervising the deaths of men, deaths on which everything is founded. Whoever decided to place the statue where it is, its back to the Capitol and its front toward the rest of the monuments and memorials on the Mall, had an unswervingly truthful eye for the symbolic use of space.

If we build something figuratively on the graves of men, such as a nation, we speak of sacrifice. If we build something literally on a place where men died, such as a shopping mall, we speak of development. During my last visit to Fredericksburg, having crossed the lost battlefield of Salem Church, where somewhere under all the stores, restaurants, and parking lots John Toffey fought in May 1863 and Oliver Cushman was killed in June 1864, I stopped briefly at a store in the Spotsylvania Mall. The cheerful young woman who waited on me asked why I was in Fredericksburg. When I told her, she said, "Oh, I love the Civil War." She then told me that she often found bullets in her backyard, which is near Todd's Tavern, the place Hancock had to turn his corps around on May 5 to reinforce Getty at the Brock Road intersection. She also said that some of the bullets "were bent" because wounded soldiers bit them during surgery. "You know that expression, 'Bite the bullet'?" she added. "Well, it's really true."

·

The photograph of the dead at Chancellorsville isn't only a picture of how the present takes place on other people's graves, however. It's also a picture of repetition, since the soldiers looking on in the photographic present of May 1864 weren't in the vicinity to build a shopping mall but to repeat the actions that had produced the skulls and bones a year before. In fact, when I learned more about the photograph, I discovered just how much repetition it involved. Bothered by the omission of the photograph from William Frassanito's *Grant and Lee: The Virginia Campaigns, 1864-1865* (1983), I took the liberty of sending the author a letter. Anyone who has spent time with Frassanito's superlative studies of Civil War photography knows enough to be suspicious of any attribution to Mathew Brady, but I wondered whether Frassanito had some reason to suspect the timing of the photo, given in the caption as sometime "during Grant's Wilderness campaign." His quick reply, for which I'm very grateful, identified the photographer as G. O. Brown from Baltimore, adding that neither the view nor the cameraman were connected with Brady and that the original caption was "Remains of unburied soldiers, one-half mile S. W. of Chancellorsville House. View taken April 1865."

In other words, by the time Brown recorded the photograph not only had thousands of men died in the Wilderness around Chancellorsville, but thousands more had died in the Wilderness a few miles farther west. If the original caption is accurate, then Brown photographed these particular remains in the area of the Chancellorsville battlefield around Fairview, but by April 1865 he also could have recorded nearly identical views at many points around Saunders Field, the Widow Tapp's farm, and the Brock Road intersection with the Orange Plank Road. Any one of these hypothetical views could have borne the caption "REMAINS OF THE DEAD IN THE WILDERNESS."

Repetition. It's impossible to think of the Wilderness without thinking of repetition, whether of events at Chancellorsville (woods burning, a general shot by his own troops), or of maneuvers during the Mine Run operations of November 1863 (Warren leading a corps across the Rapidan at Germanna Ford and heading down the Orange Turnpike towards Locust Grove). And for me it's a very small step from thinking about the local repetitions in the Wilderness to thinking about the one big repetition that matters: Could any of this happen again?

In the introduction to *The Civil War* (1990), the book based on the documentary filmscript by Geoffrey C. Ward, Ric Burns, and Ken Burns, we might find some reassurance that it couldn't: "Between 1861 and 1865, Americans made war on each other and killed each other in great numbers—if only to become the kind of country that could no longer conceive of how that was possible." Taking our cue from Robert Penn Warren's labels "the Great Alibi" and "the Treasury of Virtue," we might describe this conviction as the *Never Again* view. Although I can't afford to hire a private polling agency to back me up, I'll bet that as we head toward the sesquicentennial anniversaries of 2011–2015, a clear majority of people shopping or eating in the establishments that now crowd around Salem Church would subscribe to some version of this view. And thank goodness they do, many might add. If a clear majority thought another civil war likely, what would that statistic tell us about that state of peace in our time?

But whether they intended it or not, the language of the Burns brothers is disturbingly ambiguous. The part of the sentence after the dash doesn't say, "if only to become the kind of country where that was no longer possible." Instead, it qualifies the *Never Again* view by implying that the United States is now made up of people, not who are incapable of killing each other in great numbers, but who cannot conceive of killing each other in great numbers. And why not? With the central government so much stronger than it was in 1861 and sectionalism so much more diluted, I find it difficult to conceive how another civil war might actually happen.

This confession may say more about the limitations of my imagination, however, than about the truth or falsehood of the *Never Again* view. Three statements make me think so. The most recent comes from Charles Royster's chapter "The Anomalous War" in his prize-winning study *The Destructive War*. Royster's chapter title is ironic because the point of the chapter is that despite the comfort we get from thinking of the Civil War as an anomaly, in fact it was intrinsic to the American nation at the time. Toward the end of the chapter, Royster sums up what it was about antebellum America that led inevitably to war.

> Antebellum America was pervaded by an uncompromising
> insistence on personal autonomy, an expectation that
> opportunity and wealth must steadily expand, a demand
> that government directly serve citizens' wishes, a growing

impatience with restraints on the ambitions of individuals
or of groups. These tendencies to reject limitations and to
defy unwelcome authority knew no certain means to
resolve competing demands other than violence.

If Royster is thinking here about all the obvious analogies between antebellum American and late-twentieth-century America, he doesn't say so, but
when I drop the first word of this passage and change all the verbs from the past
to the present tense, another civil war strikes me as a little less inconceivable.

The second statement comes from the mind of Henry Fleming. Twice in
the first chapter of *The Red Badge of Courage,* young Stephen Crane's even
younger protagonist thinks to himself that he will never see the elephant, the
red animal, the blood-swollen war god that awaits him just across the Rappahannock.

Greeklike struggle would be no more. Men were better, or
more timid. Secular and religious education had effaced
the throat-grappling instinct, or else firm finance held in
check the passions.

How can we afford to go to war against each other when opportunity and
wealth must steadily expand; when there are millions of cars to buy and sell and
so many more malls and roads to build in central Virginia between Fredericksburg and the Wilderness; when Wall Street can still set so many more record
highs? Surely our common interest in a healthy economy has advanced us
beyond the primitive level of throat-grappling instincts. Surely Crane's irony
doesn't apply to us now. Surely.

The third statement, which is the oldest, comes from another young man,
this one just a little older than Crane was when he wrote his Civil War novel.
The month before he turned twenty-nine this young man, who was serving at
the time in the state House of Representatives, delivered an address on "The
Perpetuation of Our Political Institutions," the murder of an abolitionist editor
two months before still fresh in his mind.

At what point then is the approach of danger to be
expected? I answer, if it ever reach us, it must spring up
amongst us. It cannot come from abroad. If destruction be

our lot, we must ourselves be its author and finisher. As a
nation of freemen, we must live through all time, or die by
suicide.

Growing up in the early sixties, I was not at all sure that danger cannot
come from abroad. During the Cuban Missile Crisis of October 1962, my first-
grade class at Lincoln Elementary School, Madison, Wisconsin, participated
regularly in air raid drills, and each night of that tense stretch my parents deliberately stacked blankets and canned food in our small living room. Later, in fifth
grade, I learned from my history teacher and solemnly repeated at home that if
we didn't stop the Communists in Vietnam, it would be only a matter of time
until they were breaking down our door in Newark, Delaware.

Now, however, I think that the man who gave his name to my Wisconsin
elementary school was probably right, and not because I believe for a moment
that changes in eastern Europe during the 1980s and 1990s have made nuclear
weapons obsolete. The nuclear shadow has stretched over my entire lifetime,
but having made it into middle age knowing nothing but that shadow, I've also
come to see that, like the audience at the Young Men's Lyceum of Springfield,
Illinois, I need to be reminded that the scariest thing about danger is that it can
come from a direction where it's least expected. Of course I expect it to come
from abroad. Why? Because I'm one of those who cannot conceive that the
United States of America could possibly die by suicide. And yet I can think of
only four basic scenarios for the future: that "we must live through all time";
that some transatlantic or transpacific military giant will "crush us at a blow";
that some kind of environmental degradation or disaster will drastically reduce
or extinguish *homo sapiens* altogether, making the perpetuation of American
institutions irrelevant; or that we ourselves will be the author and finisher of our
destruction.

Any high school course in the rise and fall of world civilizations equips us
to rule out the first possibility. Given the historical timing of my own childhood,
I have some trouble ruling out the second as bravely as Lincoln rules out any
foreign power making a track on the Blue Ridge I can see out the window, but
I have to admit that in 1838 the chances of foreign invasion—the end of the War
of 1812 wasn't even a quarter of a century in the past—were much greater than
they are now. That leaves the third and fourth possibilities, which may at last
turn out to be versions of one another.

Why can't we conceive of authoring our own destruction, when it's nearly happened once? According to the *Never Again* view, too much has changed since 1861, but there's at least one other reason why, and that reason is simple amnesia. Riding the wave of interest that arose with the centennial, many prominent people who write about the Civil War apparently have no second thoughts about predicting that that interest will live through all time. For many reasons, I wish it were so, but interest in—or, more important, knowledge of—the war isn't automatically self-perpetuating. Anyone who thinks it is should sit down for a long talk with someone who won't reach adulthood until the sesquicentennial. According to the Census Bureau's "Population Projections of the United States by Age, Sex, Race, and Hispanic Origin: 1995–2050," as of July 1, 2015, the 150th anniversary of ratification of the Thirteen Amendment by New Hampshire, the population will reach 310,134,000, and the median age 37.3 years. It may be that the sesquicentennial will stir up another wave of interest in the war that will sweep along those on the low side of the median age, but if so, it will have to stir vigorously.

For one thing, the competition for the attention of young people has grown much fiercer, as any advertising executive will confirm. When the *American Heritage Picture History of the Civil War* first came along in 1960, it wasn't the only show in town, but it didn't have to contend with satellite-dish television, videotapes and video games, computer games and the Internet, and portable compact disc players for a share of my schoolboy attention. By the time the sesquicentennial arrives, who knows what new developments in technology and social behavior will make spending a day walking around the Wilderness feel like a pretty lukewarm activity.

And, for another thing, what will walking around in the Wilderness be like? The economic and demographic pressures to develop the area make the pressures that Lincoln put on his generals to attack the Army of Northern Virginia there look lovingly gentle by contrast. At a time when battlefield preservationists are caricatured and vilified as cranky reactionaries opposed to the steady expansion of opportunity and wealth, how optimistic can we be that people well below the median age of 37.3 will enter the year 2015 with a deep sense of being citizens of a country that really does value the physical presence of its past? It's much easier to persuade someone young of the importance of May 1864 when you're both standing in the quiet woods along the Mill Branch of Wilderness Run than it is when you're shouting at each other to be heard above six lanes of traffic roaring past Salem Church. Young people catch on fast, no matter how many patriotic pieties we drill into them. Even if they haven't read the book, they know full well that where your treasure is, there will your heart be also.

It's also impossible for me to think about the Wilderness without thinking of inconclusiveness. The most astringent statement of that inconclusiveness that I know comes from Washington Roebling, Warren's chief personal aide and a major at the time of the battle.

> The Wilderness was a useless battle fought with great loss
> and no result.

Ken Burns includes this statement in his eight-minute narrative of the Wilderness, and it's a tough statement to swallow, especially in the context of a documentary that obviously reflects its makers' belief in the redeeming virtues of the Civil War. Plenty of people would argue with Roebling, who later supervised the construction of the Brooklyn Bridge, but whatever one's assessment of Grant's strategy with respect to Union war aims, Roebling sobers us by crossing the line and daring to speak what the builders of monuments don't want to hear: It wasn't sacrifice; it was waste. Great loss qualifies as sacrifice when, and only when, something comes of it, when something gets founded on the deaths of men. If nothing comes of it, if nothing gets founded, it's waste.

Although some might be able to accept Roebling's judgment about the Wilderness—and perhaps justify paying less attention to it in wide-angle histories—many fewer of us would feel comfortable accepting his judgment with respect to the war as a whole. After all, the war gave us the Emancipation Proclamation; the Thirteenth, Fourteenth, and Fifteenth Amendments; the industrialization of the New South; and the consolidation of national identity reflected in the grammatical shift from the United States "are" to the United States "is." The war also advanced medical knowledge, the social and economic status of women, and American military might, which helped tip the balance in the world wars of the twentieth century. Whatever else, the war certainly accomplished Lincoln's war aims, first to preserve the Union and, after Sharpsburg-Antietam, to abolish slavery in the states still in rebellion after January 1, 1863.

True. All true. But like the Battle of the Wilderness, there's something inconclusive about the Civil War that makes me wonder whether it will turn out to be, in relation to something else still to come, what the Wilderness was to Spotsylvania, North Anna, Cold Harbor, and Petersburg: mere prologue. One way that Northerners patronize Southerners is to remark, with a hint of bemusement at the quaintness of the fact, how They're Still Fighting the War Down There. Never mind what this condescension reveals about a larger national tendency towards amnesia, as though the only possible justification for keeping oneself deeply aware of the past were the loss of a war, as though memory were only for losers. Despite unawareness and amnesia, whether from North, South, East, or West, there is much about the war that remains as unfinished as the fighting in Virginia was when darkness fell on Friday, May 6, 1864.

I collided with a small image of inconclusiveness when I learned recently, after some telephone calls to the Department of Veterans Affairs in Washington, that in the pension files there are still two living widows of Union soldiers. If we assume that these women, born in, say, 1920, were seventeen years old when in 1937 they married veterans who were, say, ninety (imagine that the veterans, born in 1847, were drummer boys or lied about their ages or joined the army for a few months in 1865 after they turned eighteen), then these two widows could well be alive in 2015 for the end of the sesquicentennial. When I called the United Daughters of the Confederacy in Richmond to find out about any living Confederate widows, I learned that a woman still alive in Alabama had been married to a Confederate veteran but that the U.D.C. no longer considered her a Confederate widow because she had remarried.

A country that is still paying pensions to two Civil War widows has unfinished business in a very real, immediate sense, but so does a country in which people can divide so drastically over the legacy, or legacies, of the war. In the bookstore of the Confederate Museum in New Orleans, I came across a volume called *The South Was Right!* (second edition 1994) by James Ronald Kennedy and Walter Donald Kennedy. In the final pages of this book, the Kennedys explain, "Our aim is to re-establish a constitutional republic in which everyone, including Southerners, is treated equally; or, if we fail to convince our Northern neighbors of the wisdom of such a change, then we will establish our own separate Southern nation." But the Kennedys don't limit themselves to explanations, or even to exhortations such as *"We must elect Confederate Freedom Fighters!"* in the first-person plural. Instead, there in the bookstore a block from Lee Circle they addressed me directly: "You can decide that it is time to join the ranks of the New Unreconstructed Southerners."

Meanwhile, in *Confederates in the Attic* (1998), journalist Tony Horwitz describes his visit to a classroom in which several black students, whose teacher refers to all Confederates as "criminals," voiced persistent skepticism, even cynicism, toward the proposition that the Civil War had effected substantial changes in relations between black and white in the United States. They also voiced persistent skepticism, even cynicism, toward the proposition that serious study of the war held anything of value for them. Whether one thinks these students' attitudes anomalous or typical, perceptive or shortsighted, at some level their assessment of the war echoes Washington Roebling's judgment of the Wilderness, and that echo, no matter how loud or faint, isn't a good sign for anybody.

It doesn't help to identify and dismiss as extremists both the authors of *The South Was Right!* and the teacher who refers to Confederates as criminals. It's true that all by themselves a few extremists can't make a large war that lasts several years. As the Civil War shows, it takes millions of well-meaning moderates to do that. But it's also true that millions of well-meaning moderates don't up and spontaneously combust one day. As the Civil War shows, it takes a few extremists, well-placed and visible, to help them along. Nor does it help to try to defang and declaw extreme statements with platitudes about difference and diversity. To be sure, difference and diversity enrich both conversations and countries, but they can also fray into competition, incompatibility, and estrangement. In many ways, they already have.

When I passed the Wilderness sign again the other day, I was coming from town and a visit with my friend Charles, who owns a lock of Lee's hair I'd always wanted to see. The lock came down to him from his great-grandfather, originally from Arkansas and after the war captain of the corps of cadets at the Virginia Military Institute in Lexington, not far from where Lee served as president of Washington College. On an orangish envelope measuring about 3 by 5½ inches, Charles's great-grandfather has written, "Sent to me by Gen. R. E. Lee." On a smaller envelope tucked inside it appears a note in the same hand, "A Lock of Genl. R. E. Lee's Hair." The lock itself measures about two inches long and looks like something you could sweep off the floor of a barber shop any afternoon. It's yellowish in places, perhaps with age, with several dark hairs here and there. And to think I had been expecting snowy white.

After leaving Charles's house, I took the left at the intersection from which one can see Monticello and headed north on the Constitution Route, past the turn to my own house, to visit my friend Anne, who owns a New Testament carried during the war by her great-great-great-uncle, Enos Rushton, Company E, Seventeenth Iowa Volunteers. This New Testament, bound in dark brown leather and fastened shut with a small metal clasp, measures only 3 by 4½ inches and obviously fit into Enos's pocket. The leather on the back cover has been carefully tooled into intricate designs, but the leather on the front has been worn smooth, probably from rubbing against Enos's chest. Originally from Missouri, Enos joined the army in 1861, was captured, and spent nearly a year in Andersonville prison. In 1864, he escaped from the prison with his brother Elam, traveled by night for two weeks, and rejoined the Union forces to serve until his discharge in 1865. Gingerly turning the frail pages, I found a small dark stain on the first page of John's gospel. *And the light shineth in darkness; and the darkness comprehended it not.* When I carefully closed the testament and then let it fall gently open again to wherever Enos's reading during four years of war had most deeply creased the spine, Revelation suddenly filled my palm.

A Brief Description of
the Battle of the Wilderness

MAY 1864 found Lincoln six months away from an election that would pit him against Democratic candidate George B. McClellan, his former general whom he had relieved of command in the fall of 1862. In a memorandum of August 23, 1864, more than two months into Grant's siege of Petersburg and about ten days before Atlanta fell to Sherman, Lincoln acknowledged that "it seems exceedingly probable that this Administration will not be re-elected."

> Then it will be my duty to so co-operate with the President
> elect, as to save the Union between the election and the
> inauguration; as he will have secured his election on such
> ground that he can not possibly save it afterwards.

Against this political backdrop, the outcome of the spring campaigns, east and west, could not have looked more significant. After Union victories at both Gettysburg and Vicksburg the previous July, the war in the east had stalled again after the frustrating Mine Run campaign of late 1863, a campaign that briefly took George Gordon Meade's Army of the Potomac across the Rapidan River and through the heavily wooded area known as the Wilderness.

In March 1864, Lincoln had promoted Ulysses S. Grant to lieutenant general and made him general in chief of the Armies of the United States. Although Grant retained Meade as commander of the Army of the Potomac, the new general in chief traveled east to establish his headquarters with Meade's army, spread out in winter camp north of the Rapidan from Culpeper Court House to Brandy Station. Also in March, Grant had reorganized the eastern army, eliminating the First and Third Corps and redistributing their components among the Second, Fifth, and Sixth Corps, commanded respectively by Winfield Scott Hancock, Gouverneur Warren, and John Sedgwick. Another corps, the Ninth, commanded by Ambrose Burnside, operated independently but would join the Army of the Potomac in the Wilderness, bringing with it the first black troops to fight in the Virginia theater.

Meanwhile, Robert E. Lee's Army of Northern Virginia consisted of three corps: James Longstreet's First Corps, detached and sent west during the second half of 1863 but now returned and encamped at Gordonsville; Richard Ewell's Second Corps, guarding a portion of the Rapidan fords and encamped around Orange Court House; and A. P. Hill's Third Corps, guarding other Rapidan fords and also encamped around Orange. Although different sources give different totals, Grant had at his command somewhere around 120,000 men, while Lee had at his about sixty-five thousand.

During the first hours of Wednesday, May 4, 1864, the various elements of the Army of the Potomac broke camp and headed south to cross the Rapidan once again, which they did without major obstacles, the Second Corps crossing at Ely's Ford and both the Fifth and Sixth Corps crossing farther west at Germanna Ford. Because of poor reconnaissance by James Wilson's Third Division of the Federal cavalry, the Army of the Potomac spent the night of May 4 in the Wilderness wholly unaware that Ewell's Second Corps had advanced to within a few miles, camping at Locust Grove, and that Hill's Third Corps had reached New Verdiersville. Longstreet's Corps, which had set out from Gordonsville the afternoon of May 4, would not arrive on the battlefield until the early morning of May 6.

Early on Thursday, May 5, Warren's Fifth Corps discovered the presence of Ewell's Second Corps on the Orange Turnpike. About 8:00 A.M., Wilson's cavalry engaged Thomas Rosser's Confederate cavalry at Craig's Meeting House on the Catharpin Road. Around the same time, Hill's Third Corps was making steady progress against New York cavalry down the Orange Plank Road.

At approximately 1:00 P.M., after numerous hesitations and delays, Warren's Fifth Corps attacked Ewell's Second Corps, positioned on the west side of Saunders' Field. Shortly after 4:00 P.M., having rushed south to the critical Brock Road intersection, Union General George Getty's division, detached from the Sixth Corps, advanced west of Brock Road against Hill's corps. With the arrival of Hancock's Second Corps, which had had to turn around at

Todd's Tavern and retrace its steps, a general attack soon followed. Fighting continued on both fronts until darkness.

At dawn on Friday, May 6, Ewell attacked Sedgwick's Sixth Corps, positioned on the Union right, but with little result. Fighting in the vicinity of Saunders' Field quieted by late morning. At 5:00 A.M. on the Brock Road front, Hancock attacked Hill with great success, pushing him back to the Widow Tapp's farm. Around 6:00 A.M. Longstreet's First Corps arrived in the Widow Tapp's field, and, the story goes, Lee tried to lead the Texas Brigade into battle himself, until the soldiers insisted he find safety in the rear. Longstreet's counterattack overwhelmed Hancock's troops. At about 11:00 A.M. a portion of Longstreet's command, which had traveled through the woods along an unfinished railroad cut, launched an effective attack against Hancock's left flank. Shortly before 1:00 P.M., in the confusion of the woods, Longstreet was severely wounded by his own men. At this point, the fighting along the Plank Road quieted, as Lee reorganized for another attack against Hancock, an attack that he launched shortly after 4:00 P.M. It did not succeed as Lee had hoped and ended by 5:00 P.M.

About 7:00 P.M., on the opposite flank, Confederate General John B. Gordon attacked Sedgwick's unprotected right, but darkness prevented the local rout from achieving larger success.

Early on Saturday, May 7, Grant ordered the Army of the Potomac to prepare for a night march to Spotsylvania Court House. Throughout this day the armies skirmished, and by nightfall both were moving towards Spotsylvania, Grant's army with 17,666 fewer men than had crossed the Rapidan and Lee's with somewhere between seven thousand five hundred and eleven thousand fewer than had awaited them.

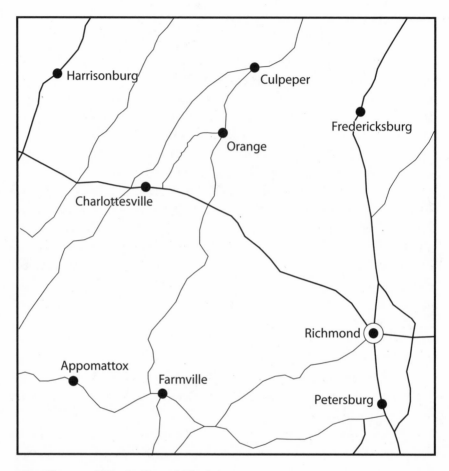

The Theater of War in Central Virginia

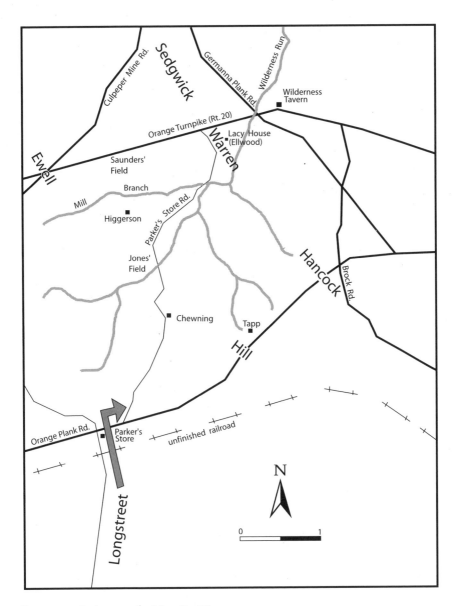

Longstreet's Approach: May 6, 1864

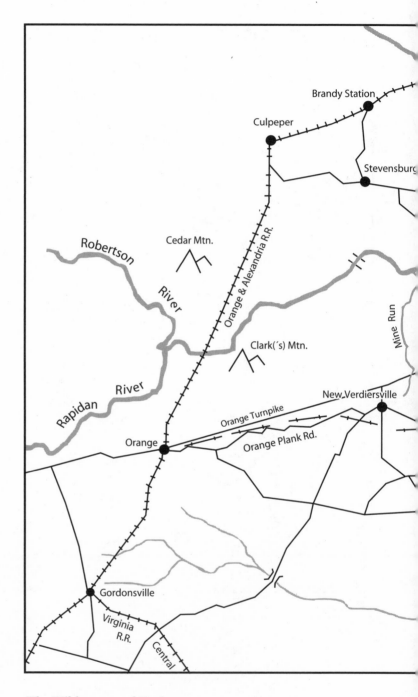

The Wilderness and Environs

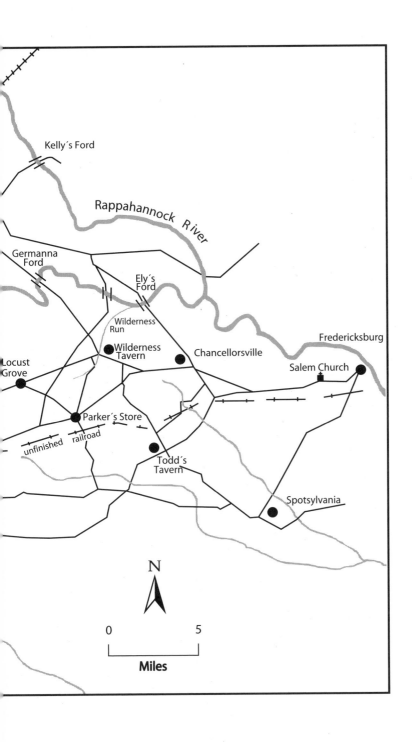

Kelly's Ford

Rappahannock River

Germanna
Ford

Ely's
Ford

Wilderness
Run

Wilderness
Tavern

Chancellorsville

Fredericksburg

Salem Church

Locust
Grove

Parker's Store

unfinished   railroad

Todd's
Tavern

Spotsylvania

N

0   5

Miles

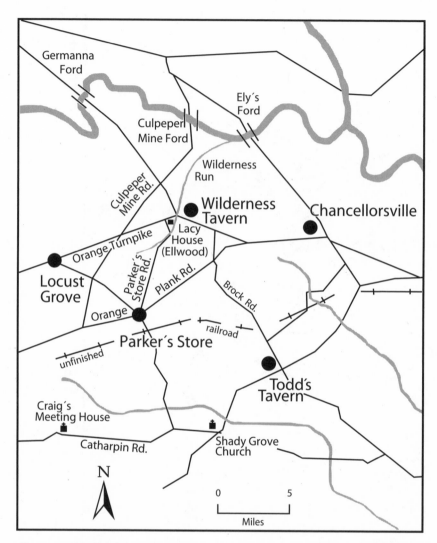

Close-up: South of the Rapidan

A Note on Sources

I've tried to make my debts and sources clear as I go, weaving them into the text itself. Having come to the end, I find that some authors and titles still remain unnamed, and I now acknowledge them with pleasure and gratitude: Mark Boatner, *Civil War Dictionary* (rev. ed. 1988); Garold L. Cole, *Civil War Eye-witnesses: An Annotated Bibliography of Books and Articles, 1955–1986* (1988); James Thomas Flexner, *The World of Winslow Homer 1836–1910* (1966); Gary W. Gallagher, ed., *The Wilderness Campaign* (1997); The Gallery Association of New York State, *Winslow Homer Prints from "Harper's Weekly"* (1977); Gerald M. Garmon, *John Reuben Thompson* (1979); Gordon Hendricks, *The Life and Works of Winslow Homer* (1979); Robert Lively, *Fiction Fights the Civil War: An Unfinished Chapter in the Literary History of the American People* (1957); David Madden and Peggy Bach, eds., *Classics of Civil War Fiction* (1991); Allan Nevins, James Robertson, Jr., Bell I. Wiley, *Civil War Books: A Critical Bibliography*, two vols. (1967–1969); Bessel A. van der Kolk, Alexander C. McFarlane, Lars Weisaeth, eds., *Traumatic Stress: The Effects of Over-whelming Experience on Mind, Body, and Society* (1996); John Wilmerding, *Winslow Homer* (1972); Steven E. Woodworth, ed., *The American Civil War: A Handbook of Literature and Research* (1996). Those who would like to skim the names of authors and books that appear in the text can do so in the index. The date of publication or composition follows at least the first appearance of any title in the text. Those in search of comprehensive bibliographies on the Battle of the Wilderness should consult the studies by Gordon Rhea and Edward Steere, in addition to Gallagher. For books on the Civil War published since the *Critical Bibliography* of Nevins, Roberston, and Wiley, see, in addition to Woodworth, Domenica M. Barbuto and Martha Kreisel, *Guide to Civil War Books: An Annotated Selection of Modern Works on the War Between the States* (1996).

Index

Italicized page numbers refer to illustrations.

Franklin, battle of, 55, 56

Franklin, Haywood, 162

Franklin's Crossing, Va., 29

Frassanito, William, 11, 13, 130, 265; *Grant and Lee: The Virginia Campaign, 1864–1865,* 265

Frazier, Charles: *Cold Mountain,* 4, 211–12, 225–26

Frederic, Harold: "A Day in the Wilderness," 212–14, 215, 217, 223; *The Deserter and Other Stories: A Book of Two Wars,* 212

Fredericksburg, first battle of, 29, 194, 226; and lost battlefield of Salem Church, 264, 266, 269

Fredericksburg, second battle of, 29

Fredericksburg and Spotsylvania National Military Park, 258

Freedom: A Documentary History of Emancipation (ed. Ira Berlin), 163

Freeman, Douglas Southall, 5, 171, 197, 201, 203. Works: *Lee's Lieutenants,* 174; *R. E. Lee,* 191, 192

Frémont, John C., 90, 97

Freud, Sigmund, 54–55, 170; *Beyond the Pleasure Principle,* 54

Frost, Robert, 239, 240; "The Black Cottage," 241; *North of Boston,* 241

Gardner, Alexander, 11, 13, 117, 209, 262; *Photographic Sketch Book of the Civil War,* 146

Garrison, William Lloyd, 260

Gaudens, Augustus St.: monument to Robert Gould Shaw and Fifty-fourth Massachusetts, 242, 244; statue of Sherman, 264

Gay, James D.: "The Battle of the Wilderness," 232–33, 235, 241, 246

Germanna Ford, 146, 152, 156, 161, 163, 165, 265, 276

Getty, George W., 66, 264, 276

Gettysburg (film), 12, 174; and reenactors, 64

Gettysburg, battle of, 3, 11, 12, 18, 30, 58, 62, 65, 66, 106, 117, 147, 174–75, 176, 177, 192, 194, 195, 209, 210, 219, 222, 226, 262, 275

Gibbon, John, 180; *Personal Recollections of the Civil War,* 167

Gibson, James, 13

Gillmore, Quincy Adams, 96

Glasgow, Ellen: *The Battle-Ground,* 212

Glory (film), 40–41

Gooding, James Henry, 164

Goodman, Joseph T., 101–2

Gordon, Caroline: "Hear the Nightingale Sing," 4

Gordon, John B., 171–73, 196, 197, 224, 256, 257, 258, 277; *Reminiscences of the Civil War,* 168, 171–73, 174, 179–80, 181, 188, 199

Gordonsville, Va., 276

Granberry, Ella, 87, 89, 93, 115

Granberry, John Cowper, 86–87, 92–93, 115, 116

Grant, Ulysses S., 3, 4, 17, 18, 27, 32, 47, 66, 70, 90, 93, 94, 97, 98, 99, 110, 114, 122, 126, 131, 145, 146, 152, 172, 178, 180, 181, 193, 196, 198, 199, 204, 213, 215, 216, 217, 218, 224, 234, 238, 247, 259, 270, 275, 276, 277; *Personal Memoirs,* 93, 167, 168, 169, 170, 174, 178–84, 188

Grant Memorial (Shrady), 264

Greenhow, Rose O'Neal, 168

Grierson, Benjamin H., 46

Griffin, Charles, 93, 193, 198–99, 204, 218

Groene, Bertram Hawthorne: *Tracing Your Civil War Ancestor,* 28–29, 30

Gurganus, Allan: *Oldest Living Confederate Widow Tells All,* 211

Hadden, R. Lee: *Reliving the Civil War: A Reenactor's Handbook,* 60, 61–62, 63–64, 65, 66

Hancock, Winfield Scott, 12, 66–67, 68, 89, 92, 101, 106, 109, 112, 113, 116, 121, 132, 134, 135, 146, 147, 179, 194, 196, 198, 199, 204, 239, 255, 256, 262, 263, 264, 276, 277

Hannum, Alberta Pierson: "Turkey Hunt," 4

Harding, Warren, 254

Harper's Magazine, 145, 234

Harper's Weekly, 118, 120–22, 134, 145–47, 152, 159, 241. Works: "Army of the Potomac—Our Wounded Escaping from the Fires in the Wilderness" (Waud), 156, 157, 158–59; "Bartlett's Brigade of Warren's Corps Charging the Enemy," 146–47, 148–49; "The Battle of the Wilderness" (anonymous poem), 218, 233–34, 235, 236,

The American South Series

Anne Goodwyn Jones and Susan V. Donaldsen, editors
Haunted Bodies: Gender and Southern Texts

M. M. Manring
Slave in a Box: The Strange Career of Aunt Jemima

Stephen Cushman
Bloody Promenade: Reflections on a Civil War Battle